IronFit®'s
Everyman Triathlons

Also by **Don Fink** and **Melanie Fink**

Be Iron Fit®, Third Edition
IronFit® Secrets for Half Iron-Distance Triathlon Success
IronFit® Triathlon Training for Women
IronFit® Strength Training and Nutrition for Endurance Athletes
IronFit®'s Marathons After 40

IronFit®'s
Everyman Triathlons

TIME-EFFICIENT TRAINING
FOR SHORT COURSE TRIATHLONS

DON FINK *and* **MELANIE FINK**

Guilford, Connecticut

An imprint of Globe Pequot

Distributed by NATIONAL BOOK NETWORK

British Library Cataloguing in Publication Information available

Library of Congress Cataloging-in-Publication Data

Names: Fink, Don, author. | Fink, Melanie, author.
Title: IronFit's Everyman Triathlons : time-efficient training for short
  course triathlons / Don Fink and Melanie Fink.
Description: Guilford, Connecticut : Lyons Press, [2018] | "Distributed by
  NATIONAL BOOK NETWORK"—T.p. verso. | Includes webography. | Includes
  bibliographical references and index.
Identifiers: LCCN 2017054018 (print) | LCCN 2017035227 (ebook) | ISBN
  9781493034475 (e-book) | ISBN 9781493032112 (paperback) | ISBN
  9781493034475 (ebook)
Subjects: LCSH: Ironman triathlon—Training. | Ironman
  triathlon—Psychological aspects.
Classification: LCC GV1060.73 (print) | LCC GV1060.73 .F5734 2018 (ebook) |
  DDC 796.42/57—dc23
LC record available at https://lccn.loc.gov/2017054018

In loving memory of Doug Clark,
Tom Fleming, and Steve Tarpinian

»CONTENTS

» INTRODUCTION

The sprint and standard distances of triathlon and duathlon are the "everyman" distances of the sport. Not only are these events the most common across North America and the world, but with the right training and information, anyone from a world-class triathlete to a weekend warrior can successfully race one. If you have a short course triathlon or duathlon dream, you have come to the right place!

There are two primary distance categories in triathlons: long course and short course. The Iron-distance (2.4-mile swim, 112-mile bike, and 26.2-mile run) and half Iron-distance (1.2-mile swim, 56-mile bike, and 13.1-mile run) are considered "long course" races, while the standard distance (1.5 km swim, 40 km bike, and 10 km run) and the sprint distance (750 meter swim, 20 km bike, and 5 km run) are considered "short course" races.

The standard distance (also referred to as the "Olympic distance") is the original triathlon format and includes a 1.5 km swim, 40 km bike, and 10 km run (which is about a 0.9-mile swim, 24.8-mile bike, and 6.2-mile run). In addition to being the distance undertaken by many thousands of triathletes worldwide, it is also the distance competed at the Olympics and by the sport's most elite triathletes in its major professional circuit, the ITU (International Triathlon Union). On the amateur side, many very popular and highly competitive regional, national, and world age group championships are competed at the standard distance.

The sprint distance is half the distance of the standard distance and usually includes a 750 meter swim, 20 km bike, and 5 km run (which is about a half-mile swim, 12.4-mile bike, and 3.1-mile run). While the distances may vary slightly from one sprint to another, most sprints are very close to these distances. On the amateur side, highly competitive regional, national, and world age group championships exist at the sprint distance.

In addition to the standard and sprint distance triathlon formats, there are also popular standard and sprint distance duathlon events. These are structured in a run-bike-run format rather than the triathlon's swim-bike-run format. The standard distance duathlon is a 10 km run, followed by a 40 km bike, and then a 5 km run (which is about a 6.2-mile run, 24.8-mile bike, and 3.1-mile run). The sprint distance duathlon consists of a 5 km run, followed by a 20 km bike, and then a 2.5 km run (which is about a 3.1-mile run, 12.4-mile bike, and 1.5-mile run). As with their triathlon counterparts, there are highly competitive regional, national, and world championships at the standard and sprint distance duathlons.

One of the reasons sprint and standard distance races are so popular is because they are not just for athletes specializing in short course events. Long course athletes compete as well. In fact, sprint and standard distance races are not only the stepping-stones to long course racing, but are also typically an integral part of the long course athlete's training and racing. Because it is only possible to race a few long course races every year, many long course triathletes choose to fill their annual racing schedules with short course events too. As a result, short course races form the center crossroad for the entire sport of triathlon.

Today the sprint and standard distances are more popular than ever, and the number of races has skyrocketed. USA Triathlon sanctions over 500 of these races in the United States, and there are many more worldwide. Several very successful race series exist at these distances too, beginning with the ITU worldwide professional series where the top pros compete side-by-side with average Joe and Jane triathletes.

Even the most powerful name in the Iron-distance world has identified the growing popularity of these distances and jumped in with a major worldwide racing series. The World Triathlon Corporation, which owns the Ironman series, is so confident in the potential growth of short course racing that it has launched a "5150" series, which, at the time of this writing, describes twenty-seven short course races worldwide. The series' name derives from the 51.50 kilometers covered in a standard distance triathlon.

The number of competing race series featuring this distance is quickly growing worldwide as well. Numerous regional race series and an even greater number of independent races coexist. TriFind.com recently listed 1,853 sprint distance races and another 563 standard distance races in the United States alone.

Why are sprint and standard distances so popular? One reason is because they are so accessible for the vast majority of busy people juggling demanding careers and important family responsibilities. While the half and full Iron-distances are achievable, they require very careful planning and much time and sacrifice to accomplish. Keeping a life balance is difficult because the training requires an enormous commitment.

The sprint and standard distances, however, can be completed by average athletes and top professionals alike. They are the "everyman" distances of triathlon. While still fun and immensely rewarding, the sprint and standard distances provide a much more accessible opportunity to compete at a high level while also maintaining a positive and sustainable lifestyle balance.

This is evident from the length of the training programs themselves. The programs for short course triathlon and duathlon in this book range from six to twelve weeks. Compare this with the thirty-week programs we designed in our book focused on the full Iron-distance and sixteen weeks in our book focused on the half Iron-distance. Sprint and standard distance triathlons and duathlons are performed at different intensity levels, with different approaches. As a result, the training differs as well. In general, you can expect the training time to be less but the intensity of the training to be more. As amazing as it may seem, if you read this book today, you could be crossing a triathlon or duathlon finish line as soon as six to twelve weeks from now.

IronFit's Everyman Triathlons provides three complete 12-week training programs (Competitive, Intermediate, and "Just Finish") for the standard distance triathlon and three complete 8-week training programs (Competitive, Intermediate, and "Just Finish") for the sprint distance triathlon. It also provides three complete 10-week training programs (Competitive, Intermediate, and "Just Finish") for the standard distance duathlon and three complete 6-week training programs (Competitive, Intermediate, and "Just Finish") for the sprint distance duathlon. In addition to the training programs, it provides everything an athlete needs to know to successfully prepare for and maximize performance at these racing distances.

As with all our books, this text is not written in a highly technical and complicated manner. Instead, it presents necessary information and training programs in an easy-to-understand and enjoyable way. After reading this book, an athlete immediately can put the information to work and get right on the road to accomplishing his or her triathlon and/or duathlon goal. *IronFit's Everyman Triathlons* provides a clear path to maximizing an athlete's success at these popular racing distances. If you want to optimize your short course performance, you have come to the right place. It's all right here—the training programs and the information you need to achieve your triathlon dream.

We start with a presentation of the eight essential training sessions for short course triathlon and duathlon. We begin not with the training programs themselves, but instead with the building blocks we use to design the perfect program. From there we discuss the crucial training principles for short course races and how to make heart rate training work for you. Without understanding the essential workouts, how they should be arranged in proper training cycles, and how they are influenced by the crucial training principles, an athlete will not optimize his or her training results but will be doing what we refer to as "junk training."

Then, with an understanding of these topics, we present twelve detailed short course training programs, each ranging from six to twelve weeks. These programs are user-friendly and can be put to immediate use by the athlete. Guidance is also provided to help athletes select the program that fits their goals and available training time.

While the twelve programs cover the specific training sessions in swimming, cycling, and running, we also provide a warm-up routine, a functional strength and core training program, and a stretching and flexibility routine, each specifically designed for success in the short course distances.

This book also presents specific training and guidance on short course triathlon's "fourth sport," the transitions known as T1 and T2, which, while key aspects of the race, are often overlooked.

From there we cover proper technique in the three sports and provide tools for improving and fine-tuning your form. Next we discuss all the needed equipment for short course success, including recommendations on the most economical ways to "buy speed." Also covered is a thorough discussion of racing strategies, race selection, and how to set exciting and motivating goals.

Finally, we present specific guidance as to exactly what an athlete should do in the off-season to best prepare for the next season and ensure continued improvement year after year.

You will also find ten motivating athlete profiles of successful athletes who have conquered the sprint and standard distances. These accounts describe some of the many athletes we have had the honor to work with over the years. You may see yourself in some of their inspiring stories. These athletes prove that amazing athletic goals are achievable—even for those with demanding careers and family responsibilities—and perhaps even more rewarding than imagined.

As we said at the outset, if you want to maximize your performance and achieve your short course triathlon and/or duathlon dream, you have come to the right place. So turn the page and let's get started!

» Triathlon and Duathlon's Most Accessible Distances

All our dreams come true, if we have the courage to pursue them. —WALT DISNEY

While short course triathlon has been with us for over forty years, it is now more popular than ever. The skyrocketing popularity of the sprint and standard distance triathlon and duathlon is one of the most exciting trends in the endurance sports world. There is a good reason why "everyone is doing it." Not only is it fun and a great way to be healthy and fit, but the races are accessible, plentiful, and easy on the budget.

The official short course distances (and their approximate equivalent in miles) are the following:

- **Standard Triathlon:** 1.5 km (0.9 mile) swim, 40 km (24.8 miles) bike, and 10 km (6.2 miles) run

- **Sprint Triathlon:** 750 meters (0.5 mile) swim, 20 km (12.4 miles) bike, and 5 km (3.1 miles) run

- **Standard Duathlon:** 10 km (6.2 miles) run, 40 km (24.8 miles) bike, and 5 km (3.1 miles) run

- **Sprint Duathlon:** 5 km (3.1 miles) run, 20 km (12.4 miles) bike, and 2.5 km (1.5 miles) run

While the exact distances of some of the many short course races vary slightly, all are at or very close to what's listed above. The reason for this is that most athletes have found these races to be the perfect distances—especially for the vast majority of athletes who also have demanding career and family responsibilities. While the full and half Iron-distances are doable, they take very careful planning and a lot of sacrifice to accomplish, often temporarily pulling the rest of life out of balance. While still substantial and challenging, the standard and sprint distances of triathlon and duathlon provide the opportunity to compete in exciting races and enjoy health and fitness, while also maintaining a good lifestyle balance.

The short course races have logistical advantages. While you may have to travel several hours to race a half or full Iron-distance triathlon, a sprint or standard distance event can likely be found locally. We live in a rural area, and a wonderful local triathlon with a twenty-five-year history starts

Alice Hector, elite age group triathlete
James Mitchell Photography

right down our street. While you may not be lucky enough to be able to walk to the starting line from your house, chances are good that with thousands of races at the sprint or standard distances, you also will have some great races nearby.

There are simple economic advantages to the race. The entry fee for many major full Iron-distance races exceeds $800, and this does not include the cost of travel and accommodations usually associated with these races. Most athletes can find a great local sprint or standard race with an entry fee of less than a quarter of this cost and practically no travel expenses. You will not have to tap into your family savings to race a short course triathlon or duathlon.

Because of these factors, the popularity of short course races will surely continue to grow. In fact, they are likely to grow at an increasing rate, as participation in triathlon continues to skyrocket worldwide. As an example of this, membership in USAT (the governing organization of triathlon in the United States) has grown by over 300 percent in the last ten years. The future of triathlon is bright, and the future of short course racing even brighter.

This accessibility and all the other factors mentioned above are exactly what brought us into the sport over twenty-five years ago. After being competitive runners for many years and experiencing a lot of the common injuries associated with that, we were beginning to cross-train. While still running, Melanie took the lead on this and began adding swimming and cycling to her training routine. Don soon followed her lead, and we were both training in all three sports.

Then one day we were visiting a fitness center in Florida and Don picked up a triathlon magazine for the first time. There was an event schedule in the back, and a sprint race in Maryland jumped out at him. Little did either of us know at the time that the simple phrase, "Hey Mel, we should try this," would lead us on an amazing journey that has continued for over twenty-five years.

We entered the race, drove to Maryland, and completed our first multisport race. Don did not even own a bike. All of his cycling was happening on a stationary bike at the gym. So he borrowed an ancient ten-speed from a friend. When he got a flat tire he didn't know how to change it. This never happened on the stationary bike at the gym. In fact, he probably got the flat because he didn't know how to properly inflate his tires in the first place. He rode the last 2 miles of the course on a flat tire!

Needless to say, our first go at triathlon was not momentous, but we absolutely loved it and were hooked. We didn't know how to train for it, we didn't know about equipment, we didn't know about race strategy—you name it, we didn't know it. We just brought what we knew from other sports to help us get by. In short, we could have really used the book you are reading right now. This hunger for knowledge, combined with the wonderful experience we enjoyed, led to our passion for triathlon training and proper preparation.

Before our drive home was over, we had already decided to sign up for a standard distance race in Delaware and a couple of duathlons hosted by the New York Triathlon club. Talk about being accessible? In our very first few months in the sport, we competed in a sprint and standard distance triathlon and a couple of duathlons all within driving distance of our home. And that was over twenty-five years ago . . . the sport is many times more accessible today.

One more important point about our first year in triathlon and duathlon: In our first standard distance race in Delaware, one of the competitors was Scott Molina. He was a top triathlete at the time and is now considered to be one of the all-time greats in the sport. Ironically, he was on the cover of that triathlon magazine we first picked up at the fitness center in Florida. That was another really cool aspect of the sport—to actually be in a race where you start shoulder-to-shoulder with the world's best. Amazingly, after over twenty-five years, that has not changed. The everyman distances of the sport still provide the exciting and motivating experience of being able to race the same races as the sport's elite.

Yes, as great as it was when we first got started, it is even better today. All the factors that attracted us to triathlon in the early days of the sport are even truer now. As easily accessible as the sport once was, it's many times more so today. There are many more races and likely to be many more within a short drive from your home. There is many times more information on how to train, what equipment you need, and resources, like the book you are now reading, to make it even easier. It is rare that this happens in a sport. Often athletes will say, "You should have been here in the good ol' days." But in this sport, while there were surely "good ol' days," they are even better today. This is truly the golden age of short course racing.

Okay, we know what you're thinking. Sure, short course triathlon and duathlon is something I would love to do. But I have family responsibilities, a challenging career, and all the other challenges of modern life; how can I train for and compete in multisport events?

We know how you feel, as we have heard this many times before—and once felt the same way ourselves. But what we have found is that it is absolutely achievable. In fact, if you do it right, everything in your life will be better as a result. Not only will you enjoy the great health and mental benefits of being a short course athlete, but your career and family life will benefit as well. The fitness, the healthy lifestyle, the motivation, it all carries over to your entire life, benefiting you and those around you.

The secret to success is to combine three crucial factors: highly effective training, highly efficient time management, and "been there, done that" knowledge. The following chapters will present proper training in great detail, as well as all the "been there, done that" knowledge for success in this sport. But first, in the following "IronFit Moment," we will explore the proven time management tips that have been the most helpful for experienced short course athletes. Then, throughout this book we will present the profiles of ten inspiring short course athletes. In addition to telling their motivating stories, we will also present many of their best time management approaches.

We continually learn of great new time management tips from our coached athletes. Many of these we will share in the ten athlete profiles in this book. But there are five specific time management approaches that are so universally employed by successful short course triathletes and duathletes that we will start our discussion on time management tips with what we call the "Big Five":

1. Train Time, Not Miles

The most successful time management tool we have experienced over the years is what we call "train time, not miles." All miles are not the same. Sometimes they take longer than expected. This makes estimating your training time more difficult. Also, an 8-mile run may be a 45-minute workout for one athlete and a 90-minute workout for another. Obviously, a training plan based in miles will not work for both of these athletes.

The most efficient way to train is by time, not distance. A 60-minute run is a 60-minute run. Put it in your day planner and plan around it just like any other appointment. All the training plans in this book are designated in time, not distance, to make planning your training time as easy as possible.

The "train time, not miles" approach is often a tough change to make for many athletes. After years of training by distance, it's hard for them to look at training in a new way and make such a fundamental change. Many athletes become what we jokingly refer to as "mileage junkies." They love the feeling of racking up mileage numbers in their training logs. But we encourage you to embrace this important concept. It will help you to greatly improve your time management and will lead to better performance and enjoyment of the sport.

(continued on next page)

(continued from previous page)

2. Indoor Training Options

While training outside is usually the most enjoyable for most athletes, it is usually not the most time efficient. The weather, darkness, setup time, and other factors can all place limitations on outdoor training. This is why many super-busy athletes do a lot of their training, especially their weekday training, indoors. You can jump on the treadmill or indoor bike at any time of the day and in any type of weather. Also, you can set up everything you need in advance of the workout and wear workout clothes suitable for indoor temperatures. For athletes living in colder climates, there is no need to bundle up with lots of layers, which is time consuming as well as inconvenient, and there is no need to train in risky and unsafe outside weather conditions. While almost all of our busiest coached athletes train outside over the weekend, many take advantage of efficient indoor training during the weekdays.

3. "Early Bird" Workouts

If at all possible, get most of your training in early. Not only are energy levels typically higher in the morning, but if you do train first thing in the morning you don't risk something unexpected arising during the day to derail your planned training sessions. Computers go down, traffic jams occur, bosses ask you to work late—you name it, it will happen. Many of the most successful busy athletes get up early, get their training in first, and then do not worry about it for the rest of the day. In fact, most comment on how great it feels. Knowing that you have it done makes you feel like the day has been a success before it has really even started.

4. Lunchtime Workouts

Midday workouts are another great time management opportunity for many athletes. This may not work for you depending on your work situation, but if you can squeeze in 45 minutes to an hour of training at lunchtime a few days a week, it greatly adds to your time efficiency. Some of our athletes have work responsibilities, like customer meetings, over lunch, and this may not always work. But most of them have at least a couple of open lunchtime slots per week when they can squeeze in a planned session. And most of our busy athletes report that their lunchtimes are at best dead time. They waste time, money, and they eat too much. A training session and a light lunch to bring back to the office is a much more efficient use of time.

5. Masters Swimming Program

This one requires a little luck. Not everyone has a local, convenient US Masters Swimming program, but if you do, it is a great time management resource. Masters Swimming programs typically have two or three scheduled sessions per week. All you need to do is to schedule around these times and then show up for each session. This is so much easier than trying to find open lane times for swimming at the pool and taking your chances on how crowded the pool will be when you get there. Your masters swim coach will have the workout planned for you, and the other swimmers in your lane will provide you with all the motivation you need.

If you have this resource, we suggest you take full advantage of it. If not, don't worry a bit. It will be a little more challenging in terms of time, but we have included everything you need in this book to get you prepared to swim in short course competitions.

Steve Levine has a busy lifestyle. He has been a highly successful doctor in osteopathic family medicine for over forty years. He and his wife have raised three grown children, and he now has three grandchildren. Steve is also an elite age group short course multisport athlete and swimmer who has been actively competing in the sport for more than fifteen years.

Steve Levine frequently wins his age group at short course races, road races, open water swims, and Masters Swimming meets, but you would never know it to talk to him. He carries himself with amazing humility. We are sure that he would scoff at us even referring to him as an elite athlete, but the fact that he has qualified for and will compete in both this year's USA Triathlon Sprint Distance National Championships and the US Masters Swimming National Championships, is all the proof you need. How many people do you know in their sixties who will be competing in the national championships in two sports this year? We are guessing that your list is pretty short.

Steve lives near the coast, and one of his favorite personal challenges is to do what we call "double race weekends." He will race an open water swim competition on a Saturday and then a triathlon on a Sunday (or vice versa) in the same weekend. The fact that he often wins his age group in both is secondary to him. He just loves the personal challenge and takes satisfaction in his double race weekends.

Steve credits his supportive wife and family for much of his success. But like most accomplished athletes, Steve also has great time management skills. In addition to utilizing many of the "Big Five" time management tips presented in this chapter, including "train in time, not miles," indoor training, "early bird" workouts, and Masters Swimming, Steve adds the following two great approaches:

Setting Up the Night Before: As Steve puts it, "I always pack my bag and lay out whatever I am going to eat or take with me the night before so in the morning I can just get right to the activity. Swim, bike, or run." This is a great approach. Have everything ready the night before. By doing so you will greatly enhance the chances that when your alarm goes off in the morning, you will get up and out the door and be into a highly productive training session before you know it.

Strategic Naps: Steve finds time to take short naps to reenergize between training, family, and career activities. This helps him to maximize the quality of his training sessions and to stay healthy overall. Most athletes make the mistake of undervaluing sleep. This is when our bodies repair themselves, build stronger, and reenergize.

Watch for Steve Levine this year at short course races, road races, open water swims, and swim meets, as he continues to amaze.

» The Eight Essential Short Course Distance Training Sessions

Success is the sum of small efforts, repeated day in and day out. —ROBERT COLLIER

This chapter presents the eight essential training sessions needed to optimally prepare for short course triathlons and duathlons. While these are not the training programs themselves, they are the essential building blocks we will use to design the perfect program.

One of the most common training mistakes we see is unfocused and non-purposeful training. Many athletes think that if they want to improve their swimming, cycling, and running they simply need to swim, cycle, and run more. So that's what they do. They fit in as many swims, bike sessions, and runs as they can, without any structure to their workouts. They throw a lot of training at the wall and see if anything sticks. This is what we call "junk training." Not only is it inefficient and risky for injury, but it also is ineffective in the long run.

Success in this sport is not just about swimming, cycling, and running every day and then showing up on race day to compete in a sprint or standard distance triathlon or duathlon. There are eight specific types of workouts that need to be included in an athlete's program to maximize training, with a specific method of execution for each. In this chapter we will clearly define each of these eight sessions in full detail and in a straightforward and easily understandable way. We explain the duration of each session, how frequently it should be completed, and at what level of training intensity. Most importantly, these workouts are fun. Training does not have to be drudgery. The essential eight sessions are designed to be both highly productive and highly enjoyable.

The standard and sprint triathlon and duathlon distance programs presented in chapters 6–9 use these eight essential training sessions and perfectly build them into each program to maximize the athlete's training benefit. We explain how these sessions are applied differently, depending on the distance and whether the athlete is training for triathlon or duathlon. We also fully explain each of the eight training sessions so that the athlete understands what he or she is doing and why. We put it all together for you, eliminating any guesswork.

Alice Hector, elite age group triathlete
James Mitchell Photography

The eight key workouts are the following:

1. *Transition Sessions (aka "Bricks")*

2. *Higher-Intensity Run Sessions*

3. *Higher-Intensity Bike Sessions*

4. *High-RPM Technique Spins*

5. *Long Aerobic Run*

6. *Long Bike Ride*

7. *The IronFit Swim Training Approach*

8. *Strategic Rest Days/Slide Days*

Following is an explanation of each of the essential eight training sessions.

1. TRANSITION SESSIONS

Transition sessions (aka "bricks") are workouts that include one or more brief periods between two sports, during which the athlete transitions from one sport to the other. The most common form this will take for triathletes is a bike-to-run transition. This usually includes a bike ride, followed by a quick change from cycling to running gear, and then a run.

A simple example of a transition session that you will see in the training programs in this book is the following:

Brick: 45 min Z2 Bike (QC) 15 min Z2 Run

We will fully present and explain the abbreviations and the heart rate zones used here later, but for now, in plain language, in the above example we begin by cycling for 45 minutes at a moderate heart rate. (Z2 is fully explained in chapter 5, but for now it is important only to understand that Z2 is a heart rate associated with a moderate level of effort.) Then we stop and quickly change from our cycling gear to our running gear (QC is explained in chapter 6, but for now it is important only to understand that it means a quick change of 5 minutes or less from the gear of one sport to the other). Last, we run for 15 minutes at a moderate heart rate.

This is the most basic example of a brick session, but as we will discuss, there are many possible versions of this highly productive workout. These can vary in length and in intensities. In most of the programs in this book, we will include one to two transition sessions per week.

Why do we present brick sessions first in our discussion? Simply because it is probably the most beneficial type of session to prepare for short course triathlon and duathlon. Being able to "run well off the bike" is a key element for short course success.

If you have not tried it yet, you will see that it is challenging to run at your best immediately after cycling. In addition to our leg muscles being fatigued from cycling, they have become used to performing in the circular cycling motion. Many of the same muscles are being used when we start to run, but they are being used in a different pattern. It takes a while for them to get used to running in an efficient way. The sooner they can do that the better. This is exactly what transition sessions do. They teach our bodies to quickly and efficiently transfer from efficient cycling to efficient running. This ability is crucial for short course triathlon success.

If you need to run for a couple of miles before getting "your running legs," you will not be very successful in a sprint triathlon with a run of 3.1 miles. Perhaps we can get away with a slower, more gradual transition in a longer triathlon, like a half or full Iron-distance race, but when it comes to short course we want to be able to run stronger and efficiently right from the start.

There is a need to train our bodies to transition from swimming to cycling as well, although it tends to be less difficult for most athletes, because swimming relies more on the arms than the legs. The legs do need to change from a kicking pattern to a circular cycling pattern, but the greater challenge in the swim-to-bike transition is the blood pooling effect caused by swimming.

After pumping blood to the muscles of the arms and shoulders for swimming, we jump on our bikes, almost completely resting our arms and shoulders. Immediately we start powering ourselves primarily with our legs. The blood now starts redirecting from the shoulders and arms to the legs. As a result, many athletes notice a slightly dizzy feeling and/or a "heavy legs" feeling when they start the bike. The fact that while we are swimming we are in a horizontal position, and then quickly rise to a vertical position as we exit the water, contributes to this feeling. As we cycle, this feeling gradually goes away as our bodies sort out the change from swimming to cycling.

While not as pronounced, the faster our bodies can acclimate to this change, the faster we can maximize our cycling speed.

While some athletes do actual swim-to-bike transition sessions, our suggestion for this one is to plan to have one of your cycling sessions right after your swim session one day a week. Bring your gear with you to the pool so you can change after your swim session—ideally within 5 minutes or less—and then get right out on your bike session. If there are indoor bikes at the same fitness center as your pool, this is another great way to approach it. After your swim session, you can quickly change to cycling clothes and jump right onto an exercise bike.

By doing this kind of quick swim-to-bike transition each week, your body will learn how to do it more efficiently, resulting in better racing results.

As you will see in the duathlon training programs in this book, we suggest double and triple transition sessions for duathlon racing success. These sessions help prepare duathletes to transition not only from bike to run, but also from run to bike, and back again.

A typical example of a double brick is the following:

Double Brick: 15 min Z2 Run (QC) 30 min Z2 Bike (QC) 15 min Z2 Run

In the above example, we begin by running for 15 minutes at a moderate heart rate. Then we stop and quickly change from our running gear to our cycling gear. Next we cycle for 30 minutes at a moderate heart rate. Then we stop and quickly change from our cycling gear to our running gear. Last, we run for 15 minutes at a moderate heart rate.

A typical example of a triple brick is the following:

Triple Brick: 15 min Z2 Run (QC) 15 min Z2 Bike (QC)
15 min Z2 Run (QC) 15 min Z2 Bike

In the above example, we begin by running for 15 minutes at a moderate heart rate. Then we stop and quickly change from our running gear to our cycling gear. Next we cycle for 15 minutes at a moderate heart rate. Then we stop and quickly change from our cycling gear to our running gear and run for 15 minutes at a moderate heart rate. We stop again and quickly change from our running gear to our cycling gear. We conclude the session by cycling for 15 minutes at a moderate heart rate.

Double and triple bricks are highly effective in duathlon training.

TIP: *While double and triple bricks are designed specifically for duathletes, it is sometimes a fun change of pace for triathletes to substitute them for regular bricks. Many of our coached athletes who live in colder winter climates like to use them for indoor training. A 1-hour double or triple brick can be a fun change from a 1-hour single brick when training indoors. You can go back and forth using a treadmill and a stationary bike trainer. The time passes quickly, and it is an enjoyable and productive training session.*

2. HIGHER-INTENSITY RUN SESSIONS

Short course triathlons and duathlons are completed at a much higher intensity level than long course races, like the half and full Iron-distances. Not surprisingly then, the training has a much greater emphasis on higher-intensity training sessions. While aerobic runs build our aerobic running base, higher-intensity run sessions build our speed and strength, which are the key to short course racing success.

Higher-intensity run sessions come in two forms: Z4 Inserts and Z4 Repeats.

Z4 Inserts: The following is an example of a higher-intensity Z4 Insert running session:

60 min Z2 (at 45 min, insert 5 min Z4)

We will fully present and explain the abbreviations and the heart rate zones used here later, but for now, in plain language, in the above example, in this 60-minute run we start off in Heart Rate Z2 (moderate intensity) and hold this heart rate zone for the first 45 minutes of the workout. Then, at 45 minutes, we increase our effort enough to raise our heart rate into Heart Rate Z4 (higher intensity). We then hold our heart rate there in Z4 for the duration of this 5-minute Z4 Insert. After the insert, we reduce our effort enough to allow our heart rate to return to Z2 (moderate intensity) for the remaining 10 minutes of the run.

The higher-intensity Z4 Inserts are a relatively long higher-intensity effort. In fact, 5 minutes, as in this example, is on the low end of the range. We use running Z4 Inserts of up to 15 minutes in the training programs later in this book.

Z4 Repeats: Now that we have discussed higher-intensity Z4 Inserts, the following is an example of a higher-intensity Z4 Repeats running session:

60 min Z2 (at 10 min, insert 10 x 2 min Z4 @ 1 min jog)

In this 60-minute run session, we start off running in Heart Rate Z2 (moderate intensity). Then, 10 minutes into the run, we increase our effort level enough to bring our heart rate up into Heart Rate Z4 (higher intensity) for a total of 2 minutes. Then, exactly 2 minutes from the time we first started trying to achieve Z4, we slow down enough to bring our heart rate down into an easy (low intensity) jog. As soon as we have jogged for exactly 1 minute, we again increase our effort level sufficiently to raise our heart rate back up into Z4 for 2 minutes. We continue this same sequence of 2 minutes of Z4 followed by 1 minute of easy jog for a total of ten complete cycles. Once we have completed all ten times, we adjust our effort level to again return to Z2 and complete the remainder of the 60-minute run (which is 20 minutes) in Z2.

Higher-intensity run sessions are highly effective training sessions for short course triathlon and duathlon. We will include one to two of these sessions per week in most of the programs in this book.

3. HIGHER-INTENSITY BIKE SESSIONS

As discussed in the previous section about higher-intensity run training, short course triathlons and duathlons are completed at a much higher intensity level than long course races like the half and full Iron-distances. Accordingly, the training needs to have a much greater emphasis on higher-intensity training as well. Similar to the situation with running, aerobic cycling sessions build our aerobic cycling base, but it is higher-intensity bike sessions that build our speed and strength, the keys to short course success.

Higher-intensity bike sessions come in three forms: Z4 Inserts, Z4 Repeats, and Z4 Hill Repeats.

Z4 Inserts: The following is an example of a higher-intensity Z4 Insert bike session:

1:30 hr Z2 (at 1:15, insert 10 min Z4)

We will fully present and explain the abbreviations and the heart rate zones used here later, but for now, in plain language, in the above example, in this 90-minute bike session we start off in Heart Rate Z2 (moderate intensity) and hold this heart rate zone for the first 1 hour and 15 minutes of the workout. Then, at the 1 hour and 15-minute point, we increase our effort enough to raise our heart rate into Heart Rate Z4 (higher intensity). We then hold our heart rate in Z4 for the duration of this 10-minute Z4 Insert. After the insert, we reduce our effort sufficiently to allow our heart rate to return to Z2 (moderate intensity) for the remaining 5 minutes of the bike session.

The higher-intensity Z4 Inserts are a relatively long higher-intensity effort. In fact, 10 minutes, as in this example, is on the mid-to-low end of the range. We use cycling Z4 Inserts up to 30 minutes in the training programs later in this book. This is significantly longer than the 15-minute maximum for these sessions on the running side.

In the programs later in this book, we will often use bike Z4 Inserts just before the run portion of some transition sessions. The following is an example of this:

Brick: 60 min Z2 (at 45 min insert 10 min Z4) Bike (QC), 30 min Z2 Run

This is a great type of session for triathlon and duathlon race preparation. As we mentioned earlier, one of the great benefits of transition (brick) sessions is that they teach our bodies to quickly transition from cycling to running. We can challenge our bodies even more by including a Z4 Insert right before the transition. As a result, this is an important and beneficial session when properly designed into an overall program.

Z4 Repeats: *Now that we have discussed higher-intensity Z4 Inserts, the following is an example of a higher-intensity Z4 Repeats cycling session:*

60 min Z2 (at 10 min, insert 6 x 4 min Z4 @ 2 min spin)

In this 60-minute cycling session, we start off cycling in Heart Rate Z2 (moderate intensity). Then, 10 minutes into the session, we increase our effort level sufficiently to raise our heart rate up into Heart Rate Z4 (higher intensity) for a total of 4 minutes. Then, exactly 4 minutes from the time we first started trying to achieve Z4, we slow down enough to bring our heart rate into an easy Heart Rate Z1 (low intensity) spin. As soon as we have spun for exactly 2 minutes, we again increase our effort level enough to raise our heart rate back up into Z4 for 4 minutes. We continue this same sequence of 4 minutes of Z4 followed by 2 minutes of easy spin for a total of six complete cycles. Once we have completed the six cycles, we adjust our effort level to again return to Z2 and complete the remainder of the 60-minute ride (which is 14 minutes) in Z2.

Z4 Hill Repeats: *Z4 Hill Repeats are a slight variation from Z4 Repeats. They are great for developing cycling power and are especially helpful when training for a race with a hilly bike course. The following is an example of a Z4 Hill Repeat session:*

60 min Z2 (at 10 min, insert 5 x 3 min Z4 Hill Repeats @ easy spin back down)

We start this 60-minute workout by cycling in Heart Rate Z2 (moderate intensity) for 10 minutes. Ideally, there is a good training hill in your area that you can cycle to the base of within this 10-minute period. Then, at exactly 10 minutes into this session, we cycle up the hill in Heart Rate Z4 (higher intensity) for 3 minutes. Once completing the 3 minutes, we safely turn around and cycle easily back to the bottom of the hill. We repeat this same sequence up and down the hill five times. Then we complete the time that remains in the 60-minute ride in Z2. The amount of this final portion in Z2 will vary depending on how long it took us to cycle easily back down the hill after each time we cycled up the hill for 3 minutes.

These sessions are very challenging, and we suspect you may be cursing us while you are doing them, but there is nothing better for building your anaerobic cycling power and speed. Furthermore, there is nothing better for building your hill climbing strength and confidence as well.

Higher-intensity cycling sessions are highly productive training sessions for short course triathlon and duathlon. We will include one to two of these sessions per week in most of the programs in this book.

TIP: *You may have noticed that while we discussed Z4 Hill Repeats as one of the higher-intensity sessions on the cycling side, we did not include a similar type of session on the running side. It has been our experience that running Z4 Hill Repeats can be risky for injury for most athletes, and the risk is usually greater than the reward. Having said this, if you are an athlete who rarely gets injured and feel strongly that you would like to include these types of run sessions, we provide guidance on how to do so later in this book. We also provide alternative approaches to building your hill running strength.*

4. HIGH-RPM TECHNIQUE SPINS

High-RPM spins are cycling sessions where we spin the pedals at a relatively high cadence of about 100–105 revolutions per minute (RPM), but we do so at a low-intensity effort level with a heart rate of Z1. To do this we must be in a very easy gear (low resistance) to allow us to spin the pedals quickly while keeping our heart rate down at a fairly low level. These sessions are best completed either cycling on flat terrain or on an indoor bike trainer. We live in a relatively hilly area so we mostly do these on the trainer.

The following is an example of a high-RPM technique spin session:

60 min Z1 (at 100–105 revolutions per minute)

Most athletes do not realize the great value of these high-RPM spins because of the comfortably low heart rate. In typical "triathlete logic," if it doesn't hurt, it cannot possibly have any benefit. After working with hundreds and hundreds of endurance athletes, we often have to laugh at this good old triathlete reasoning because, of course, this is not the case.

In fact, high-RPM sessions are truly synergistic training and have two major benefits: improved technique and active recovery.

High-RPM spins help us to develop highly efficient cycling form. We want to be spinning the pedals in a circular pattern, not mashing them down and pulling them up. "Spinning circles" is the most efficient way to cycle. The important point is, however, that it is very difficult to achieve a high cadence like 100–105 RPM unless you are spinning circles. If you find that you have difficulty spinning your pedals at this high of a cadence, this might be an especially important training session for you. But even if you are very accomplished at spinning circles at a high cadence, these sessions are beneficial in building and maintaining good cycling form.

In addition to improving technique, these are excellent sessions for recovery. The combination of the high cadence and low resistance helps legs to recover and freshen for the next day's training. As you will see in the training programs in this book, when these sessions are included, they are usually positioned among the other workouts of the week where they can maximize this benefit—often after a very hard session and/or right before going into a rest day. They serve to jump-start our recovery and send us into our rest day with our bodies ready to fully recover and absorb all the good benefits of our training.

High-RPM spin sessions are helpful for short course athletes. Along with our higher-intensity cycling workouts, these sessions work to build an unbeatable combination of speed and efficiency. Accordingly, most training programs in this book include one high-RPM spin session per week.

5. LONG AEROBIC RUN

The definition of a long aerobic run is usually any low- to moderate-intensity run of 90 minutes or more, but for purposes of training for short course triathlons and duathlons, we consider a long aerobic run to be any run of 60 minutes or more that is completed at a moderate heart rate. Not needing as many longer, time-consuming training sessions is one of the many advantages of short course training versus long course training. We will explain heart rate zones in chapter 5 and show you how to calculate your personal zones, but for now, our moderate heart zones will be Zone 1 and Zone 2 (Z1 and Z2).

Our long aerobic runs are to be completed at a moderate level of effort and are designed to build our aerobic capacity. Many athletes make the mistake of going too hard on all their workouts. As we will discuss later in this book, this results in performance stagnation and even injury. Our foundation needs to be a solid aerobic base, and that is exactly what these longer, more moderate runs provide.

Most athletes find long aerobic runs to be fun. There is not the pressure of higher-intensity sessions. Holding a moderate level of effort is much easier than holding a high level of effort. While we often need to get mentally up for a higher-intensity training session, this is not the case for low- to moderate-intensity sessions. Long aerobic runs are much more relaxing mentally and physically. Old-school runners often refer to these sessions as LSD: long slow distance. If you love running—and we do—these can be the most enjoyable sessions. You will find that most of the training programs in this book include one long aerobic run per week.

6. LONG BIKE RIDE

The definition of a long ride is similar to the long aerobic run. It is typically any ride of 90 minutes or more at a moderate, or mostly moderate, intensity. For purposes of training for short course triathlons and duathlons, we will consider it any ride of 60 minutes or more that is completed at a mostly moderate heart rate. We will explain heart rate zones in chapter 5 and show you how to calculate yours, but for now, our moderate heart zones will be Zone 1 and Zone 2 (Z1 and Z2).

Most of our long rides are to be completed at a moderate level of effort and are designed primarily to build our aerobic capacity. Many athletes make the mistake of going too hard on all their workouts. As we will discuss later in this book, this results in performance stagnation and even injury. Our foundation needs to be a solid aerobic base, and that is exactly what these longer, mostly moderate rides provide.

The one exception is that sometimes a Z4 Insert (higher intensity) is included in these long rides. You will see examples of this in the training programs later in his book. When that is the case, it is important to work the Z4 Insert hard, resulting in a higher heart rate, but to keep the remainder of the ride moderate and fully aerobic.

Long rides are great sessions for getting outside and enjoying nature and the outdoors. While many athletes do the higher-intensity sessions as indoor training for time management and efficiency, the long rides are great to do outside.

Long rides are another highly beneficial training session for short course triathlons and duathlons, and you will find that most of the training programs in this book include one long ride per week.

7. THE IRONFIT SWIM TRAINING APPROACH

Swimming in short course triathlon is certainly an endurance sport—no question about it. But swimming is far more reliant on technique than are cycling and running. As we like to joke, swimming has more in common with golf and tennis than it does with cycling and running. The reason for this is that while technique is important for running and cycling, in swimming it is the major determinant of performance.

Water is nine times denser than air, so passing through it takes far more energy. Athletes with poor, inefficient technique end up wasting valuable energy on the swim, leaving them much more tired than optimal when they move on to the bike and run. As we like to say, triathlon is a finite equation. What you use during the swim takes away from what is available for the bike and run. Ultimately, you want to achieve the optimal level of effort in each of the three sports to maximize performance. The key to triathlon is to learn how to swim efficiently and to get from point "a" to point "b" as quickly and as efficiently as possible.

In general, in our Masters Swimming programs over the years and in the many masters programs we have visited during our travels, we find that athletes swim too hard too much of the time. It is as if athletes are training for one all-out swimming effort, as opposed to the first leg of a three-sport race.

The approach we suggest to our trained athletes is to focus on efficiency over speed. The beauty of this approach is that over time they find that they achieve both efficiency and speed. While they focus on technique, they gradually become faster as well, without increasing their effort level. Any time you can increase speed without increasing effort is golden in the sport of triathlon.

Having a good local US Masters Swimming program with an experienced open water coach is a great asset. If you are fortunate enough to have that available to you, you may want to take full advantage of it. But if you do not have a great program nearby, do not worry. The swim sessions, technique guidance, and training approach we present in this book are all you need to improve your swim and get you ready for short course competitions.

We suggest swim training sessions in the following format:

- Warm-up

- Technique Drills

- Main Sets

- Technique Drills

- Cooldown

A simple example of a swim session in this format is the following:

200 meter warm-up, 6 x 50 meter drills, main set: 10 x 100 meters
@ 15 seconds rest, 6 x 50 meter drills, 200 cooldown

Note how the main set is sandwiched by technique drills. The warm-up, drills, and cooldown are at a 65–75 percent perceived effort, and even the main sets are only at an 80–85 percent effort, and sometimes up to 90–95 percent for shorter efforts. We really do not suggest any "all-out" swimming because this leads to fatigued, sloppy form. We want to keep everything fresh and efficient.

By the way, in a triathlon you should never be swimming "all-out." This can often spoil your race. You will start the bike too fatigued and will not be maximizing the finite equation we mentioned earlier. We train to be efficient because that is how we want to race.

This proven approach to triathlon swimming is built into all the training programs in the book, and there are dozens of suggested swim sessions presented for your use.

8. STRATEGIC REST DAYS/SLIDE DAYS

"Type A" triathletes do not like to take rest days. We understand this, as we once felt the same way. We thought that if we were not training every day, we were not improving. What we have come to understand is that strategic rest days greatly increase an athlete's success.

In fact, proper rest days are absolutely essential to optimizing our training. Our bodies simply need the proper amount of time to recover and absorb the good benefits of our training. Many athletes cannot ever get their minds around this, and they are continually frustrated by injury and performance stagnation. The rest day should be considered no different than any other key workout. With our coached athletes we often jokingly refer to it as "the non-workout workout."

There are one or two weekly rest days strategically built into all the training programs presented in this book. We say "strategically" because they are placed among the other workouts in the week at a point where they will prove most beneficial.

Another great benefit of having planned rest days is that they also help with time management. As you will see in the training programs in this book, we refer to our rest days as "Rest Days/Slide Days." In other words, we encourage you to use rest days to help adjust your training to be able to complete it all each week. You can "slide" your rest days forward or back by one day to help your training schedule work better around your overall schedule on a particular week.

For example, if Monday is your usual Rest Day/Slide Day but you realize you have a commitment on Tuesday that will prevent you from training that day, simply slide Tuesday's training session forward to Monday. Designate Tuesday as your rest day for that week.

All the workouts are designed in a specific order for good reason, and we want to avoid "flipping" them during the week. Instead, if something comes up and you cannot get a planned workout in on the specified day, simply slide your Rest Day/Slide Day forward or back one day to accommodate the situation. This allows you to get all your training sessions in while keeping them in the order in which they are intended, and still getting the benefit of your rest days.

The three 12-week training programs (Competitive, Intermediate, and "Just Finish") for the standard distance triathlon, three 8-week training programs for the sprint distance triathlon, three 10-week training programs for the standard distance duathlon, and three 6-week training programs for the sprint distance duathlon presented in this book all use these eight essential training sessions and build them into each program to maximize the athlete's training benefit. We have designed these programs to entirely eliminate the guesswork. Just follow the program each day while enjoying the challenge and the journey.

Everything was going according to plan. In fact, Nataliya Schouten was on an amazing winning streak. Not only was she healthy and clicking off her training day after day, but she seemed to be setting personal records every time she raced.

On May 23, Don's email to Nataliya began with:

"Hi Nataliya, Congratulations again on all of your amazing recent racing success . . . PRs in both the 10K and Half . . . AWESOME!! I am so happy for you and so proud of you . . ."

Unfortunately, Nataliya's email back to Don had an ominous tone:

"Hi Don . . . on a not so happy note, I got bad news on Tuesday indicating I may be having some major health issues. I am going for more testing today, and I hope it is OK. However, we may have to modify my training schedule accordingly. If the diagnosis is confirmed, I will most likely not be able to do any of the races this summer. I hope for the best though. Nataliya"

While Don also hoped for the best, the next email he received from Nataliya confirmed his worst fears:

"Hi Don, I just found out I have breast cancer. I will be undergoing a surgery and possibly radiation and chemotherapy. My oncologist thinks I can continue exercising but I have to cut it in half. So I haven't done anything since my race. Can you please change my plan to make it more maintenance at this time? I am going to continue training but I will not be able to race until cancer is gone. Have you had an athlete continuing training with cancer? Nataliya"

While Don felt shocked and saddened by the news, he also felt inspired by this amazing athlete. After having received what may have been the worst news of her life, she did not appear to be at all discouraged. In fact, she not only was committed to persevering over this challenge, but was hoping and planning on training right through it. Nataliya clearly did not view her illness as a time to fold up her tent and go home. Instead, she saw it as a time to dig deep and battle through. It was clear to Don that she was a person of incredible strength and positive attitude.

Don was not the only one to notice this. In fact, everyone around her quickly realized this as well. A couple of weeks later, after Nataliya had surgery and started going through treatments, she wrote,

"I am in good spirits and surprised everyone with my iron will and positive attitude. I know you will find it funny (as nobody else does), when my doctor announced I have cancer, the first words out of my mouth were: 'Darn it, I will not be able to do a half Ironman in July, will I?' My doctor replied with 'This really should be the least of your worries now.'"

At her request, we introduced Nataliya to other athletes we coach who had successfully survived cancer and returned to competitive athletics. While she gained strength from these contacts, she also reached out to others still going through treatment to help share her strength and support with them as well.

As we are sure you have suspected at this point, not only did Nataliya beat cancer, but she did it in almost record time and was back into competition in amazingly short order.

On September 24, less than four months after her initial diagnosis, Nataliya celebrated her victory over cancer by completing the super sprint distance Lake Geneva Triathlon in Williams Bay, Wisconsin. It was an amazing personal victory and never did a sprint distance triathlon feel so good!

Like most successful triathletes, Nataliya has become an expert at time management. She utilizes many of the "Big Five" time management techniques from chapter 1, especially "train time, not miles," "early bird" training, and indoor training. Nataliya found "train time, not miles" to be the most challenging to adopt. As Nataliya puts it, "I was a 'mileage junkie' before I joined your program. This required me to change my entire mindset and approach to training. I attribute a lot

(continued on next page)

(continued from previous page)

of my athletic success to this approach since it took the 'mileage' pressure away and let me concentrate on my workouts better."

In addition to using several of the "Big Five," Nataliya has developed many of her own great time management approaches. One of the most impressive is how she managed her ever-changing energy levels while battling cancer. As Nataliya told us, "Since I was diagnosed with cancer, I had an additional challenge I had to overcome to successfully and consistently continue my training. I developed brain fog and fatigue as a result of surgery and medications administered that lasted several months. There were many times I had no energy to get out of bed, let alone exercise. I had to completely revamp my training time because "early bird" training was not always an option. I call my approach 'no excuses when feeling good.' Basically, I figured out the windows of opportunity for me to exercise during the day. I had two or three time slots available depending on the day. I would set the alarm for my usual training time in the morning. If I woke up and had no energy to train, I would use my next training time slot when I felt better to make up my training time. I told myself if I feel good during one of my designated training windows, I have no excuse to not use it. This approach worked very well for me and made my recovery miraculously quick."

Watch for Nataliya Schouten at sprint and standard distance triathlons in the future. She is that very fast triathlete smiling all the way!

» Short Course Distance Training Cycles and Training Races

Change your thoughts and you change your world. —NORMAN VINCENT PEALE

One of the most common mistakes we see with self-coached short course athletes is that they don't take full advantage of training cycles. They pretty much train the same way most of the time regardless of whether their next race is in five months, five weeks, or five days. They either repeat the same group of workouts continuously year-round or they do whatever workouts the local triathlon club, running club, cycling club, or masters swim program are offering.

If the local triathlon club does a long ride every Sunday morning, you do a long ride every Sunday morning. If the local running club does a higher-intensity track session every Wednesday evening, you do a higher-intensity track session every Wednesday evening. While these sessions may be the optimal workout for you some of the time, it is unlikely that they are the right workouts for you all of the time, or even most of the time. And sometimes, they may be exactly the opposite of what you should be doing to maximize your performance.

Typically, this approach of participating in whatever group training sessions are available to you locally will have some initial effectiveness, but then fitness improvements soon level off. This leads to frustration. What used to work no longer does. This is a wasteful and inefficient way to train and usually leads to performance stagnation at best and injury at worse. This approach does not take advantage of the power of training cycles and our bodies' natural way of becoming stronger and faster. A much better way to train is by taking advantage of the magic of training cycles.

THE THREE TRAINING CYCLES

There are three training cycles that occur simultaneously in a great overall training plan: the weekly training cycle, the "A Race" training cycle, and the annual training cycle. If built correctly into your training program, training cycles provide truly synergistic training that will help you to break through to new levels of performance.

This is why properly designing the optimal training plan is so challenging. Each individual workout in a training plan should not stand alone. Instead, it should be designed to be the optimal workout to maximize the training benefit within all three training cycles. Each workout selected for a specific day should be the best possible one in conjunction with each of the other training sessions around it, to maximize the training benefit within all three training cycles.

As you will see, the three training cycles work together to maximize racing performance and help keep an athlete improving year after year.

WEEKLY TRAINING CYCLE

The weekly training cycle is our weekly pattern of training sessions—the actual sequence in which we do our workouts and on which day of the week. This doesn't mean that we do the exact same workout on the same day of each week. It means we generally do the same type of workout on the same day of most weeks. There are two reasons why this makes sense.

First, our workouts need to be properly ordered and spaced to maximize their effectiveness. A well-designed weekly training cycle with proper ordering and spacing of workouts will result in truly synergistic training. However, just doing your workouts randomly throughout the week is more likely to result in performance stagnation and/or injury.

Alice Hector, elite age group triathlete
James Mitchell Photography

Second, your training schedule needs to efficiently fit into your overall schedule, including your work, family, and other responsibilities. Having a regular weekly training cycle helps you to better plan around your workouts and better coordinate your training with all your other responsibilities.

All the training programs in this book are designed to maximize the benefit of the weekly training cycle.

"A RACE" TRAINING CYCLE

The "A Race" training cycle is centered on one specific major race coming up. Each "A Race" cycle can range from several weeks to several months, and while it may include some additional races, it is primarily focused on preparing for one major race. The training programs in chapters 6–9 are examples of "A Race" training cycles. They can be adjusted to include some possible training races (e.g., a road race, a cycling time trial, an open water swim, or another triathlon or duathlon), but the entire cycle is geared toward preparing for and maximizing performance at one specific "A Race."

Most athletes will have from one to five "A Race" training cycles in a year. Because short course racing requires less time to prepare for and recover from, most short course athletes tend to be at the higher end of this range.

"A Race" training cycles include various specific training phases. The programs in chapters 6–9 all suggest a base building phase of four to eight weeks before beginning the actual program. This phase will be practically all aerobic (Heart Rate Z1 to Z2) and will focus on working with the athlete's body to gradually and safely build his or her aerobic base and endurance. Typically, the base building phase will gradually build the athlete's training hours up to the approximate hours in the first week of the training program.

Once the base has been established, each program will then introduce higher-intensity training, and then both the higher-intensity portions and overall durations will gradually build. These will be our most challenging weeks as we focus on strength, endurance, and speed. This is the peak training phase of the "A Race" training cycle.

Then, with seven to nine days to go prior to the "A Race," depending on the program, we will transition into our pre-race taper phase. Most athletes don't properly approach the pre-race taper phase. It's not the time to squeeze in any training you missed. As we like to say at this point, "The hay is in the barn." The taper is the time for the athlete to get rested, sharp, and race-ready. We want to gather our energy both physically and mentally and prepare ourselves for a 100 percent effort on race day.

ANNUAL TRAINING CYCLE

The annual training cycle is the big picture. It's your road map for preparing for and achieving all your goals for the entire year. It is likely to include from one to five "A Race" cycles, and it is also likely to include an off-season training and maintenance phase (which is covered in chapter 16). For some athletes, their annual training cycle may even change which sport it focuses on throughout the year. For example, while an athlete's "A Races" may be short course triathlons in the spring and summer, they may be road races in the fall and indoor swim meets in the winter.

The important point is that all three training cycles need to work together to maximize an athlete's racing performances, to help keep the athlete healthy, and to help keep the athlete improving year after year. As coaches, when we design our athletes' training schedule, we always want to be looking at this big picture. We don't want to just design a workout that seems to fit in today. What we really want to do is design each workout with all three cycles in mind. We want it to be the best training session for our weekly cycle, our "A Race" cycle, and our annual cycle. When we can accomplish this, we have truly synergistic and beneficial training.

MAXIMIZING THE BENEFIT OF TRAINING RACES

As mentioned earlier, "A Race" training cycles typically include additional races other than the "A Race" itself. These races, however, should be selected with a purpose in mind, and they should be designed to contribute to our preparation for the "A Race," not take away from it.

For example, if you have never swum an open water race before, it would obviously make sense to include one in your preparation before you attempt your first short course triathlon. Doing so would give you valuable open water experience and greater confidence on race day.

To take an extreme example on the other side: If you have never run a road race before, it would not be a good idea to schedule a marathon for the weekend before your short course triathlon or duathlon. It would ruin your planned pre-race taper phase, and instead of being rested, physically fresh, and mentally sharp on race day, you would more likely be tired, stiff, and sore.

The point is that the type of practice race and its timing are key. We will now consider the possible race options, whether or not they are a good fit for you, and, if so, how best to build them into your training plan.

For most athletes, there are up to four types of optional training races to consider including during your training programs. These are a road race, a bike time trial, an open water swim, or another short course triathlon or duathlon. Depending on the athlete, each race has the potential of providing specific elements that will benefit the athlete in his or her "A Race" preparation. Of course, each race needs to be properly timed and built into the athlete's training program in a way that makes the program work best overall.

In the following sections, we will present each of the four possible practice races and provide information to help you to decide whether or not you should include them. If you do include them, we explain how best to build them into your training schedule. We will also provide tips to help you locate suitable races in your geographical area and also suggest substitutions if you cannot locate the right race at the right time.

ROAD RACES

Road races are often not a high-priority practice race for most triathletes, as most triathletes come from a running background and have plenty of road racing experience. These athletes are usually best served to skip this one, as continued training, not racing, would be more beneficial. But for those who have never run a race before, it's a great confidence builder to complete a short road race prior to a short course triathlon. While the same generally holds true for duathlon, road races are of greater value in duathlon training, as typically more than half your time in a duathlon is spent running.

If you do decide that a practice road race is right for you, we generally suggest a 10K for standard distance triathletes and duathletes, and a 5K for sprint distance triathletes and duathletes.

In chapter 6, we will present more suggestions on how to adjust your training program to properly include a road race. Later in this chapter we provide tips on locating an appropriate race near you.

CYCLING TIME TRIALS

Cycling time trials can be a helpful practice race for some triathletes and duathletes. These are usually structured as timed 100 percent solo efforts, and many cycling clubs across the country offer these competitions. While you can, of course, do a 100 percent cycling effort on your own if you prefer, an organized event will usually provide a safer closed-road situation and the added motivation of friendly competition. This is something to consider if you do not have a great deal of bike racing experience.

If you do decide that a practice cycling time trial is right for you, we generally suggest a distance of around 10–40 km for standard distance triathletes and duathletes, and 5–25 km for sprint distance triathletes and duathletes.

In chapter 6, we will present more suggestions on how to adjust your training program to properly include a cycling time trial. Later in this chapter we provide tips on locating an appropriate race near you.

OPEN WATER SWIMS

Obviously, practice open water swim competitions are not suggested for duathletes, but for triathletes who do not come from a swimming background, these are usually very beneficial. If swimming is your weakest of the three sports, we highly suggest you try to include an open water swim if possible. Even if you are a strong swimmer, there is a big difference between swimming in a pool and open water, and you may still benefit from one.

If you do decide a practice open water swim competition is right for you, we generally suggest a distance of around 750 meters (about 0.5 mile) to 1.5 km (about 1 mile) for sprint and standard distance triathletes, respectively. The greatest challenge when looking for a race, however, may be logistics. We have been fortunate to live near the ocean and lakes and always have a large selection of open water races available to us. Depending on where you live and your proximity to open water, this may or may not be a realistic option for you.

In chapter 6, we will present more suggestions on how to adjust your training program to properly include an open water swim competition. Later in this chapter we provide tips on locating an appropriate race near you.

SPRINT DISTANCE TUNE-UPS FOR STANDARD DISTANCE RACES

For those training for a standard distance triathlon or duathlon, a sprint distance triathlon or duathlon may be a helpful practice race. This is especially true for newer short course athletes who have not raced many or any triathlons or duathlons before—though less from the standpoint of conditioning and more from the standpoint of experience and testing out all your race day routines: pre-race, race, and post-race. It's a great opportunity to practice everything just like you plan to on race day and then take a much higher confidence level with you into your standard distance "A Race."

In chapter 6, we will present more suggestions on how to adjust your training program to properly include a sprint distance competition. In the next section of this chapter, we provide tips on locating an appropriate race near you.

LOCATING PRACTICE RACES

However many of these training races you decide to include in your training program, our suggestion is to try to keep it as simple as possible. Trips to races involving a lot of travel time and expense may not be worth it. Try to find practice races in your area that you may even be able to drive to the morning of the race. We are lucky to live in an area where all four of these racing options are frequently available within an hour's drive from our home. We realize that is not the case for a lot of athletes. To the extent possible, try to minimize the travel time and expense and weigh the pros and cons before signing up for a race far out of your area.

There are surely great local sources for race information in your area. These include race listing websites, local running and cycling clubs, bike shops, and the local US Masters Swimming program. There are also some good sources that cover races across the United States and beyond. Here are a few to consider:

Road Race Events

- Coolrunning.com

- Runningintheusa.com

- Runnersworld.com

Cycling Time Trial Events

- Active.com

- USAcycling.org

- Cyclingnews.com

Open Water Swimming Events

- Active.com

- Openwaterswimming.com

- USMS.org

Triathlon and Duathlon Events

- Active.com

- Trifind.com

- USAtriahlon.org

For athletes based outside North America, we have included additional websites in Appendix B.

» IRONFIT SUCCESS STORY:
Bryan Mendelson

Bryan Mendelson has a demanding career in automotive management, and he and his wife have four children—three of whom are triplets. That is surely enough to keep anyone extremely busy, but Bryan has also been a successful endurance athlete and triathlete for over ten years.

Even after ten years, Bryan continues to increase his fitness and take his performances to new levels. Bryan has successfully competed in all distances of triathlon from sprint to Iron-distance and has had success at all levels, including top ten finishes in sprint races and top two finishes in long course. Bryan also excels at road racing and recently set a new personal best in the marathon.

How does Bryan do it? A demanding career, four children including triplets, and he continues to not only make it look relatively easy, but also raises the bar.

As with many successful endurance athletes, Bryan is a master of time management.

As one of our coached athletes, he trains by time, not distance, and also utilizes the other "Big Five" time management techniques presented in chapter 1, especially "early bird" workouts and indoor training.

Bryan gets up early most days and gets his training sessions in before going to work. He enjoys the satisfaction of having his workout accomplished before the day has even begun, and he avoids the risk of some unanticipated event during the day that prevents him from getting his training in. Bryan lays out the necessary clothing and equipment the night before so he can wake up and get quickly into his training session.

Bryan lives in the northeastern United States, so cold weather and daylight training hours are often challenges, especially during the winter. Bryan does a portion of his training indoors, which allows him to train around weather and daylight issues, and is a more efficient way to complete morning sessions.

In addition to the "Big Five," Bryan also utilizes the following great approaches:

Planning Ahead: Bryan carefully plans ahead by considering his training, work, and family schedule together, and he identifies conflicts early. This allows him the necessary time to make smart adjustments that will keep everything working together smoothly.

Utilizing Rest Day/Slide Days: Part of his planning success is his effective use of Rest Day/Slide Days. Bryan uses the approach described earlier about how to slide rest days forward or back in his schedule to make everything fit in.

Focus on Nutrition: Bryan also has a consistent focus on good nutrition, both in terms of molding his body for endurance sports success and also consuming the right things at the right times to energize his body before training sessions, to sustain his energy during sessions, and for recovery after sessions.

Watch for Bryan Mendelson at the races this year, continually building his performances and making the endurance sports lifestyle look easy.

The Crucial Training Principles for Short Course Success

The five S's of sports training are: stamina, speed, strength, skill, and spirit; but the greatest of these is spirit. —KEN DOHERTY

There are three crucial training principles that will greatly increase your potential for short course racing success. To embrace them you will eliminate years of trial and error and possibly even injury. We wish we fully understood these three principles over twenty-five years ago. We are sure we would have avoided countless setbacks and re-starts along our own multisport journey.

As you will see, these principles have been built into all of the twelve training programs presented in this book. We guess you could say that you don't really need to bother separately with them. Yet they are so important we suggest that you read this to help you approach each type of session correctly and with a clearer understanding of how the individual sessions of each training week are not only interconnected, but dependent on each other.

The three crucial principles we will present are the following:

- Overload Principle

- Training Volume

- Hard Day/Easy Day

We will start with the most important of all, the overload principle.

OVERLOAD PRINCIPLE

Probably the most common error we see self-trained athletes make is not embracing the overload principle in their training. Often the type of people who get into a sport like triathlon or duathlon are referred to as "Type A" personalities. They are driven to achieve their goals and they believe hard work and sacrifice are the way to get there. We, of course, admire them for this, but unfortunately this positive quality drifts into a mindset of "more is always better" and the "no pain, no gain" approach. We often joke that many triathletes and duathletes think that if they are not suffering they can't be getting better.

Don understands this entirely as he used to feel the same way early in his endurance sports career. He believed that outworking everyone else, even to the point of pushing through pain, was the key to breaking through to new levels of performance.

But Don learned what all athletes eventually learn who embrace this philosophy. All the "more is always better" and "no pain, no gain" approaches ever get you is physically injured and mentally burned out. As we now coach our successful athletes, we don't want to necessarily work "harder" than our competitors, we want to work smarter. This all starts with the overload principle.

The American Council on Exercise defines the overload principle as: "One of the principles of human performance that states that beneficial adaptations occur in response to demands applied to the body at levels beyond a certain threshold (overload), but within the limits of tolerance and safety." In simplest terms, our bodies either need to work harder, or in a different way than they are used to working, in order to improve.

If we regularly do the exact same volume of training, we will eventually hit a plateau and fitness and performance will no longer improve. In fact, it will become stagnant and eventually probably even decline.

We need to introduce gradual "overloads" to our training volume to stimulate improvement. We include the word gradual because this will only work if the proper amount of overload is introduced.

Alice Hector, elite age group triathlete
James Mitchell Photography

If too much of an overload occurs, it can cause a breakdown and no improvement will be gained. Conversely, if the overload is too modest, it will not be enough to stimulate growth. The overload needs to be just the right amount to stimulate desired fitness improvements. We refer to this as gradual adaption.

The overload principle is built into all the training programs presented in this book.

TRAINING VOLUME

The second principle we will discuss is one that almost all athletes believe they understand, but in practice, we find that few actually do. It is widely misunderstood.

What is meant by training volume? Most athletes do not actually know. Many equate the volume of training with the duration of training. For example, they believe that to increase volume one needs to increase the duration of the workouts.

Actually, *volume* is the combination of training duration, training frequency, and training intensity:

Volume = Duration x Frequency x Intensity

To the surprise of many athletes, volume is not the same thing as duration. Duration is actually just one of three of the variables of volume. As a first step to understanding training volume, let's discuss each of the three components.

Duration is measured in time. For example, a 45-minute run or a 60-minute bike ride. That is what we mean by duration and all of the training programs in this book indicate a specific duration for every bike and run training session.

Frequency is measured in times per week. For example, a particular week in some of the programs in this book may indicate two swims, three bike sessions, and three run sessions. Our frequencies are simply two swim sessions per week, three bike sessions per week, and three run sessions per week.

Intensity is measured in heart rate or level of perceived effort. The higher the heart rate, the higher the intensity, and, conversely, the lower the heart rate, the lower the intensity. Likewise, the higher the perceived effort, the higher the intensity, and the lower the perceived effort the lower the intensity. All of the training programs in this book indicate specific heart rate zones for each bike and run session, and specific levels of perceived effort for all swim sessions.

The important point to understand about volume is that an increase in any of these three represents an increase in training volume.

HARD DAY/EASY DAY

The hard day/easy day concept relates to many of the concepts we have just discussed. If you had a very hard run yesterday and finished your usual running course in your fastest time ever, what should today's workout be?

In typical triathlete logic it should be the same workout and you should go a little harder and see if you can set a new personal record.

But this is, of course, a big mistake. It's not working with our body, it's working against it. After a high-intensity and/or high-duration run day, we need to give our body time to recover and fully absorb the benefits of that session. Our bodies want to react to that training session by building back stronger than before. By working your body again in the exact same way, you break it down, not allowing it to build back up.

After a hard run day, you should have an easy run day or not a run day at all. After a high-intensity run day, we are better off focusing on a different type of session that allows for the recovery our bodies need—perhaps a moderate run or a moderate bike session. It can even be a higher-intensity bike session, as long as you don't link too many consecutive higher-intensity days together.

This concept is built into all of the programs in this book. You will see that we never do two days in a row of higher-intensity sessions in the same sport, and we never do more than three days of higher-intensity sessions in a row of any sport. By doing so, we will work with our bodies to more fully absorb the good benefits of our training while reducing the chance of injury.

Even though the concepts of the overload principle, training volume, and the hard day/easy day are built into each of the programs in this book, it is helpful to keep them in mind as you approach each workout. As we like to say, there is a method to our madness. When a session is designed to be 100 percent at a moderate level of intensity, then that is truly the best approach. "Triathlete logic" may say that if Don and Mel say moderate intensity is good for this workout, then higher intensity would be even better. Please ignore these feelings and stick with the program as designed. It will keep you positively progressing toward your goal while also helping to avoid injury.

IRONFIT SUCCESS STORY:
Bill Diemer

Bill Diemer has a demanding career as a chemist, and he and his wife have four young children. That is surely enough to keep anyone extremely busy, but Bill has also been a successful triathlete for over thirteen years.

Not only has Bill had a long and successful endurance sports career, but he continues to build his fitness and improve his performances. Even after all these years, he recently lowered his best standard distance triathlon time by 20 minutes and finished in the top two in his age group at a competitive sprint distance triathlon. Bill even includes a long course race from time to time and has broken 12 hours in the full Iron-distance. Despite his busy and demanding life and all the challenges

(continued on next page)

(continued from previous page)

along the way, Bill continues to raise the bar and set an amazing example for those wanting to live the endurance sports lifestyle.

Bill utilizes all of the "Big Five" time management approaches presented in chapter 1.

As one of our coached athletes, he trains by time rather than distance and when possible he utilizes Masters Swimming programs. When he can't, he uses the IronFit swimming approach presented in chapter 2 and the type of swim workouts presented in chapter 6.

Bill does a portion of his training indoors, which he finds to be more time-efficient and allows him to work around weather issues and daylight constraints. Bill also gets up early most days and gets a portion of his training in before the family is up. Not only do these early morning sessions ensure that he can check off his daily training before the day even gets started, but it allows him more time with his family when they all get up.

Bill also takes advantage of lunchtime training sessions, usually doing his runs. As with many athletes, Bill finds running to be the easiest type of session to do from work because it requires the least equipment and setup of the three sports.

In addition to the "Big Five," Bill also utilizes a great approach we refer to as the "family meeting." Bill coordinates his training and racing plans well in advance with his wife so they can make sure that everything is always covered and there are no surprises. We often see many of our most successful coached athletes utilizing some form of the "family meeting." It is a great way to keep everyone onboard and supportive of your endurance sports goals and lifestyle.

Watch for Bill Diemer at the races this year, continually building his performances and making the endurance sports lifestyle look easy.

» Heart Rate Training for Short Course Distances

Well done is better than well said.
—BENJAMIN FRANKLIN

There is no better way to improve the efficiency and benefit of your training time than through heart rate training. If you embrace just one crucial concept from this book, it should be the importance of proper heart rate training. Doing so can lead to years of improved performance and enjoyment from the sport—while ignoring it often leads to performance stagnation and injury.

Based on the observation that the vast majority of triathletes and duathletes you see training are wearing some sort of heart rate monitor, you could easily conclude that everyone is doing it. But the reality is that few actually are. Most athletes view the data from their heart rate monitor as interesting information, but don't use it to guide their training in any way.

Most athletes mistakenly go by "feel" when they are training. There are several reasons for this, but the most common is the belief that their bodies will tell them what intensity level is right for their training. We believe that you should always listen to your body, but if you rely on it entirely to determine your intensity level, you will end up doing a lot of "junk training." This wasteful, purposeless training does not maximize the fitness benefit of your training time.

We will not focus on a lot of complicated scientific theories and technical talk in this book. After coaching hundreds of athletes for many years, we know that this is not what most athletes want. What athletes want is to know exactly what they need to do each day to achieve their goals, and they want a plan that they can immediately put into action. And that is exactly what this book provides.

Having said this, we will offer a brief and to-the-point explanation of what is behind effective heart rate training.

AEROBIC VERSUS ANAEROBIC

The body's two main energy systems are the following:

- **Aerobic Energy System:** An energy system that utilizes oxygen and stored fat to power physical activity. This system can support activity for prolonged periods of time, as stored fat and oxygen are available in almost endless supply. Even a very lean triathlete or duathlete, with a body fat percentage in the single digits, has enough stored fat to run several short course races back-to-back.

- **Anaerobic Energy System:** An energy system that utilizes glycogen (stored sugar) to power muscle activity. This system cannot support activity for long periods of time, as the body stores sugar in relatively small quantities.

While both of these energy systems work at the same time, the ratio of the two systems changes as the level of activity changes. The intensity of our training activity determines the ratio at which we are drawing from each system. The higher the intensity, the more anaerobic the activity. The lower the intensity, the more aerobic the activity.

Heart rate is an excellent indicator of where we are in the spectrum of aerobic and anaerobic ratios. At lower heart rates, the mix is more aerobic. At higher heart rates, the mix is more anaerobic. As our effort level and heart rate increases, the mix becomes more anaerobic.

For example, we race short course races at a higher level of intensity than half and full Iron-distance triathlons. Therefore, short course races are more anaerobic than long course races.

The important point to understand is that an effective heart rate training program gets you training at the proper intensity level at the right time, which serves to develop both your aerobic and anaerobic systems.

Alice Hector, elite age group triathlete
James Mitchell Photography

As mentioned earlier, the majority of athletes train at the wrong intensity most of the time, resulting in highly ineffective training; this is why we call it "junk training." The most successful triathletes and duathletes understand that we need to put out a very big effort on our "hard days," and that we need to restrain our effort to a moderate level on "easy days." A good heart rate training program has the athlete in the proper heart rate zone at the right time, resulting in highly effective training.

ESTIMATING YOUR HEART RATE ZONES

The most accurate way to determine your maximum heart rate and heart rate training zones is to have it professionally tested. If this is not possible, we suggest our simple five-step approach, which we have successfully used with our coached athletes.

➤➤ *Step 1:*

The first step is to calculate an estimate of your maximum heart rate (MHR) for running by using one of two popular formulas, one for men and the other for women. We find that these tests provide accurate results for most athletes we coach, but there are some who are either a little above or below these results. We start with these formulas in Step 1 and then in Steps 2–5 determine if we need to fine-tune the results.

The formulas for estimating MHR for running are the following:

For Men: 220 – Your Age = MHR
For Women: 226 – Your Age = MHR

The following is an example for a forty-five-year-old male and a forty-five-year-old female:

Male: 220 – 45 = 175 MHR
Female: 226 – 45 = 181 MHR

➤➤ *Step 2:*

Once we have an estimation of MHR for running, we double-check it with a running field test. We find the best field test is a 5K race. If that is not possible, we suggest either a 5 km or 3-mile 100 percent effort solo time trial. The MHR achieved during this test is a very good indication of an athlete's MHR for running.

The best places to complete this field test as a solo effort are on a running track, an accurate treadmill, or a safe measured course.

➤➤ *Step 3:*

Once we have completed the running field test and have either confirmed or adjusted our running MHR, we can use our running MHR to determine the four run training zones (Z1, Z2, Z3, and Z4) for use with the training plans presented in chapters 6–9 and 16, using the following calculations:

Zone 4: 90–95 percent of MHR (anaerobic training)
Zone 3: 86–89 percent of MHR (middle zone)
Zone 2: 75–85 percent of MHR (higher-end aerobic training)
Zone 1: 65–74 percent of MHR (lower-end aerobic training)

As an example, for a forty-five-year-old male athlete with an estimated 175 MHR, his heart rate zones for running would be as follows:

Z4: 90–95 percent of 175 MHR = 157–166 beats per minute (BPM)
Z3: 86–89 percent of 175 MHR = 150–156 BPM
Z2: 75–85 percent of 175 MHR = 131–149 BPM
Z1: 65–74 percent of 175 MHR = 114–130 BPM

›› Step 4:

Now that we have our running heart rate zones, we will estimate our MHR and heart rate zones for cycling by multiplying each by 95 percent. Due to the differences between running and cycling, for most athletes, cycling MHR and all cycling training zones are typically about 5 percent lower.

Following is an estimate for the same forty-five-year-old male athlete's MHR for cycling and his cycling training zones based on his running heart rate zones:

Cycling MHR = 175 BPM run MHR x 95 percent = 166 BPM
Cycling Z4 = 157–166 BPM run Z4 x 95 percent = 150–158 BPM
Cycling Z3 = 150–156 BPM run Z4 x 95 percent = 143–149 BPM
Cycling Z2 = 131–149 BPM run Z4 x 95 percent = 125–142 BPM
Cycling Z1 = 114–130 BPM run Z4 x 95 percent = 108–124 BPM

›› Step 5:

Now that we have an estimation of cycling MHR and cycling training zones, we double-check our results in the final step with a cycling field test. We find the best field test is a 15-minute 100 percent effort time trial. The MHR achieved during this test is a very good indication of an athlete's MHR for cycling. If it indicates something other than the 166 BPM from the above formula, then we would adjust the cycling training zones accordingly.

The best place to complete the cycling field test as a solo effort is on a safe measured course that is closed to traffic. Certain accurate indoor bike trainers (e.g., Computrainer) provide the needed data for this test and provide a safe alternative to doing this test out on the streets. If you do your field test on an indoor trainer, we suggest you do future tests on the same trainer for the most accurate comparison.

That's it! With the successful completion of these five steps, we now have the heart rate zones needed for all the training programs in chapters 6–9 and 16.

» AN IRONFIT MOMENT:
Lactate Threshold

Many athletes hear the term *lactate threshold*, but few really understand what it is and what it means in the context of effective training. Lactate threshold is the heart rate level at which lactate begins to accumulate at a faster rate in the muscles than the body can clear.

Lactate is produced in our bodies when performing physical activity. The accumulation of lactate has a negative impact on the muscles' ability to perform. Lactate threshold is not a constant. It changes relatively quickly for several reasons, including changes in your fitness level. Daily variations of up to several heartbeats per minute are common.

Another way to look at lactate threshold is that it is approximately the heart rate that a well-trained athlete can maintain for about a 1-hour 100 percent effort. This can be helpful to know, as it implies that for any distance you race that takes you less than 1 hour to complete, you should be mostly at a heart rate higher than your lactate threshold; and for any distance that takes you longer than 1 hour to complete, you should be mostly at a heart rate under your lactate threshold.

TRAINING BY "FEEL" AND THE DREADED "GRAY ZONE"

For each race distance there is an optimal mix of training intensities that an athlete should train in to maximize the benefit of his or her training time, as well as to avoid stagnation and even injury. Effective training for short course triathlon and duathlon is no exception. The training programs in this book are designed with these principles in mind to provide highly effective time-efficient training.

But, as we discussed earlier, many athletes do not correctly utilize heart rate training and instead train by "feel." What we find with these athletes is that over time all their training begins to gravitate to the same narrow range of heart rates.

On the one hand, moderate aerobic training (Z1 to Z2) feels too easy to them. They apply typical triathlete and duathlete logic, which says that if it does not hurt it can't be good, and they push harder. They think that "if Z2 is good, Z3 must be even better." So instead of locking in on Z2 for a "Z2 workout," they push harder and raise their heart rates up into the lower portion of Z3.

On the other hand, very high-intensity (Z4) training feels too hard, especially if they are still tired from going Z3 instead of Z2 the day before. They back off a little, and instead of pushing into Z4, they settle with upper Z3.

In short, the anaerobic training feels too hard and the aerobic training feels too easy, so they gravitate to the middle of the two for the majority of their training, which is Z3. This is what we call "gray zone" training. Gray zone athletes are not training either the aerobic system or anaerobic system well. All their training sessions fall within a fairly narrow range of heart rates.

When you consider this with real logic (rather than "triathlete and duathlete logic"), you can see why this approach is so flawed. In the example we provided for the forty-five-year-old male athlete, his Z3 run training zone goes from 150–156 BPM. This is a spread of only 6 beats per minute. How can it possibly make sense that all your training should be within a 6 BPM range? After a while, all you are doing is training in that range and not much else.

One additional reason why athletes get caught in the "gray zone" trap is because at first it seems to work. To an untrained athlete new to the sport, this approach will usually result in some initial training gains. But eventually the athlete's performance begins to stagnate, which leads to frustration at best and injury at worst.

This is often when these frustrated athletes come to us for coaching. The training that used to work for them no longer does. They are not improving anymore and they tend to be injured a lot. They are looking for the missing piece to help them break through to the next level.

We are often excited to see this as coaches, because we know that if we can persuade them to embrace proper heart rate training, they will have the breakthrough they desire. Typically these athletes have great untapped potential, and the way to realize this potential is through a proper heart rate training approach.

The answer to this question depends on several factors, most importantly your experience level, your level of competitiveness, and how much flexibility you desire in your training.

Various trends sweep the endurance sports world from time to time. Currently watts-based training for the bike is one of them. Many of even the most novice athletes seem to think that it is some kind of magic bullet that will instantly put them on the starting line at the sprint or standard distance world championships.

Athletes often tell us that they "train with power." When we ask them exactly what they mean by this, we learn that they have a power meter on their bike, and they casually take note of how many watts they are generating during some of their training. After telling us this, they often ask a question like, "I usually do my bike workout around 180 watts, is that good?" There is a simple two-word answer to that question: "It depends." These athletes are not really doing watts-based training. What they are actually doing is merely riding with a power meter and taking note of their wattage.

True power training involves conducting proper power testing on a regular basis, setting and frequently updating power levels, and performing very specific training sessions based on these levels. We have been training many of our elite coached athletes using watts-based training for many years, and while these athletes have been very successful with it, we have also learned that true power training is not for everyone. Many find that it is too technical and too restrictive for their liking. These athletes prefer the greater flexibility of our approach to heart rate training.

Unlike the heart rate training approach presented earlier, where training zones are based on maximum heart rate (MHR), proper training with watts is based on an athlete's *functional threshold power* (FTP). It's helpful to think of FTP as being sort of the watts equivalent of lactate threshold. The challenge to this is that our FTP is always changing as compared to MHR, which is very stable with only gradual changes over time. While changes in MHR should be looked at on a year-to-year basis, changes in FTP are frequent. They change month to month, week to week, and even day to day. As a result, to effectively train with watts-based power levels, the athlete needs to constantly re-test his or her power levels. While this is fine with many of the elite athletes we coach, we find that few age group athletes have the time or incentive to complete such frequent tests. We have had much greater success with heart rate training for the vast majority of athletes.

Please consider also that while we have coached many athletes with watts on the bike who have qualified for everything from the sprint and standard distance world championships to the Ironman World Championships, we have trained just as many who accomplished the same, but preferred to use our heart rate training system for the bike as well as the run. In fact, we have trained top elite athletes who have won their age group at the Hawaii Ironman and other major world-class events who trained with heart rate zones, not power levels.

We suggest you consider these factors when deciding if you want to invest the money in a power meter and do this type of training.

For "Just Finish" and intermediate-level athletes, we suggest you use the heart rate training system presented in this book. If you are an experienced competitive athlete, you will still be very successful with the heart rate training system, but if you decide you want to try watts-based training, we suggest you do so under the guidance of an experienced coach. In Appendix A we have a list of suggested books, including some good ones that deal specifically with power training. You may want to check these out as well.

There is another option for those who already have a power meter. It's what we refer to as the "gateway to power training." Use the heart rate system in this book, but determine what your approximate watts-equivalent ranges are for Z1, Z2, Z3, and Z4. By doing this, you can monitor your workouts with both heart rate and watts. Once you have some experience with this, you will be in a much better position to decide if you want to transition into a complete watts-based approach on the bike or stick with a heart rate approach.

Susan Winkelried has a very busy life. With a husband, two teenage boys, two very active family dogs, and a job as a substitute teacher, it's amazing that she is also an elite-level endurance athlete. After more than thirteen years in the sport, Susan has been successful at building her skills and performance and gradually climbing through the competitive ranks. She now successfully competes in all triathlon distances from sprint to full Iron-distance, and all running distances from 5K to marathon.

What is even more amazing, given all the success she has had, is that she never participated in athletics at all until she was nearly forty. She was not always the elite performer she is today. Through her strong determination and embrace of smart, efficient training principles, she now almost makes it look easy.

One of Susan's proudest breakthrough achievements is her podium finish at the standard distance Atlantic City International Triathlon. It was a strange weather day for August in New Jersey, with cold temperatures and ferocious storm-like winds. Susan took it all in stride and battled the whole way from start to finish—right onto the awards podium.

In addition to time-efficient training, Susan is a master of time management. She uses many of the "Big Five" time management tips presented in chapter 1, especially "train time, not miles" and indoor training. She has also perfected many of her own approaches.

Susan does not have a Masters Swimming program that fits into her schedule, so she swim trains on her own using the IronFit swim approach presented in this book. Susan is a great example of how successful this approach can be.

Following are some of Susan's best time management approaches:

- Susan blocks out time for her workouts when her boys are in school. These are the least busy times of the day and offer the greatest opportunity for her to focus on getting the most from her training.

- Susan has three separate gear bags for each sport, each in a different color. She packs all that she will need—clothes, gear, and even sports drinks and nutrition—well in advance, usually the night before. This way there is no scurrying around at the last minute before a workout. She just grabs the right bag and goes.

- Susan has installed shoe organizers in both her garage and hall closet to keep her gear organized and ready for action. The one hanging in the garage is used for bike gear (e.g., extra cartridges, tubes, lube, etc.), running shoes, running visors and hats, and extra swim goggles and swim caps. The one hanging in the hall closet, which is climate controlled, is used for training clothes, training nutrition items, calf sleeves, various glove options, and other similar items.

Watch for Susan Winkelried as she continues to improve her performances and make the endurance sports lifestyle look easy!

» 12-Week Standard Distance Triathlon Training Programs

Accept the challenges so you can feel the exhilaration of victory.

—GEORGE S. PATTON

This chapter includes three detailed 12-week standard distance triathlon (1.5 km swim, 40 km bike, and 10 km run) training programs. Each program is based on the number of hours an athlete has available to train. The Competitive Program includes an average of 10 and a peak of 12 weekly hours; the Intermediate Program includes an average of 7.5 and a peak of 9 weekly hours; and the "Just Finish" Program includes an average of 5 and a peak of 6 weekly hours. All you need to do is simply select the program that best fits your goals, competitiveness, level of experience, and available training time.

Each program explains exactly what to do each and every day throughout the 12-week period. There are no complicated formulas or overly general workout descriptions. Having worked with hundreds of athletes over the years, we know that this is not what most athletes want. Athletes want clear direction on exactly what they need to do and when. That is what this chapter provides. The programs are designed to be efficient, productive, and enjoyable.

Following is a summary comparison of the three 12-week programs:

Training Program	Average Hours/Week	Peak Hours/Week	Total Hours (Approx.)
Competitive	10	12	120
Intermediate	7.5	9	90
"Just Finish"	5	6	60

First, consider the time management techniques presented in chapter 1 and the athlete profiles presented throughout this book. Next, conservatively estimate your available weekly training time. Once you have completed this analysis, simply select the program that best fits your goals, experience level, and available training time.

ABBREVIATIONS FOR TRAINING PROGRAMS

Following is an explanation of the abbreviations used in each of the training programs in this book:

- **Z1:** Heart Rate Zone 1 (heart rate zones are explained in chapter 5)

- **45 min:** Forty-five minutes

- **1:30 hr:** One hour and 30 minutes

- **100+RPM:** Pedal bike at a cadence of 100 or more pedal revolutions per minute.

- **Trans or "Brick":** Transition sessions are a combined bike/run session, where we transition from one sport to the other in 5 minutes or less (transition sessions are discussed in chapter 2).

- **Double Trans:** Double transition sessions are combined run/bike/run sessions, where we transition from one sport to the other in 5 minutes or less (transition sessions are discussed in chapter 2). There are two transitions: the first from running to cycling and the second from cycling back to running.

- **Triple Trans:** Triple transition sessions are combined run/bike/run/bike sessions, where we transition from one sport to the other in 5 minutes or less (transition sessions are discussed in chapter 2). There are a total of three transitions: the first from running to cycling, the second from cycling back to running, and the third from running back to cycling.

- **QC:** Quickly change from cycling gear to running gear or from running gear to cycling gear.

- **Z1 to Z2:** Train at a heart rate anywhere within Zone 1 and Zone 2 (heart rate zones are discussed in chapter 5).

- **60 min Z2 (at 45 min, insert 10 min Z4):** Begin the 60-minute session in your Z2 heart rate. At 45 minutes into the session, increase your heart rate to Z4 (by increasing your effort level) for 10 minutes. At the completion of the 10 minutes, return to Z2 for the remaining 5 minutes of the session.

- **PU:** Pickups are temporary increases in effort by about 10–15 percent.

- **Spin:** Easy recovery cycling in an easier gear

- **Jog:** Easy recovery running at a slower pace

- **Sample Bike Training Session: 60 min Z2 (at 10 min, insert 5 x 4 min Z4 @ 2 min spin):** Begin your 60-minute bike session at a pace that will maintain a Z2 heart rate. At 10 minutes into the session, increase your heart rate to Z4 (by increasing your effort level) for 4 minutes, and then decrease gearing for an easy 2-minute spin. Repeat this sequence five times. After completing five sequences, return to a Z2 heart rate for the remainder of the bike session, which in this example will be 20 minutes.

- **Sample Run Training Session: 60 min Z2 (at 10 min, insert 4 x 6 min Z4 @ 3 min jog):** Begin your 60-minute run at a pace that will maintain a Z2 heart rate. At 10 minutes into the run, increase your effort enough to maintain a Z4 heart rate for a period of 6 minutes. After the 6 minutes, slow down to an easy 3-minute jog, bringing your heart rate back down to Z1 or Z2. Repeat this sequence four times. After completing four sequences, return to a Z2 heart rate for the remainder of the run, which in this example will be 14 minutes.

- **WU:** Easy warm-up

- **CD:** Easy cooldown

- **DR:** Swim drills (swim drills are presented in chapter 12)

NOTES TO SWIM SESSIONS
IN TRAINING PROGRAMS

Perceived Effort: It is suggested you use the following perceived effort levels with the swim sessions:

- Warm-up, drills (see chapter 12 for swim drills), and cooldown should be at a perceived effort of about 65–75 percent.

- Main swim sets should be at a perceived effort of about 80–85 percent.

- Main swim sets indicated as "Fast" should be at a perceived effort of about 90–95 percent.

The following is an example of how to read a swim session workout:

300 WU, 6 x 50 drills @ 10 sec, 10 x 50 @ 10 sec,
5 x 150 @ 15 sec, 6 x 50 drills @ 10 sec, 200 CD

1. Start by swimming an easy 300 yards/meters (65–75 percent perceived effort).

2. Then select one or more drills from chapter 12 and swim it for 50 yards/meters. Rest for 10 seconds at the wall after completing the 50-yard/meter drill and then repeat this entire sequence for a total of six times, each time swimming 50 yards/meters of the drill and taking a 10-second rest after (65–75 percent perceived effort).

3. Then swim 50 yards/meters and stop at the wall for a 10-second rest. Repeat this entire sequence for a total of ten times (80–85 percent perceived effort).

4. Then swim 150 yards/meters and stop at the wall for a 15-second rest. Repeat this entire sequence for a total of five times (80–85 percent perceived effort).

5. Then select one or more drills from chapter 12 and swim it for 50 yards/meters. Rest for 10 seconds at the wall after completing the 50-yard/meter drill and then repeat this entire sequence for a total of six times, each time swimming 50 yards/meters of the drill and taking a 10 second rest after (65–75 percent perceived effort).

6. Finish by swimming an easy 200 yards/meters (65–75 percent perceived effort).

Following are our three 12-week training programs and full explanations of each, starting with the 12-week Competitive Program.

COMPETITIVE TRAINING PROGRAM FOR STANDARD DISTANCE TRIATHLONS

The Competitive Program is for the experienced athlete who wants to maximize his or her potential and has available time to train for an average of about 10 hours a week, with several peak weeks of about 12 hours. The total combined training time over the 12-week period is approximately 120 hours, so we like to refer to this as the "120-hour triathlon plan."

If you are already in your racing season and in good form, you can begin the program immediately after your last race. The first week is fully aerobic, which will help to complete your recovery and firm up your aerobic base. Then in the second week, we will include easy pickups on both the cycling and running sides to prepare you to transition into our higher-intensity sessions.

From there our higher-intensity sessions and duration will build and become more challenging. We start at about 8.5 hours of training in the first week and then gradually build to about 12 hours in the seventh week. This amount assumes two swims of about 1 hour per week, but this program also includes an optional third swim, which adds another hour to these totals. If swimming is your weakest of the three sports, it will be very helpful to include the third swim if possible.

As presented, short course triathlon is completed at a much higher intensity level than long course races, so as expected, standard distance training includes a greater focus on higher-intensity Z4 training. Weeks 3–10 will each have four sessions that will include Z4 training sessions, including two bike sessions and two run sessions. Our quantity of Z4 training will gradually build and peak in week 8 at just over 105 minutes combined.

Our longest sessions in the twelve weeks will be three 3-hour transition sessions in weeks 6–10. Our longest runs of the twelve weeks will be three 2-hour sessions in weeks 5, 7, and 9 of the program.

This 12-week program includes one Rest Day/Slide Day per week. See the section in chapter 2 explaining the concept of Rest Day/Slide Days and how best to use them for optimal time management.

With nine days to go before our race, we will transition into a crisp taper phase to have us rested, sharp, and race-ready. Our durations will gradually decrease and our intensities will be no higher than Z2 during these last nine days. At this point, the most challenging training has been completed, and it is time to taper wisely and become physically and mentally energized.

If you are not coming off a race or you have not already built up to or close to 8.5 hours of training per week before starting the Competitive Program, it is suggested that you do so. Depending on your starting point, complete four to eight weeks of moderate aerobic exercise to properly prepare to begin the program. If you are starting from scratch, we suggest you start with two easy weekly swims of about 30 minutes, three easy bike sessions of about 30–45 minutes, and three easy run sessions of 30–45 minutes. Then, over the four- to eight-week period, make gradual increases each week until you are comfortably up to, or close to, the 8.5-hour level. Once there, you are ready to begin with the first week of the 12-week program.

COMPETITIVE PROGRAM

The following chart details the 12-week Competitive Program:

COMPETITIVE PROGRAM
STANDARD DISTANCE TRIATHLON

Week 1	Swim	Bike	Run
M	#1 opt	Rest Day/Slide Day	Rest Day/Slide Day
T	Off	Off	45 min Z2
W	#2	Trans: 45 min Z2 (QC)	15 min Z2
R	Off	45 min Z2	Off
F	#3	Off	45 min Z2
S	Off	Trans: 1:15 hr Z2 (QC)	15 min Z2
S	Off	30 min Z1 (100+ RPM)	1:15 hr Z1 to Z2
Totals: 8:30 hr	2:00+ hr	3:15 hr	3:15 hr
Week 2	**Swim**	**Bike**	**Run**
M	# 4 opt	Rest Day/Slide Day	Rest Day/Slide Day
T	Off	Off	45 min Z2 (at 10 min, insert 5 x 1 min PU @ 1 min jog)
W	#5	Trans: 45 min Z2 (QC)	15 min Z2
R	Off	60 min Z2 (at 10 min, insert 5 x 1 min PU @ 1 min spin)	Off
F	#6	Off	60 min Z2 (at 45 min, insert 5 x 1 min PU @ 1 min jog)
S	Off	Trans: 1:30 hr Z2 (at 1:15, insert 5 x 1 min PU @ 1 min spin) (QC)	15 min Z2
S	Off	30 min Z1 (100+ RPM)	1:30 hr Z1 to Z2
Totals: 9:30 hr	2:00+ hr	3:45 hr	3:45 hr

COMPETITIVE PROGRAM
STANDARD DISTANCE TRIATHLON

Week 3	Swim	Bike	Run
M	#7 opt	Rest Day/Slide Day	Rest Day/Slide Day
T	Off	Off	60 min Z2 (at 10 min, insert 8 x 2 min Z4 @ 1 min jog)
W	#8	Trans: 45 min Z2 (QC)	15 min Z2
R	Off	60 min Z2 (at 10 min, insert 5 x 4 min Z4 @ 2 min spin, then 5 x 2 min Z4 @ 1 min spin)	Off
F	#9	Off	60 min Z2 (at 45 min, insert 5 min Z4)
S	Off	Trans: 1:45 hr Z2 (at 1:30, insert 5 min Z4) (QC)	30 min Z2
S	Off	45 min Z1 (100+ RPM)	1:30 hr Z1 to Z2
Totals: 10:30 hr	2:00+ hr	4:15 hr	4:15 hr
Week 4	**Swim**	**Bike**	**Run**
M	#10 opt	Rest Day/Slide Day	Rest Day/Slide Day
T	Off	Off	60 min Z2 (at 10 min, insert 7 x 3 min Z4 @ 1.5 min jog)
W	#11	Trans: 45 min Z2 (QC)	15 min Z2
R	Off	60 min Z2 (at 10 min, insert 15 x 2 min Z4 Hill Repeats @ spin back down)	Off
F	#12	Off	60 min Z2 (at 45 min, insert 7.5 min Z4)
S	Off	Trans: 1:45 hr Z2 (at 1:30, insert 10 min Z4) (QC)	30 min Z2
S	Off	45 min Z1 (100+ RPM)	1:45 hr Z1 to Z2
Totals: 10:45 hr	2:00+ hr	4:15 hr	4:30 hr

COMPETITIVE PROGRAM
STANDARD DISTANCE TRIATHLON

Week 5	Swim	Bike	Run
M	#13 opt	Rest Day/Slide Day	Rest Day/Slide Day
T	Off	Off	60 min Z2 (at 10 min, insert 6 x 4.5 min Z4 @ 2 min jog)
W	#14	Trans: 45 min Z2 (QC)	15 min Z2
R	Off	60 min Z2 (at 10 min, insert 4 x 5 min Z4 @ 3 min spin, then 5 x 2 min Z4 @ 1 min spin)	Off
F	#15	Off	60 min Z2 (at 45 min, insert 10 min Z4)
S	Off	Trans: 1:45 hr Z2 (at 1:25, insert 15 min Z4) (QC)	30 min Z2
S	Off	45 min Z1 (100+ RPM)	2:00 hr Z1 to Z2
Totals: 11:00 hr	2:00+ hr	4:15 hr	4:45 hr
Week 6	Swim	Bike	Run
M	#16 opt	Rest Day/Slide Day	Rest Day/Slide Day
T	Off	Off	60 min Z2 (at 10 min, insert 5 x 6 min Z4 @ 3 min jog)
W	#17	Trans: 45 min Z2 (QC)	15 min Z2
R	Off	60 min Z2 (at 10 min, insert 12 x 2.5 min Z4 Hill Repeats @ spin back down)	Off
F	#1	Off	60 min Z2 (at 40 min, insert 12.5 min Z4)
S	Off	Trans: 2:15 hr Z2 (at 1:50, insert 20 min Z4) (QC)	45 min Z2
S	Off	45 min Z1 (100+ RPM)	1:30 hr Z1 to Z2
Totals: 11:15 hr	2:00+ hr	4:45 hr	4:30 hr

COMPETITIVE PROGRAM
STANDARD DISTANCE TRIATHLON

Week 7	Swim	Bike	Run
M	#2 opt	Rest Day/Slide Day	Rest Day/Slide Day
T	Off	Off	60 min Z2 (at 10 min, insert 4 x 7.5 min Z4 @ 3.5 min jog)
W	#3	Trans: 45 min Z2 (QC)	15 min Z2
R	Off	60 min Z2 (at 10 min, insert 2 x 7.5 min Z4 @ 3.5 min spin, then 3 x 5 min Z4 @ 3 min spin)	Off
F	#4	Off	60 min Z2 (at 40 min, insert 15 min Z4)
S	Off	Trans: 2:15 hr Z2 (at 1:45, insert 25 min Z4) (QC)	45 min Z2
S	Off	60 min Z1 (100+ RPM)	2:00 hr Z1 to Z2
Totals: 12:00 hr	2:00+ hr	5:00 hr	5:00 hr
Week 8	Swim	Bike	Run
M	#5 opt	Rest Day/Slide Day	Rest Day/Slide Day
T	Off	Off	60 min Z2 (at 10 min, insert 6 x 3 min Z4 @ 1.5 min jog, then 6 x 2 min Z4 @ 1 min jog)
W	#6	Trans: 45 min Z2 (QC)	15 min Z2
R	Off	60 min Z2 (at 10 min, insert 10 x 3 min Z4 Hill Repeats @ spin back down)	Off
F	#7	Off	60 min Z2 (at 15 min, insert 15 min Z4)
S	Off	Trans: 2:15 hr Z2 (at 1:40, insert 30 min Z4) (QC)	45 min Z2
S	Off	60 min Z1 (100+ RPM)	1:30 hr Z1 to Z2
Totals: 11:30 hr	2:00+ hr	5:00 hr	4:30 hr

COMPETITIVE PROGRAM
STANDARD DISTANCE TRIATHLON

Week 9	Swim	Bike	Run
M	#8 opt	Rest Day/Slide Day	Rest Day/Slide Day
T	Off	Off	60 min Z2 (at 10 min, insert 4 x 4.5 min Z4 @ 2 min jog, then 6 x 2 min Z4 @ 1 min jog)
W	#9	Trans: 45 min Z2 (QC)	15 min Z2
R	Off	60 min Z2 (at 10 min, insert 1 x 10 min Z4 @ 5 min spin, then 5 x 4 min Z4 @ 2 min spin)	Off
F	#10	Off	60 min Z2 (at 40 min, insert 15 min Z4)
S	Off	Trans: 2:15 hr Z2 (at 1:40, insert 30 min Z4) (QC)	45 min Z2
S	Off	60 min Z1 (100+ RPM)	2:00 hr Z1 to Z2
Totals: 12:00 hr	2:00+ hr	5:00 hr	5:00 hr
Week 10	**Swim**	**Bike**	**Run**
M	#11 opt	Rest Day/Slide Day	Rest Day/Slide Day
T	Off	Off	60 min Z2 (at 10 min, insert 3 x 6 min Z4 @ 3 min jog, then 6 x 2 min Z4 @ 1 min jog)
W	#12	Trans: 45 min Z2 (QC)	15 min Z2
R	Off	60 min Z2 (at 10 min, insert 8 x 3.5 min Z4 Hill Repeats @ spin back down)	Off
F	#13	Off	60 min Z2 (at 15 min, insert 15 min Z4)
S	Off	Trans: 2:15 hr Z2 (at 1:40, insert 30 min Z4) (QC)	45 min Z2
S	Off	60 min Z1 (100+ RPM)	1:30 hr Z1 to Z2
Totals: 11:30 hr	2:00+ hr	5:00 hr	4:30 hr

COMPETITIVE PROGRAM
STANDARD DISTANCE TRIATHLON

Week 11	Swim	Bike	Run
M	#14 opt	Rest Day/Slide Day	Rest Day/Slide Day
T	Off	Off	60 min Z2 (at 10 min, insert 3 x 7.5 min Z4 @ 3.5 min jog, then 3 x 2 min Z4 @ 1 min jog)
W	#15	Trans: 45 min Z2 (QC)	15 min Z2
R	Off	60 min Z2 (at 10 min, insert 5 x 4 min Z4 @ 2 min spin, then 5 x 2 min Z4 @ 1 min spin)	Off
F	#16	Off	60 min Z2 (at 45 min, insert 10 min Z4)
S	Off	Trans: 1:15 hr Z2 (QC)	15 min Z2
S	Off	30 min Z1 (100+ RPM)	60 min Z1 to Z2
Totals: 9:00 hr	2:00+ hr	3:30 hr	3:30 hr
Week 12	**Swim**	**Bike**	**Run**
M	Off	Rest Day/Slide Day	Rest Day/Slide Day
T	Off	Off	45 min Z1 to Z2 (at 10 min, insert 5 x 1 min PU @ 1 min jog)
W	1/2 hr easy	Trans: 45 min Z1 to Z2 (QC)	15 min Z1 to Z2
R	Off	60 min Z1 (at 10 min, insert 5 x 1 min PU @ 1 min spin)	Off
F	1/2 hr easy	Off	40 min Z1 (at 10 min, insert 5 x 1 min PU @ 1 min jog)
S	Off	15 min Z1—easy bike safety check	20 min Z1—easy (in a.m.)
S	RACE!!!	RACE!!! (Standard Distance Triathlon)	RACE!!! (Standard Distance Triathlon)
Totals: 5:00 hr	1:00+ hr	2:00 hr (+ Race)	2:00 hr (+ Race)

SWIM SESSIONS FOR THE COMPETITIVE PROGRAM

Our swims for the Competitive Program will be approximately 3,000 yards or meters in length, which is a workout distance most athletes can complete within 1 hour. Our suggestion is that if you need to lengthen the session to last a full hour, simply extend the warm-up and/or cooldown portion as needed. If, however, you find you need to shorten the session to make it fit into an hour, reduce the main sets as needed but keep the warm-up, drills, and cooldown the same.

Following are our seventeen swim sessions (of approximately 3,000 yards/meters) that are to be used with the Competitive Programs:

3,000 YARDS/METERS (APPROX.)

W/O	W/UP	Drills@10sec	Main Set	Drills@ 10 sec	C/D
1	300	8 x 50	2 x [6 x 100 @ 15 sec, 4 x 75 @ 15 sec, 2 x 50 @ 10 sec]	2 x 100	200
2	300	8 x 50	4 x [250 Pull @ 20 sec, 150 @ 15 sec, 50 @ 15 sec]	6 x 50	200
3	300	8 x 50	5 x [50 @ 10 sec, 75 @ 10 sec, 100 @ 15 sec, 125 @ 15 sec]	7 x 50	200
4	300	8 x 50	6 x [25 @ 10 sec, 75 @ 15 sec, 125 @ 15 sec, 75 @ 10 sec, 25 @ 10 sec]	150 Kick w/ fins	200
5	300	8 x 50	4 x 200 Pull @ 20 sec, 4 x 150 @ 15 sec, 4 x100 @ 10 sec, 4 x 50 @ 10 sec	4 x 50	200
6	300	8 x 50	4 x 150 @ 15 sec, 300 Kick w/fins @ 10 sec, 5 x 100 @ 15 sec, 200 Kick w/fins, 4 x 50 @ 15 sec, 100 Kick w/fins @ 10 sec	4 x 50	200
7	300	6 x 50	2 x [4 x 75 @ 15 sec, 300 Pull @ 15 sec, 4 x 50 @ 15 sec, 200 Pull @ 15 sec]	200 Kick w/ fins	200
8	300	4 x 100	2 x [200 Pull @ 10 sec, 2 x 100 @ 15 sec, 150 Pull @ 10 sec, 2 x 75 @ 10 sec, 100 Pull @ 10 sec, 2 x 50 @ 10 sec]	6 x 50	200
9	300	6 x 50	2 x [2 x 25 @ 10 sec, 3 x 50 @ 10 sec, 4 x 75 @ 10 sec, 5 x 100 @ 15 sec]	200 Kick w/ fins	200
10	300	3 x 100	3 x [150, 75, 50, 25 all @ 10 sec], then 2 x [200, 150, 100, 50 all @ 15 sec]	6 x 50	200
11	300	6 x 50	2 x [200 Kick, 200 Pull, 200 all @ 15 sec], then 3 x [100 Kick, 100 Pull, 100 all @ 10 sec]	4 x 50	200
12	300	4 x 75	6 x 25 @ 10 sec, 6 x 50 @ 10 sec, 6 x 75 @ 10 sec, 4 x 125 @ 15 sec, 4 x 150 @ 20 sec	4 x 50	200
13	300	6 x 50	2 x [2 x 150 @ 10 sec, 3 x 50 Fast @ 15 sec, 4 x 100 @ 10 sec, 8 x 25 Fast @ 10 sec]	100 Kick w/ fins	200
14	300	6 x 50	8 x 50 (25 Fast, 25 Easy), 8 x 75 (25 Fast, 50 Easy), 6 x 100 (50 Fast, 50 Easy), 4 x 150 (75 Fast, 75 Easy)	100 Kick w/ fins	200
15	300	6 x 50	3 x [50, 75, 100, 125 all @ 15 sec], then 4 x [25, 50, 75, 100 all @ 10 sec]	200 Kick w/ fins	200
16	300	6 x 50	2x [100 Pull @ 10 sec, 8 x 25 Fast @ 10 sec, 100 Pull @ 10 sec, 4 x 50 Fast @ 15 sec, 100 Pull @ 10 sec, 4 x 75 Fast @ 15 sec, 100 Pull]	100 Kick w/ fins	200
17	300	6 x 50	10 x 25 @ 10 sec, 8 x 50 @ 10 sec, 6 x 100 @ 15 sec, 4 x 125 @ 15 sec, 2 x 150 @ 15 sec	150 Kick w/ fins	200

The second of our three 12-week training programs for the standard distance triathlon is the Intermediate Program.

INTERMEDIATE TRAINING PROGRAM FOR STANDARD DISTANCE TRIATHLONS

The Intermediate Program is for the athlete who fits best between the Competitive Program and the "Just Finish" Program, both in terms of goals and competitiveness, and has available time to train for an average of about 7.5 hours a week, with several peak weeks of about 9 hours. The total combined training time over the 12-week period is approximately 90 hours, so we like to refer to this as the "90-hour triathlon plan."

If you are already in your racing season and in good form, you can begin the program immediately after your race. The first week is fully aerobic, which will help to complete your recovery and firm up your aerobic base. Then in the second week, we will include easy pickups, on both the cycling and running sides, to prepare you to transition into higher-intensity sessions.

From there our higher-intensity sessions and durations will build and become more challenging. We start at about 6.25 hours of training in the first week and then gradually build each week to about 9 hours in the seventh week. This amount assumes two swims per week starting at about 45 minutes each in the first week and then increasing to 1 hour per week in the fifth week.

As presented, short course triathlon is completed at a much higher intensity level than long course races, so as expected, standard distance training includes a greater focus on higher-intensity Z4 training. Weeks 3–10 will each have three sessions that will include Z4 training sessions, including two bike sessions and one run session. Our quantity of Z4 training will gradually build and peak in week 8 at close to 80 minutes combined.

Our longest sessions in the twelve weeks will be three 2.5-hour transition sessions in weeks 7–10 of the program. Our longest runs of the twelve weeks will be 1.5-hour sessions and will also occur in weeks 7–10.

This 12-week program includes two Rest Day/Slide Days per week. See the section in chapter 2 explaining the concept of Rest Day/Slide Days and how best to use them for optimal time management. This program also includes weekly optional high-RPM cycling technique sessions.

With nine days to go before our race, we will transition into our crisp taper phase to have us rested, sharp, and race-ready. Our durations will gradually decrease and our intensities will be no higher than Z2 during these last nine days. At this point, the most challenging training has been completed, and it is time to taper wisely and become physically and mentally energized.

If you are not coming off a race, or you have not already built up to, or close to, 6.25 hours of training per week before starting the Intermediate Program, it is suggested that you do so. Depending on your starting point, complete four to eight weeks of moderate aerobic exercise to properly prepare to begin the program. If you are starting from scratch, we suggest you start with two easy weekly swims of about 30 minutes, three easy bike sessions of about 30 minutes, and three easy run sessions of 15–30 minutes. Then, over the four- to eight-week period, make gradual increases each week until you are comfortably up to, or close to, the 6.25-hour level. Once there, you are ready to begin with the first week of the 12-week program.

INTERMEDIATE PROGRAM

The following chart details the 12-week Intermediate Program:

INTERMEDIATE PROGRAM
STANDARD DISTANCE TRIATHLON

Week 1	Swim	Bike	Run
M	#25 opt	Rest Day/Slide Day	Rest Day/Slide Day
T	Off	Off	45 min Z2
W	#26	Trans: 45 min Z2 (QC)	15 min Z2
R	Off	45 min Z2	Off
F	Or #25 opt	Rest Day/Slide Day	Rest Day/Slide Day
S	Off	Trans: 1:00 hr Z2 (QC)	15 min Z2
S	Off	Optional: 0–30 min Z1 (100+ RPM)	1:00 hr Z1 to Z2
Totals: 6:15 hr	1:30+ hr	2:30+ hr	2:15 hr
Week 2	Swim	Bike	Run
M	#27 opt	Rest Day/Slide Day	Rest Day/Slide Day
T	Off	Off	60 min Z2 (at 10 min, insert 5 x 1 min easy PUs @ 1 min jog)
W	#28	Trans: 45 min Z2 (QC)	15 min Z2
R	Off	45 min Z2 (at 10 min, insert 5 x 1 min easy PUs @ 1 min spin)	Off
F	Or #27 opt	Rest Day/Slide Day	Rest Day/Slide Day
S	Off	Trans: 1:15 hr Z2 (at 1:00, insert 10 min Z4) (QC)	15 min Z2
S	Off	Optional: 0–30 min Z1 (100+ RPM)	1:00 hr Z1 to Z2
Totals: 6:45 hr	1:30+ hr	2:45+ hr	2:30 hr

INTERMEDIATE PROGRAM
STANDARD DISTANCE TRIATHLON

Week 3	Swim	Bike	Run
M	#29 opt	Rest Day/Slide Day	Rest Day/Slide Day
T	Off	Off	60 min Z2 (at 45 min, insert 5 min Z4)
W	#30	Trans: 45 min Z2 (QC)	15 min Z2
R	Off	60 min Z2 (at 10 min, insert 4 x 4 min Z4 @ 2 min spin, then 3 x 2 min Z4 @ 1 min spin)	Off
F	Or #29 opt	Rest Day/Slide Day	Rest Day/Slide Day
S	Off	Trans: 1:30 hr Z2 (at 1:15, insert 5 min Z4) (QC)	15 min Z2
S	Off	Optional: 0–30 min Z1 (100+ RPM)	1:15 hr Z1 to Z2
Totals: 7:30 hr	1:30+ hr	3:15+ hr	2:45 hr
Week 4	**Swim**	**Bike**	**Run**
M	#31 opt	Rest Day/Slide Day	Rest Day/Slide Day
T	Off	Off	60 min Z2 (at 10 min, insert 6 x 3 min Z4 @ 1.5 min jog)
W	#32	Trans: 45 min Z2 (QC)	15 min Z2
R	Off	60 min Z2 (at 10 min, insert 12 x 2 min Z4 Hill Repeats @ spin back down)	Off
F	Or #31 opt	Rest Day/Slide Day	Rest Day/Slide Day
S	Off	Trans: 1:30 hr Z2 (at 1:15, insert 10 min Z4) (QC)	15 min Z2
S	Off	Optional: 0–30 min Z1 (100+ RPM)	1:15 hr Z1 to Z2
Totals: 7:30 hr	1:30+ hr	3:15+ hr	2:45 hr

INTERMEDIATE PROGRAM
STANDARD DISTANCE TRIATHLON

Week 5	Swim	Bike	Run
M	#18 opt	Rest Day/Slide Day	Rest Day/Slide Day
T	Off	Off	60 min Z2 (at 45 min, insert 10 min Z4)
W	#19	Trans: 45 min Z2 (QC)	15 min Z2
R	Off	60 min Z2 (at 10 min, insert 3 x 5 min Z4 @ 3 min spin, then 4 x 2 min Z4 @ 1 min spin)	Off
F	Or #18 opt	Rest Day/Slide Day	Rest Day/Slide Day
S	Off	Trans: 1:45 hr Z2 (at 1:25, insert 15 min Z4) (QC)	30 min Z2
S	Off	Optional: 0–30 min Z1 (100+ RPM)	1:15 hr Z1 to Z2
Totals: 8:30 hr	2:00+ hr	3:30+ hr	3:00 hr
Week 6	Swim	Bike	Run
M	#20 opt	Rest Day/Slide Day	Rest Day/Slide Day
T	Off	Off	60 min Z2 (at 10 min, insert 5 x 4.5 min Z4 @ 2 min jog)
W	#21	Trans: 45 min Z2 (QC)	15 min Z2
R	Off	60 min Z2 (at 10 min, insert 10 x 2.5 min Z4 Hill Repeats @ spin back down)	Off
F	Or #20 opt	Rest Day/Slide Day	Rest Day/Slide Day
S	Off	Trans: 1:45 hr Z2 (at 1:20, insert 20 min Z4) (QC)	30 min Z2
S	Off	Optional: 0–30 min Z1 (100+ RPM)	1:15 hr Z1 to Z2
Totals: 8:30 hr	2:00+ hr	3:30+ hr	3:00 hr

INTERMEDIATE PROGRAM
STANDARD DISTANCE TRIATHLON

Week 7	Swim	Bike	Run
M	#22 opt	Rest Day/Slide Day	Rest Day/Slide Day
T	Off	Off	60 min Z2 (at 40 min, insert 15 min Z4)
W	#23	Trans: 45 min Z2 (QC)	15 min Z2
R	Off	60 min Z2 (at 10 min, insert 1 x 7.5 min Z4 @ 3.5 min spin, then 3 x 5 min Z4 @ 3 min spin)	Off
F	Or #22 opt	Rest Day/Slide Day	Rest Day/Slide Day
S	Off	Trans: 2:00 hr Z2 (at 1:30, insert 25 min Z4) (QC)	30 min Z2
S	Off	Optional: 0–30 min Z1 (100+ RPM)	1:30 hr Z1 to Z2
Totals: 9:00 hr	2:00+ hr	3:45+ hr	3:15 hr
Week 8	Swim	Bike	Run
M	#24 opt	Rest Day/Slide Day	Rest Day/Slide Day
T	Off	Off	60 min Z2 (at 10 min, insert 4 x 6 min Z4 @ 3 min jog)
W	#18	Trans: 45 min Z2 (QC)	15 min Z2
R	Off	60 min Z2 (at 10 min, insert 8 x 3 min Z4 Hill Repeats @ spin back down)	Off
F	Or #24 opt	Rest Day/Slide Day	Rest Day/Slide Day
S	Off	Trans: 2:00 hr Z2 (at 1:25, insert 30 min Z4) (QC)	30 min Z2
S	Off	Optional: 0–30 min Z1 (100+ RPM)	1:30 hr Z1 to Z2
Totals: 9:00 hr	2:00+ hr	3:45+ hr	3:15 hr

INTERMEDIATE PROGRAM
STANDARD DISTANCE TRIATHLON

Week 9	Swim	Bike	Run
M	#19 opt	Rest Day/Slide Day	Rest Day/Slide Day
T	Off	Off	60 min Z2 (at 40 min, insert 15 min Z4)
W	#20	Trans: 45 min Z2 (QC)	15 min Z2
R	Off	60 min Z2 (at 10 min, insert 1 x 10 min Z4 @ 3 min spin, then 3 x 4 min Z4 @ 2 min spin)	Off
F	Or #19 opt	Rest Day/Slide Day	Rest Day/Slide Day
S	Off	Trans: 2:00 hr Z2 (at 1:25, insert 30 min Z4) (QC)	30 min Z2
S	Off	Optional: 0–30 min Z1 (100+ RPM)	1:30 hr Z1 to Z2
Totals: 9:00 hr	2:00+ hr	3:45+ hr	3:15 hr
Week 10	Swim	Bike	Run
M	#21 opt	Rest Day/Slide Day	Rest Day/Slide Day
T	Off	Off	60 min Z2 (at 10 min, insert 3 x 7.5 min Z4 @ 3.5 min jog)
W	#22	Trans: 45 min Z2 (QC)	15 min Z2
R	Off	60 min Z2 (at 10 min, insert 6 x 3.5 min Z4 Hill Repeats @ spin back down)	Off
F	Or #21 opt	Rest Day/Slide Day	Rest Day/Slide Day
S	Off	Trans: 2:00 hr Z2 (at 1:25, insert 30 min Z4) (QC)	30 min Z2
S	Off	Optional: 0–30 min Z1 (100+ RPM)	1:30 hr Z1 to Z2
Totals: 9:00 hr	2:00+ hr	3:45+ hr	3:15 hr

INTERMEDIATE PROGRAM
STANDARD DISTANCE TRIATHLON

Week 11	Swim	Bike	Run
M	#23 opt	Rest Day/Slide Day	Rest Day/Slide Day
T	Off	Off	60 min Z2 (at 40 min, insert 15 min Z4)
W	#24	Trans: 45 min Z2 (QC)	15 min Z2
R	Off	60 min Z2 (at 10 min, insert 3 x 4 min Z4 @ 2 min spin, then 5 x 2 min Z4 @ 1 min spin)	Off
F	Or #23 opt	Rest Day/Slide Day	Rest Day/Slide Day
S	Off	Trans: 1:15 hr Z2 (QC)	15 min Z2
S	Off	Optional: 0–30 min Z1 (100+ RPM)	60 min Z1 to Z2
Totals: 7:30 hr	2:00+ hr	3:00+ hr	2:30 hr
Week 12	**Swim**	**Bike**	**Run**
M	Off	Rest Day/Slide Day	Rest Day/Slide Day
T	Off	Off	45 min Z1 to Z2 (at 10 min, insert 5 x 1 min easy PUs @ 1 min jog)
W	1/2 hr easy	Trans: 30 min Z1 to Z2 (QC)	15 min Z1 to Z2
R	Off	45 min Z1 (at 10 min, insert 5 x 1 min easy PUs @ 1 min spin)	Off
F	1/2 hr easy	Rest Day/Slide Day	Rest Day/Slide Day
S	Off	15 min Z1—easy bike safety check	30 min Z1—easy (in a.m.)
S	RACE!!	RACE!!! (Standard Distance Triathlon)	RACE!!! (Standard Distance Triathlon)
Totals: 4:00 hr	1:00+ hr	1:30 hr (+ Race)	1:30 hr (+ Race)

SWIM SESSIONS FOR THE INTERMEDIATE PROGRAM

Our swims through the first four weeks will each be approximately 2,000 yards or meters in length, which is a workout distance most athletes can complete within 45 minutes. Our swims will then increase to 2,500 yards or meters starting in the fifth week, which is a workout distance most athletes can complete in 60 minutes. Our suggestion is that if you need to lengthen the session to last a full 45 or 60 minutes, simply extend the warm-up and/or cooldown portion as needed. If, however, you find you need to shorten the session to make it fit into 45 or 60 minutes, reduce the main sets as needed, but keep the warm-up, drills, and cooldown the same.

Following are our fifteen swim sessions (sessions 25–32 are approximately 2,000 yards/meters and sessions 18–24 are approximately 2,500 yards/meters) that are to be used with the Intermediate Programs in this book:

2,500 YARDS/METERS (APPROX.)

W/O	W/UP	Drills@10sec	Main Set	Drills @ 10 sec	C/D
18	200	8 x 50	2 x [3 x 100 @ 15 sec, 4 x 75 @ 15 sec, 2 x 50 @ 10 sec]	6 x 50	200
19	200	8 x 50	4 x [50 @ 10 sec, 75 @ 15 sec, 100 @ 15 sec, 125 @ 20 sec]	6 x 50	200
20	200	8 x 50	10 x 25 @ 10 sec, 6 x 50 @ 10 sec, 4 x 75 @ 15 sec, 2 x 125 @ 20 sec, 2 x 150 @ 20 sec	6 x 50	200
21	200	8 x 50	2 x 200 Pull @ 30 sec, 3 x 150 @ 20 sec, 4 x100 @ 15 sec, 5 x 50 @ 10 sec	6 x 50	200
22	200	8 x 50	2 x [150, 75, 50, 25 all @ 10 sec], then 2 x [200, 150, 100, 50 all @ 15 sec]	4 x 50	200
23	200	8 x 50	4 x 150 @ 15 sec, 200 Kick w/fins @ 10 sec, 4 x 100 @ 15 sec, 200 Kick w/fins @ 10 sec, 4 x 50 @ 15 sec	4 x 50	200
24	200	6 x 50	2 x [2 x 150 @ 10 sec, 4 x 50 Fast @ 15 sec, 2 x 100 @ 10 sec, 4 x 25 Fast @ 10 sec]	4 x 50	200

2,000 YARDS/METERS (APPROX.)

W/O	W/UP	Drills@10sec	Main Set	Drills @ 10 sec	C/D
25	200	8 x 50	2 x 25 @ 10 sec, 3 x 50 @ 10 sec, 4 x 75 @ 10 sec, 5 x 100 @ 15 sec	4 x 50	200
26	200	8 x 50	3 x 100 @ 15 sec, 4 x 75 @ 15 sec, 6 x 50 @ 10 sec	6 x 50	200
27	200	8 x 50	3 x [50 @ 10 sec, 75 @ 15 sec, 100 @ 15 sec, 125 @ 20 sec]	6 x 50	200
28	200	8 x 50	6 x 25 @ 10 sec, 5 x 50 @ 10 sec, 4 x 100 @ 15 sec, 2 x 150 @ 20 sec	4 x 50	200
29	200	6 x 50	1 x 200 Pull @ 30 sec, 3 x 150 @ 20 sec, 4 x100 @ 15 sec, 4 x 50 @ 10 sec	4 x 50	200
30	200	6 x 50	2 x [150, 75, 50, 25 all @ 10 sec], then 2 x [150, 100, 50 all @ 15 sec]	4 x 50	200
31	200	6 x 50	3 x 150 @ 15 sec, 100 Kick w/Fins @ 10 sec, 3 x 100 @ 15 sec, 100 Kick w/Fins @ 10 sec, 4 x 50 @ 15 sec	4 x 50	200
32	200	6 x 50	2 x [1 x 150 @ 10 sec, 4 x 50 Fast @ 15 sec, 1 x 100 @ 10 sec, 4 x 25 Fast @ 10 sec]	4 x 50	200

The final of our three 12-week training programs for the standard distance triathlon is the "Just Finish" Program.

"JUST FINISH" TRAINING PROGRAM FOR STANDARD DISTANCE TRIATHLONS

The "Just Finish" Program is for the athlete who has limited time available to train, but would like to be able to complete a standard distance triathlon safely, in good health, and in good spirits. The "Just finish" athlete needs to have available time to train for an average of about 5 hours a week, with several peak weeks of about 6 hours. The total combined training time over the 12-week period is approximately 60 hours, so we like to refer to this as the "60-hour triathlon plan."

If you are already in your racing season and in good form, you can begin the program immediately after your race. The first week is fully aerobic, which will help to complete your recovery and firm up your aerobic base. Then in the second week, we will include easy pickups, on both the cycling and running sides, to prepare you to transition into or higher-intensity sessions.

From there our higher-intensity sessions and duration will build and become more challenging. We start at about 4.5 hours of training in the first week and then gradually build to about 6 hours in the seventh week. This amount assumes two swims per week of about 45 minutes per session.

As presented, short course triathlon is completed at a much higher intensity level than long course races, so as expected, standard distance training includes a greater focus on higher-intensity Z4 training. Weeks 3–10 will each have three sessions that will include Z4 training sessions, including two bike sessions and one run session. Our quantity of Z4 training will gradually build and peak in week 9 at about 65 minutes combined.

Our longest sessions in the twelve weeks will be 2-hour transition sessions in weeks 7–10 of the program. Our longest runs of the twelve weeks will be 1-hour sessions and will occur in weeks 3–10.

This 12-week program includes two Rest Day/Slide Days per week. See the section in chapter 2 explaining the concept of Rest Day/Slide Days and how best to use them for optimal time management. This program also includes optional high-RPM cycling technique sessions.

With nine days to go before our race, we will transition into our crisp taper phase to have us rested, sharp, and race-ready. Our durations will gradually decrease and our intensities will be no higher than Z2 during these last nine days. At this point, the most challenging training has been completed, and it is time to taper wisely and become physically and mentally energized.

In chapter 14 we present a specific racing strategy for "Just Finish" athletes, which we suggest you consider.

If you are not coming off a race or you have not already built up to, or close to, 4.5 hours of training per week before starting the "Just Finish" Program, it is suggested that you do so. Depending on your starting point, complete four to eight weeks of moderate aerobic exercise to properly prepare to begin the program. If you are starting from scratch, we suggest you start with two weekly easy swims of about 15–30 minutes, two easy bike sessions of about 15–30 minutes, and two easy run sessions of 15–30 minutes. Then, over the four- to eight-week period, make gradual increases each week until you are comfortably up to, or close to, the 4.5-hour level. Once there, you are ready to begin with the first week of the 12-week program.

"JUST FINISH" PROGRAM

The following chart details the 12-week "Just Finish" Program:

"JUST FINISH" PROGRAM
STANDARD DISTANCE TRIATHLON

Week 1	Swim	Bike	Run
M	#25 opt	Rest Day/Slide Day	Rest Day/Slide Day
T	Off	45 min Z2	Off
W	#26	Off	Off
R	Off	Off	45 min Z2
F	Or #25 opt	Rest Day/Slide Day	Rest Day/Slide Day
S	Off	45 min Z2	Off
S	Off	Optional: 0–30 min Z1 (100+ RPM)	45 min Z1 to Z2
Totals: 4:30 hr	1:30+ hr	1:30+ hr	1:30 hr
Week 2	Swim	Bike	Run
M	#27 opt	Rest Day/Slide Day	Rest Day/Slide Day
T	Off	45 min Z2 (at 10 min, insert 5 x 1 min easy PUs @ 1 min spin)	Off
W	#28	Off	Off
R	Off	Off	45 min Z2 (at 10 min, insert 5 x 1 min easy PUs @ 1 min jog)
F	#27 opt	Rest Day/Slide Day	Rest Day/Slide Day
S	Off	60 min Z2 (at 45 min, insert 5 x 1 min easy PUs @ 1 min spin)	Off
S	Off	Optional: 0–30 min Z1 (100+ RPM)	45 min Z1 to Z2
Totals: 4:45 hr	1:30+ hr	1:45+ hr	1:30 hr

"JUST FINISH" PROGRAM
STANDARD DISTANCE TRIATHLON

Week 3	Swim	Bike	Run
M	#29 opt	Rest Day/Slide Day	Rest Day/Slide Day
T	Off	45 min Z2 (at 10 min, insert 3 x 4 min Z4 @ 2 min spin, then 3 x 2 min Z4 @ 1 min spin)	Off
W	#30	Off	Off
R	Off	Off	45 min Z2 (at 30 min, insert 5 min Z4)
F	#29 opt	Rest Day/Slide Day	Rest Day/Slide Day
S	Off	1:00 hr Z2 (at 45 min, insert 5 min Z4)	Off
S	Off	Optional: 0–30 min Z1 (100+ RPM)	60 min Z1 to Z2
Totals: 5:00 hr	1:30+ hr	1:45+ hr	1:45 hr
Week 4	**Swim**	**Bike**	**Run**
M	#31 opt	Rest Day/Slide Day	Rest Day/Slide Day
T	Off	45 min Z2 (at 10 min, insert 8 x 2 min Z4 Hill Repeats @ spin back down)	Off
W	#32	Off	Off
R	Off	Off	45 min Z2 (at 30 min, insert 7.5 min Z4)
F	#31 opt	Rest Day/Slide Day	Rest Day/Slide Day
S	Off	1:15 hr Z2 (at 60 min, insert 10 min Z4)	Off
S	Off	Optional: 0–30 min Z1 (100+ RPM)	60 min Z1 to Z2
Totals: 5:15 hr	1:30+ hr	2:00+ hr	1:45 hr

"JUST FINISH" PROGRAM
STANDARD DISTANCE TRIATHLON

Week 5	Swim	Bike	Run
M	#25 opt	Rest Day/Slide Day	Rest Day/Slide Day
T	Off	45 min Z2 (at 10 min, insert 2 x 5 min Z4 @ 3 min spin, then 4 x 2 min Z4 @ 1 min spin)	Off
W	#26	Off	Off
R	Off	Off	45 min Z2 (at 30 min, insert 10 min Z4)
F	#25 opt	Rest Day/Slide Day	Rest Day/Slide Day
S	Off	Trans: 1:15 hr Z2 (at 55 min, insert 15 min Z4) (QC)	15 min Z2
S	Off	Optional: 0–30 min Z1 (100+ RPM)	60 min Z1 to Z2
Totals: 5:30 hr	1:30+ hr	2:00+ hr	2:00 hr
Week 6	Swim	Bike	Run
M	#27 opt	Rest Day/Slide Day	Rest Day/Slide Day
T	Off	45 min Z2 (at 10 min, insert 6 x 2.5 min Z4 Hill Repeats @ spin back down)	Off
W	#28	Off	Off
R	Off	Off	45 min Z2 (at 25 min, insert 12.5 min Z4)
F	#27 opt	Rest Day/Slide Day	Rest Day/Slide Day
S	Off	Trans: 1:15 hr Z2 (at 50 min, insert 20 min Z4) (QC)	30 min Z2
S	Off	Optional: 0–30 min Z1 (100+ RPM)	60 min Z1 to Z2
Totals: 5:45 hr	1:30+ hr	2:00+ hr	2:15 hr

"JUST FINISH" PROGRAM
STANDARD DISTANCE TRIATHLON

Week 7	Swim	Bike	Run
M	#29 opt	Rest Day/Slide Day	Rest Day/Slide Day
T	Off	45 min Z2 (at 10 min, insert 1 x 7.5 min Z4 @ 3.5 min spin, then 5 x 2 min Z4 @ 1 min spin)	Off
W	#30	Off	Off
R	Off	Off	45 min Z2 (at 25 min, insert 15 min Z4)
F	#29 opt	Rest Day/Slide Day	Rest Day/Slide Day
S	Off	Trans: 1:30 hr Z2 (at 1:00 hr, insert 25 min Z4) (QC)	30 min Z2
S	Off	Optional: 0–30 min Z1 (100+ RPM)	60 min Z1 to Z2
Totals: 6:00 hr	1:30+ hr	2:15+ hr	2:15 hr
Week 8	**Swim**	**Bike**	**Run**
M	#31 opt	Rest Day/Slide Day	Rest Day/Slide Day
T	Off	45 min Z2 (at 10 min, insert 5 x 3 min Z4 Hill Repeats @ spin back down)	Off
W	#32	Off	Off
R	Off	Off	45 min Z2 (at 25 min, insert 15 min Z4)
F	#31 opt	Rest Day/Slide Day	Rest Day/Slide Day
S	Off	Trans: 1:30 hr Z2 (at 55 min, insert 30 min Z4) (QC)	30 min Z2
S	Off	Optional: 0–30 min Z1 (100+ RPM)	60 min Z1 to Z2
Totals: 6:00 hr	1:30+ hr	2:15+ hr	2:15 hr

"JUST FINISH" PROGRAM
STANDARD DISTANCE TRIATHLON

Week 9	Swim	Bike	Run
M	#25 opt	Rest Day/Slide Day	Rest Day/Slide Day
T	Off	45 min Z2 (at 10 min, insert 1 x 10 min Z4 @ 5 min spin, then 4 x 2 min Z4 @ 1 min spin)	Off
W	#26	Off	Off
R	Off	Off	45 min Z2 (at 25 min, insert 15 min Z4)
F	#25 opt	Rest Day/Slide Day	Rest Day/Slide Day
S	Off	Trans: 1:30 hr Z2 (at 55 min, insert 30 min Z4) (QC)	30 min Z2
S	Off	Optional: 0–30 min Z1 (100+ RPM)	60 min Z1 to Z2
Totals: 6:00 hr	1:30+ hr	2:15+ hr	2:15 hr
Week 10	**Swim**	**Bike**	**Run**
M	#27 opt	Rest Day/Slide Day	Rest Day/Slide Day
T	Off	45 min Z2 (at 10 min, insert 4 x 3.5 min Z4 Hill Repeats @ spin back down)	Off
W	#28	Off	Off
R	Off	Off	45 min Z2 (at 25 min, insert 15 min Z4)
F	#27 opt	Rest Day/Slide Day	Rest Day/Slide Day
S	Off	Trans: 1:30 hr Z2 (at 55 min, insert 30 min Z4) (QC)	30 min Z2
S	Off	Optional: 0–30 min Z1 (100+ RPM)	60 min Z1 to Z2
Totals: 6:00 hr	1:30+ hr	2:15+ hr	2:15 hr

"JUST FINISH" PROGRAM
STANDARD DISTANCE TRIATHLON

Week 11	Swim	Bike	Run
M	#29 opt	Rest Day/Slide Day	Rest Day/Slide Day
T	Off	45 min Z2 (at 10 min, insert 4 x 4 min Z4 @ 2 min spin)	Off
W	#30	Off	Off
R	Off	Off	45 min Z2 (at 25 min, insert 15 min Z4)
F	#29 opt	Rest Day/Slide Day	Rest Day/Slide Day
S	Off	Trans: 60 min Z2 (QC)	15 min Z2
S	Off	Optional: 0–30 min Z1 (100+ RPM)	45 min Z1 to Z2
Totals: 5:00 hr	1:30+ hr	1:45+ hr	1:45 hr
Week 12	**Swim**	**Bike**	**Run**
M	Off	Rest Day/Slide Day	Rest Day/Slide Day
T	Off	45 min Z2 (at 10 min, insert 5 x 1 min easy PUs @ 1 min spin)	Off
W	1/2 hr easy	Off	Off
R	Off	Off	45 min Z2 (at 10 min, insert 5 x 1 min easy PUs @ 1 min jog)
F	1/2 hr easy	Rest Day/Slide Day	Rest Day/Slide Day
S	Off	30 min Z1—easy bike safety check	30 min Z1—easy (in a.m.)
S	RACE!!!	RACE!!! (Standard Distance Triathlon)	RACE!!! (Standard Distance Triathlon)
Totals: 3:30 hr	1:00+ hr	1:15 hr (+ Race)	1:15 hr (+ Race)

SWIM SESSIONS FOR THE "JUST FINISH" PROGRAM

Our swim session will each be approximately 2,000 yards or meters in length, which is a workout distance most athletes can complete within 45 minutes. Our suggestion is that if you need to lengthen the session to last 45 minutes, simply extend the warm-up and/or cooldown portion as needed. If, however, you find you need to shorten the session to make it fit into 45 minutes, reduce the main sets as needed, but keep the warm-up, drills, and cooldown the same.

The eight swim sessions of approximately 2,000 yards/meters that are to be used with the "Just Finish" Programs can be found on page 78.

GUIDELINES FOR ADJUSTING THE TRAINING PROGRAMS FOR PRACTICE RACES

As discussed in chapter 3, while not essential, you may want to include one or more practice races prior to your sprint or standard distance triathlon or duathlon. There are pros and cons of doing so, depending on the unique situation of the athlete. See chapter 3 for additional information on which, if any, practice races would be best for you.

If you do decide to include practice races, please consider the following guidelines for adjusting the training schedule to accommodate them:

- **Open Water Swim:** As discussed in chapter 3, a training race up to 1 mile may be beneficial for some triathletes. It can be substituted in for any of the planned swims. Because open water swims are typically on Saturday or Sunday mornings, our suggestion is to simply complete it in the morning before your other bike and/or run training planned for that day, and to count it toward any of your planned swim sessions. Any weekend between week 2 and two weeks before your race date is fine for an open water swim practice race. We don't suggest tapering for this particular training race, but we do suggest completing it at a racing intensity. No other practice races should be planned for the same week as the practice open water swim race.

- **Road Races:** As discussed in chapter 3, a training race of 5–10 km may be beneficial to some sprint and standard distance triathletes and duathletes. The best time to include one of these races would be any weekend between week 3 and two weeks before your race date. Simply substitute the race in as all, or a portion of, your weekly long aerobic run session, and then complete any time remaining on that session any time that day after the race. We don't suggest tapering for this particular training race, but we do suggest completing it at a racing intensity. No other practice races should be planned for the same week as a 5–10 km practice road race.

- **Cycling Time Trial:** As discussed in chapter 3, a cycling time trial of 5–40 km may be beneficial to some sprint and standard distance triathletes and duathletes. The best time to include one of these races would be any weekend between week 3 and two weeks before your race date. Simply substitute the race in as all or a portion of your weekly long bike session, and then complete any time remaining on that session any time that day after the race. We don't suggest tapering for this particular training race, but we do suggest completing it at a racing intensity. No other practice races should be planned for the same week as a 5–40 km practice cycling time trial.

- **Sprint Distance Triathlon or Duathlon:** As discussed in chapter 3, a sprint triathlon or duathlon may be beneficial to some standard distance triathletes and duathletes. The best time to include one of these races would be any weekend between week 3 and two weeks before your race date. Simply substitute the race in as all or a portion of either your weekly long bike session or long aerobic run session, and then complete any time remaining on that session any time that day after the race. We don't suggest tapering for this particular training race, but we do suggest completing it at a racing intensity. No other practice races should be planned for the same week as a practice sprint triathlon or duathlon race.

GUIDELINES FOR ADJUSTING TRAINING PROGRAM FOR MISSED WORKOUTS

What if you miss a period of training due to an illness, a work-related trip, or any other reason? After not training for several days, we do not want to risk injury by immediately jumping back into our program where we left off. We want to ease back in safely, at just the right rate of increase to get us back on track to achieving our goals.

You should always first attempt to use the Rest Day/Slide Days to prevent missed workouts as discussed earlier. If that is not possible to account for the missed workouts, please consider the guidelines below.

1. **One to Two Days of Missed Training:** If you miss one to two days of training for any reason and cannot fit the missed sessions in by using the Rest Day/Slide Days, just skip them. Missing one or two workouts is never going to matter in the long run, but trying to play catch-up and doubling up workouts is risky and could result in setbacks.

2. **Three to Four Days of Missed Training:** Rejoin your training program (again, skip the missed days), but when you rejoin do only half the scheduled training on the first day back, resuming full training on the second day back.

3. **Five to Six Days of Missed Training:** Rejoin your training program (again, skip the missed days), but when you rejoin do one-third of the scheduled training on the first two days back, and two-thirds of the scheduled training on the next two days back. Resume full training on the fifth day back.

4. **Seven or More Days of Missed Training:** Reconsider the timing of your goal and consider a major redesign of your training program.

GUIDELINES FOR CROSS-TRAINING THROUGH INJURY

If you miss training due to a minor injury, check with your doctor to see if a cross-training alternative can be substituted in to keep you on schedule. For example, if your doctor determines that running will aggravate your injury, but the elliptical machine will not, consider substituting in elliptical sessions for your runs until you return to 100 percent good health.

Now that we have presented our three standard distance triathlon training programs, we will move on to chapter 7 where we will present three sprint distance triathlon training programs.

» 8-Week Sprint Distance Triathlon Training Programs

What you get by achieving your goals is not as important as what you become by achieving them. —**ZIG ZIGLAR**

This chapter includes three detailed 8-week sprint distance triathlon (750 meter swim, 20 km bike, and 5 km run) training programs. Each program is based on the number of hours an athlete has available to train. The Competitive Program includes an average of 9 and a peak of 11 weekly hours; the Intermediate Program includes an average of 6.5 and a peak of 8 weekly hours; and the "Just Finish" Program includes an average of 4 and a peak of 5 weekly hours. All you need to do is simply select the program that best fits your goals, competitiveness, level of experience, and available training time.

Each program explains exactly what to do each and every day throughout the 8-week period. There are no complicated formulas or overly general workout descriptions. Having worked with hundreds of athletes over the years, we know that this is not what most athletes want. Athletes want clear direction on what they need to do and when. That is exactly what this chapter provides. The programs are designed to be efficient, productive, and enjoyable.

Following is a summary comparison of our three 8-week training programs:

Training Program	Average Hours/Week	Peak Hours/Week	Total Hours (Approx.)
Competitive	9	11	75
Intermediate	6.5	8	55
"Just Finish"	4	5	35

First, consider the time management techniques presented in chapter 1 and the athlete profiles presented throughout this book, then conservatively estimate your weekly training time availability. Once you have completed this analysis, simply select the program that best fits you, your goals, your experience level, and your available training time.

ABBREVIATIONS FOR TRAINING PROGRAMS

An explanation of the abbreviations used in each of training programs in this book can be found on pages 60–61 in chapter 6.

NOTES TO SWIM SESSIONS IN TRAINING PROGRAMS

Perceived Effort: It is suggested you use the following perceived effort levels with the swim sessions:

- Warm-up, drills (see chapter 12 for swim drills), and cooldown should be at a perceived effort of about 65–75 percent.

- Main swim sets should be at a perceived effort of about 80–85 percent.

- Main swim sets indicated as "Fast" should be at a perceived effort of about 90–95 percent.

The following is an example of how to read a swim session workout:

300 WU, 6 x 50 drills @ 10 sec, 10 x 50 @ 10 sec,
5 x 150 @ 15 sec, 6 x 50 drills @ 10 sec, 200 CD

1. Start by swimming an easy 300 yards/meters (65–75 percent perceived effort).

2. Then select one or more drills from chapter 12 and swim it for 50 yards/meters. Rest for 10 seconds at the wall after completing the 50-yard/meter drill and then repeat this entire sequence for a total of six times, each time swimming 50 yards/meters of the drill and each time taking a 10-second rest after (65–75 percent perceived effort).

3. Then swim 50 yards/meters and stop at the wall for a 10-second rest. Repeat this entire sequence for a total of ten times (80–85 percent perceived effort).

4. Then swim 150 yards/meters and stop at the wall for a 15-second rest. Repeat this entire sequence for a total of five times (80–85 percent perceived effort).

5. Then select one or more drills from chapter 12 and swim it for 50 yards/meters. Rest for 10 seconds at the wall after completing the 50 yard/meter drill and then repeat this entire sequence for a total of six times, each time swimming 50 yards/meters of the drill and taking a 10-second rest after (65–75 percent perceived effort).

6. Finish by swimming an easy 200 yards/meters (65–75 percent perceived effort).

Following are our three 8-week training programs and full explanations of each, starting with the 8-week Competitive Program.

COMPETITIVE TRAINING PROGRAM FOR SPRINT DISTANCE TRIATHLONS

The Competitive Program is for the experienced athlete who wants to maximize his or her potential and has available time to train for an average of about 9 hours a week, with several peak weeks of about 11 hours. The total combined training time over the 8-week period is approximately 75 hours, so we like to refer to this as the "75-hour sprint triathlon plan."

If you are already in your racing season and in good form, you can begin the program immediately after your last race. The first week is fully aerobic, which will help to complete your recovery and firm up your aerobic base. Then in the second week we will include easy pickups, on both the cycling and running sides, to prepare you to transition into our higher-intensity sessions.

From there our higher-intensity sessions and duration will build and become more challenging. We start at about 8 hours of training in the first week, and then gradually build to about 11 hours in the fifth week. This amount assumes two swims of about 1 hour per week, but this program also includes an optional third swim, which adds another hour to these totals. If swimming is your weakest of the three sports, it will be very helpful to include the third swim if possible.

As presented, short course triathlon is completed at a much higher intensity level than long course races, so as expected, sprint distance training includes a greater focus on higher-intensity Z4 training. Weeks 3–6 will each have four sessions that will include Z4 training sessions, including two bike sessions and two run sessions. Our quantity of Z4 training will gradually build and peak in week 6 at about 105 minutes combined.

Our longest sessions in the eight weeks will be three 2.5-hour transition sessions in weeks 5 and 6. Our longest runs of the eight weeks will be three 90-minute sessions in weeks 4, 5, and 6 of the program.

This 8-week program includes one Rest Day/Slide Day per week. See the section in chapter 2 explaining the concept of Rest Day/Slide Days and how best to use them for optimal time management.

With nine days to go before our race, we will transition into our crisp taper phase to have us rested, sharp, and race-ready. Our durations will gradually decrease and our intensities will be no higher than Z2 during these last nine days. At this point, the most challenging training has been completed, and it is time to taper wisely and become physically and mentally energized.

If you are not coming off a race or you have not already built up to, or close to, 8 hours of training per week before starting the Competitive Program, it is suggested that you do so. Depending on your starting point, complete four to eight weeks of moderate aerobic exercise to be properly prepared to begin the program. If you are starting from scratch, we suggest you start with two easy weekly swims of about 30 minutes, three easy bike sessions of about 30–45 minutes, and three easy run sessions of 30–45 minutes. Then, over the four- to eight-week period, make gradual increases each week until you are comfortably up to, or close to, the 8-hour level. Once there, you are ready to begin with the first week of the 8-week program.

COMPETITIVE PROGRAM

The following chart details the 8-week Competitive Program:

COMPETITIVE PROGRAM
SPRINT DISTANCE TRIATHLON

Week 1	Swim	Bike	Run
M	#1 opt	Rest Day/Slide Day	Rest Day/Slide Day
T	Off	Off	45 min Z2
W	#2	Trans: 45 min Z2 (QC)	15 min Z2
R	Off	45 min Z2	Off
F	#3	Off	45 min Z2
S	Off	Trans: 1:00 hr Z2 (QC)	15 min Z2
S	Off	30 min Z1 (100+ RPM)	60 min Z1 to Z2
Totals: 8:00 hr	2:00+ hr	3:00 hr	3:00 hr
Week 2	Swim	Bike	Run
M	# 4 opt	Rest Day/Slide Day	Rest Day/Slide Day
T	Off	Off	60 min Z2 (at 10 min, insert 5 x 1 min PU @ 1 min jog)
W	#5	Trans: 45 min Z2 (QC)	15 min Z2
R	Off	60 min Z2 (at 10 min, insert 5 x 1 min PU @ 1 min spin)	Off
F	#6	Off	45 min Z2 (at 30 min, insert 5 min Z4)
S	Off	Trans: 1:15 hr Z2 (at 60 min, insert 10 min Z4) (QC)	15 min Z2
S	Off	30 min Z1 (100+ RPM)	1:15 hr Z1 to Z2
Totals: 9:00 hr	2:00+ hr	3:30 hr	3:30 hr

COMPETITIVE PROGRAM
SPRINT DISTANCE TRIATHLON

Week 3	Swim	Bike	Run
M	#7 opt	Rest Day/Slide Day	Rest Day/Slide Day
T	Off	Off	60 min Z2 (at 10 min, insert 10 x 2 min Z4 @ 1 min jog)
W	#8	Trans: 45 min Z2 (QC)	15 min Z2
R	Off	60 min Z2 (at 10 min, insert 5 x 4 min Z4 @ 2 min spin, then 5 x 2 min Z4 @ 1 min spin)	Off
F	#9	Off	60 min Z2 (at 45 min, insert 7.5 min Z4)
S	Off	Trans: 1:30 hr Z2 (at 1:10, insert 15 min Z4) (QC)	30 min Z2
S	Off	45 min Z1 (100+ RPM)	1:15 hr Z1 to Z2
Totals: 10:00 hr	2:00+ hr	4:00 hr	4:00 hr
Week 4	Swim	Bike	Run
M	#10 opt	Rest Day/Slide Day	Rest Day/Slide Day
T	Off	Off	60 min Z2 (at 10 min, insert 7 x 3 min Z4 @ 1.5 min jog)
W	#11	Trans: 45 min Z2 (QC)	15 min Z2
R	Off	60 min Z2 (at 10 min, insert 15 x 2 min Z4 Hill Repeats @ spin back down)	Off
F	#12	Off	60 min Z2 (at 45 min, insert 10 min Z4)
S	Off	Trans: 1:45 hr Z2 (at 1:20, insert 20 min Z4) (QC)	30 min Z2
S	Off	45 min Z1 (100+ RPM)	1:30 hr Z1 to Z2
Totals: 10:30 hr	2:00+ hr	4:15 hr	4:15 hr

COMPETITIVE PROGRAM
SPRINT DISTANCE TRIATHLON

Week 5	Swim	Bike	Run
M	#13 opt	Rest Day/Slide Day	Rest Day/Slide Day
T	Off	Off	60 min Z2 (at 10 min, insert 6 x 4.5 min Z4 @ 2 min jog)
W	#14	Trans: 45 min Z2 (QC)	15 min Z2
R	Off	60 min Z2 (at 10 min, insert 2 x 7.5 min Z4 @ 3.5 min spin, then 3 x 5 min Z4 @ 3 min spin)	Off
F	#15	Off	60 min Z2 (at 40 min, insert 12.5 min Z4)
S	Off	Trans: 2:00 hr Z2 (at 1:30, insert 25 min Z4) (QC)	30 min Z2
S	Off	60 min Z1 (100+ RPM)	1:30 hr Z1 to Z2
Totals: 11:00 hr	2:00+ hr	4:45 hr	4:15 hr
Week 6	**Swim**	**Bike**	**Run**
M	#16 opt	Rest Day/Slide Day	Rest Day/Slide Day
T	Off	Off	60 min Z2 (at 10 min, insert 5 x 6 min Z4 @ 3 min jog)
W	#17	Trans: 45 min Z2 (QC)	15 min Z2
R	Off	60 min Z2 (at 10 min, insert 12 x 2.5 min Z4 Hill Repeats @ spin back down)	Off
F	#1	Off	60 min Z2 (at 40 min, insert 15 min Z4)
S	Off	Trans: 2:00 hr Z2 (at 1:25, insert 30 min Z4) (QC)	30 min Z2
S	Off	60 min Z1 (100+ RPM)	1:30 hr Z1 to Z2
Totals: 11:00 hr	2:00+ hr	4:45 hr	4:15 hr

COMPETITIVE PROGRAM
SPRINT DISTANCE TRIATHLON

Week 7	Swim	Bike	Run
M	#2 opt	Rest Day/Slide Day	Rest Day/Slide Day
T	Off	Off	60 min Z2 (at 10 min, insert 4 x 7.5 min Z4 @ 3.5 min jog)
W	#3	Trans: 45 min Z2 (QC)	15 min Z2
R	Off	60 min Z2 (at 10 min, insert 1 x 10 min Z4 @ 5 min spin, then 5 x 4 min Z4 @ 2 min spin)	Off
F	#4	Off	60 min Z2 (at 45 min, insert 10 min Z4)
S	Off	Trans: 1:45 hr Z2 (QC)	45 min Z2
S	Off	30 min Z1 (100+ RPM)	60 min Z1 to Z2
Totals: 10:00 hr	2:00+ hr	4:00 hr	4:00 hr
Week 8	Swim	Bike	Run
M	Off	Rest Day/Slide Day	Rest Day/Slide Day
T	Off	Off	45 min Z1 to Z2 (at 10 min, insert 5 x 1 min PU @ 1 min jog)
W	1/2 hr easy	Trans: 45 min Z1 to Z2 (QC)	15 min Z1 to Z2
R	Off	60 min Z1 (at 10 min, insert 5 x 1 min PU @ 1 min spin)	Off
F	1/2 hr easy	Off	40 min Z1 (at 10 min, insert 5 x 1 min PU @ 1 min jog)
S	Off	15 min Z1—easy bike safety check	20 min Z1—easy (in a.m.)
S	RACE!!!	RACE!!! (Sprint Distance Triathlon)	RACE!!! (Sprint Distance Triathlon)
Totals: 5:00 hr	1:00+ hr	2:00 hr (+ Race)	2:00 hr (+ Race)

SWIM SESSIONS FOR THE COMPETITIVE PROGRAM FOR SPRINT DISTANCE TRIATHLONS

Our swims for the Competitive Program will be approximately 3,000 yards or meters in length, which is a workout distance most athletes can complete within 1 hour. Our suggestion is that if you need to lengthen the session to last a full hour, simply extend the warm-up and/or cooldown portion as needed. If, however, you find you need to shorten the session to make it fit into an hour, reduce the main sets as needed but keep the warm-up, drills, and cooldown the same.

The seventeen swim sessions (of approximately 3,000 yards/meters) that are to be used with the Competitive Programs in this book can be found on page 70 in chapter 6.

The second of our three 8-week training programs for the sprint distance triathlon is the Intermediate Program.

INTERMEDIATE TRAINING PROGRAM FOR SPRINT DISTANCE TRIATHLONS

The Intermediate Program is for the athlete who fits best between the Competitive Program and the "Just Finish" Program, both in terms of goals and competitiveness, and has available time to train for an average of about 6.5 hours a week, with several peak weeks of about 8 hours. The total combined training time over the 8-week period is approximately 55 hours, so we like to refer to this as the "55-hour sprint triathlon plan."

If you are already in your racing season and in good form, you can begin the program immediately after your race. The first week is fully aerobic, which will help to complete your recovery and firm up your aerobic base. Then in the second week, we will include easy pickups, on both the cycling and running sides, to prepare you to transition into our higher-intensity sessions.

From there our higher-intensity sessions and duration will build and become more challenging. We start at about 5.5 hours of training in the first week and then gradually build each week to about 8 hours in the fifth week. This amount assumes two swims per week starting at about 45 minutes each in the first four weeks and then increasing to 1 hour each in the fifth week.

As presented, short course triathlon is completed at a much higher intensity level than long course races, so as expected, sprint distance training includes a greater focus on higher-intensity Z4 training. Weeks 3–6 will each have three sessions that will include Z4 training sessions, including two bike sessions and one run session. Our quantity of Z4 training will gradually build and peak in week 5 at about 77 minutes combined.

This 8-week program includes two Rest Day/Slide Days per week. See the section in chapter 2 explaining the concept of Rest Day/Slide Days and how best to use them for optimal time management. This program also includes optional high-RPM cycling technique sessions.

Our longest sessions in the eight weeks will be three 2-hour transition sessions in weeks 4–6 of the program. Our longest runs of the eight weeks will be 1-hour sessions and will occur in weeks 2–6.

With nine days to go before our race, we will transition into our crisp taper phase to have us rested, sharp, and race-ready. Our durations will gradually decrease and our intensities will be no higher than Z2 during these last nine days. At this point, the most challenging training has been completed, and it is time to taper wisely and become physically and mentally energized.

If you are not coming off a race or you have not already built up to, or close to, 5.5 hours of training per week before starting the Intermediate Program, it is suggested that you do so. Depending on your starting point, complete four to eight weeks of moderate aerobic exercise to be properly prepared to begin the program. If you are starting from scratch, we suggest you start with two easy weekly swims of about 30 minutes; three easy bike sessions of about 30 minutes; and three easy run sessions of 15–30 minutes. Then, over the four- to eight-week period, make gradual increases each week until you are comfortably up to, or close to, the 5.5-hour level. Once there, you are ready to begin with the first week of the 8-week program.

INTERMEDIATE PROGRAM

The following chart details the 8-week Intermediate Program:

INTERMEDIATE PROGRAM
SPRINT DISTANCE TRIATHLON

Week 1	Swim	Bike	Run
M	#25 opt	Rest Day/Slide Day	Rest Day/Slide Day
T	Off	Off	45 min Z2
W	#26	Trans: 30 min Z2 (QC)	15 min Z2
R	Off	45 min Z2	Off
F	Or #25 opt	Rest Day/Slide Day	Rest Day/Slide Day
S	Off	Trans: 45 min Z2 (QC)	15 min Z2
S	Off	Optional: 0–30 min Z1 (100+ RPM)	45 min Z1 to Z2
Totals: 5:30 hr	1:30+ hr	2:00+ hr	2:00 hr
Week 2	**Swim**	**Bike**	**Run**
M	#27 opt	Rest Day/Slide Day	Rest Day/Slide Day
T	Off	Off	45 min Z2 (at 10 min, insert 5 x 1 min PU @ 1 min jog)
W	#28	Trans: 30 min Z2 (QC)	15 min Z2
R	Off	60 min Z2 (at 10 min, insert 5 x 1 min PU @ 1 min spin)	Off
F	Or #27 opt	Rest Day/Slide Day	Rest Day/Slide Day
S	Off	Trans: 1:00 hr Z2 (at 45 min, insert 10 min Z4) (QC)	15 min Z2
S	Off	Optional: 0–30 min Z1 (100+ RPM)	60 min Z1 to Z2
Totals: 6:15 hr	1:30+ hr	2:30+ hr	2:15 hr

INTERMEDIATE PROGRAM
SPRINT DISTANCE TRIATHLON

Week 3	Swim	Bike	Run
M	#29 opt	Rest Day/Slide Day	Rest Day/Slide Day
T	Off	Off	60 min Z2 (at 10 min, insert 7 x 3 min Z4 @ 1.5 min jog)
W	#30	Trans: 45 min Z2 (QC)	15 min Z2
R	Off	60 min Z2 (at 10 min, insert 4 x 4 min Z4 @ 2 min spin, then 3 x 2 min Z4 @ 1 min spin)	Off
F	Or #29 opt	Rest Day/Slide Day	Rest Day/Slide Day
S	Off	Trans: 1:15 hr Z2 (at 55 min, insert 15 min Z4) (QC)	15 min Z2
S	Off	Optional: 0–30 min Z1 (100+ RPM)	60 min Z1 to Z2
Totals: 7:00 hr	1:30+ hr	3:00+ hr	2:30 hr
Week 4	**Swim**	**Bike**	**Run**
M	#31 opt	Rest Day/Slide Day	Rest Day/Slide Day
T	Off	Off	60 min Z2 (at 45 min, insert 10 min Z4)
W	#32	Trans: 45 min Z2 (QC)	15 min Z2
R	Off	60 min Z2 (at 10 min, insert 12 x 2 min Z4 Hill Repeats @ spin back down)	Off
F	Or #31 opt	Rest Day/Slide Day	Rest Day/Slide Day
S	Off	Trans: 1:30 hr Z2 (at 1:05, insert 20 min Z4) (QC)	30 min Z2
S	Off	Optional: 0–30 min Z1 (100+ RPM)	60 min Z1 to Z2
Totals: 7:30 hr	1:30+ hr	3:15+ hr	2:45 hr

INTERMEDIATE PROGRAM
SPRINT DISTANCE TRIATHLON

Week 5	Swim	Bike	Run
M	#18 opt	Rest Day/Slide Day	Rest Day/Slide Day
T	Off	Off	60 min Z2 (at 10 min, insert 6 x 4.5 min Z4 @ 2 min jog)
W	#19	Trans: 45 min Z2 (QC)	15 min Z2
R	Off	60 min Z2 (at 10 min, insert 2 x 7.5 min Z4 @ 3.5 min spin, then 2 x 5 min Z4 @ 3 min spin)	Off
F	Or #18 opt	Rest Day/Slide Day	Rest Day/Slide Day
S	Off	Trans: 1:30 hr Z2 (at 1:00, insert 25 min Z4) (QC)	30 min Z2
S	Off	Optional: 0–30 min Z1 (100+ RPM)	60 min Z1 to Z2
Totals: 8:00 hr	2:00+ hr	3:15+ hr	2:45 hr
Week 6	**Swim**	**Bike**	**Run**
M	#20 opt	Rest Day/Slide Day	Rest Day/Slide Day
T	Off	Off	60 min Z2 (at 40 min, insert 15 min Z4)
W	#21	Trans: 45 min Z2 (QC)	15 min Z2
R	Off	60 min Z2 (at 10 min, insert 10 x 2.5 min Z4 Hill Repeats @ spin back down)	Off
F	Or #20 opt	Rest Day/Slide Day	Rest Day/Slide Day
S	Off	Trans: 1:30 hr Z2 (at 55 min, insert 30 min Z4) (QC)	30 min Z2
S	Off	Optional: 0–30 min Z1 (100+ RPM)	60 min Z1 to Z2
Totals: 8:00 hr	2:00+ hr	3:15+ hr	2:45 hr

INTERMEDIATE PROGRAM
SPRINT DISTANCE TRIATHLON

Week 7	Swim	Bike	Run
M	#22 opt	Rest Day/Slide Day	Rest Day/Slide Day
T	Off	Off	60 min Z2 (at 10 min, insert 5 x 6 min Z4 @ 3 min jog)
W	#23	Trans: 45 min Z2 (QC)	15 min Z2
R	Off	60 min Z2 (at 10 min, insert 1 x 10 min Z4 @ 5 min spin, then 5 x 4 min Z4 @ 2 min spin)	Off
F	Or #22 opt	Rest Day/Slide Day	Rest Day/Slide Day
S	Off	Trans: 1:00 hr Z2 (QC)	15 min Z2
S	Off	Optional: 0–30 min Z1 (100+ RPM)	45 min Z1 to Z2
Totals: 7:00 hr	2:00+ hr	2:45+ hr	2:15 hr
Week 8	**Swim**	**Bike**	**Run**
M	Off	Rest Day/Slide Day	Rest Day/Slide Day
T	Off	Off	45 min Z1 to Z2 (at 10 min, insert 5 x 1 min PU @ 1 min jog)
W	1/2 hr easy	Trans: 30 min Z1 to Z2 (QC)	15 min Z1 to Z2
R	Off	45 min Z1 (at 10 min, insert 5 x 1 min PU @ 1 min spin)	Off
F	1/2 hr easy	Rest Day/Slide Day	Rest Day/Slide Day
S	Off	15 min Z1—easy bike safety check	30 min Z1—easy (in a.m.)
S	RACE!!!	RACE!!! (Sprint Distance Triathlon)	RACE!!! (Sprint Distance Triathlon)
Totals: 4:00 hr	1:00+ hr	1:30 hr (+ Race)	1:30 hr (+ Race)

SWIM SESSIONS FOR THE INTERMEDIATE PROGRAM FOR SPRINT DISTANCE TRIATHLONS

Our swims through the first four weeks will all be approximately 2,000 yards or meters in length, which is a workout distance most athletes can complete within 45 minutes. Our swims will then increase to 2,500 yards or meters starting in the fifth week, which is a workout distance most athletes can complete in 60 minutes. Our suggestion is that if you need to lengthen the session to last a full 45 or 60 minutes, simply extend the warm-up and/or cooldown portion as needed. If, however, you find you need to shorten the session to make it fit into 45 or 60 minutes, reduce the main sets as needed, but keep the warm-up, drills, and cooldown the same.

The fifteen swim sessions that are to be used with the Intermediate Programs in this book can be found on page 78 in chapter 6.

The final of our three 8-week training programs for the sprint distance triathlon is the "Just Finish" Program.

"JUST FINISH" TRAINING PROGRAM FOR SPRINT DISTANCE TRIATHLONS

The "Just Finish" program is for the athlete who has limited time available to train, but would like to be able to complete a sprint distance triathlon safely, in good health, and in good spirits. The "Just finish" athlete needs to have available time to train for an average of about 4 hours a week, with several peak weeks of about 5 hours. The total combined training time over the 8-week period is approximately 35 hours, so we like to refer to this as the "35-hour sprint triathlon plan."

If you are already in your racing season and in good form, you can begin the program immediately after your race. The first week is fully aerobic, which will help to complete your recovery and firm up your aerobic base. Then in the second week, we will include easy pickups, on both the cycling and running sides, to prepare you to transition into our higher-intensity sessions.

From there our higher-intensity sessions and duration will build and become more challenging. We start at about 4 hours of training in the first week and then gradually build to about 5 hours in the fifth week. This amount assumes two swims per week of about 45 minutes per session.

As presented, short course triathlon is completed at a much higher intensity level than long course races, so as expected, sprint distance training includes a greater focus on higher-intensity Z4 training. Weeks 3–6 will each have three sessions that will include Z4 training sessions, including two bike sessions and one run session. Our quantity of Z4 training will gradually build and peak in week 5 at over 50 minutes combined.

Our longest sessions in the eight weeks will be 1-hour bike sessions in weeks 5–7 of the program. Our longest runs of the eight weeks will be 45-minute sessions and will occur in weeks 3–7.

This 8-week program includes two Rest Day/Slide Days per week. See the section in chapter 2 explaining the concept of Rest Day/Slide Days and how best to use them for optimal time management. This program also includes optional high-RPM cycling technique sessions.

With nine days to go before our race, we will transition into our crisp taper phase to have us rested, sharp, and race-ready. Our durations will gradually decrease and our intensities will be no higher than Z2 during these last nine days. At this point, the most challenging training has been completed, and it is time to taper wisely and become physically and mentally energized.

In chapter 14 we present a specific racing strategy for "Just Finish" athletes, which we suggest you consider.

If you are not coming off a race or you have not already built up to or close to 4 hours of training per week before starting the "Just Finish" Program, it is suggested that you do. Depending on your starting point, complete four to eight weeks of moderate aerobic exercise to be properly prepared to begin the program. If you are starting from scratch, we suggest you start with two weekly easy swims of about 15–30 minutes, two easy bike sessions of about 15–30 minutes, and two easy run sessions of 15–30 minutes. Then, over the four- to eight-week period, make gradual increases each week until you are comfortably up to, or close to, the 4-hour level. Once there, you are ready to begin with the first week of the 8-week program.

"JUST FINISH" PROGRAM

The following chart details the 8-week "Just Finish" Program:

"JUST FINISH" PROGRAM
SPRINT DISTANCE TRIATHLON

Week 1	Swim	Bike	Run
M	#25 opt	Rest Day/Slide Day	Rest Day/Slide Day
T	Off	Off	30 min Z2
W	#26	Trans: 15 min Z2 (QC)	15 min Z2
R	Off	30 min Z2	Off
F	Or #25 opt	Rest Day/Slide Day	Rest Day/Slide Day
S	Off	30 min Z2	Off
S	Off	Optional: 0–30 min Z1 (100+ RPM)	30 min Z1 to Z2
Totals: 4:00 hr	1:30+ hr	1:15+ hr	1:15 hr
Week 2	Swim	Bike	Run
M	#27 opt	Rest Day/Slide Day	Rest Day/Slide Day
T	Off	Off	30 min Z2 (at 10 min, insert 5 x 1 min PU @ 1 min jog)
W	#28	Trans: 15 min Z2 (QC)	15 min Z2
R	Off	30 min Z2 (at 10 min, insert 5 x 1 min PU @ 1 min spin)	Off
F	Or #27 opt	Rest Day/Slide Day	Rest Day/Slide Day
S	Off	45 min Z2 (at 30 min, insert 10 min Z4)	Off
S	Off	Optional: 0–30 min Z1 (100+ RPM)	30 min Z1 to Z2
Totals: 4:15 hr	1:30+ hr	1:30+ hr	1:15 hr

"JUST FINISH" PROGRAM
SPRINT DISTANCE TRIATHLON

Week 3	Swim	Bike	Run
M	#29 opt	Rest Day/Slide Day	Rest Day/Slide Day
T	Off	Off	30 min Z2 (at 10 min, insert 4 x 3 min Z4 @ 1.5 min jog)
W	#30	Trans: 15 min Z2 (QC)	15 min Z2
R	Off	30 min Z2 (at 10 min, insert 3 x 4 min Z4 @ 2 min spin)	Off
F	Or #29 opt	Rest Day/Slide Day	Rest Day/Slide Day
S	Off	45 min Z2 (at 25 min, insert 15 min Z4)	Off
S	Off	Optional: 0–30 min Z1 (100+ RPM)	45 min Z1 to Z2
Totals: 4:30 hr	1:30+ hr	1:30+ hr	1:30 hr
Week 4	**Swim**	**Bike**	**Run**
M	#31 opt	Rest Day/Slide Day	Rest Day/Slide Day
T	Off	Off	30 min Z2 (at 15 min, insert 10 min Z4)
W	#32	Trans: 15 min Z2 (QC)	15 min Z2
R	Off	45 min Z2 (at 10 min, insert 6 x 2 min Z4 Hill Repeats @ spin back down)	Off
F	Or #31 opt	Rest Day/Slide Day	Rest Day/Slide Day
S	Off	45 min Z2 (at 20 min, insert 20 min Z4)	Off
S	Off	Optional: 0–30 min Z1 (100+ RPM)	45 min Z1 to Z2
Totals: 4:45 hr	1:30+ hr	1:45+ hr	1:30 hr

"JUST FINISH" PROGRAM
SPRINT DISTANCE TRIATHLON

Week 5	Swim	Bike	Run
M	#25 opt	Rest Day/Slide Day	Rest Day/Slide Day
T	Off	Off	30 min Z2 (at 10 min, insert 3 x 4.5 min Z4 @ 2 min jog)
W	#26	Trans: 15 min Z2 (QC)	15 min Z2
R	Off	45 min Z2 (at 10 min, insert 3 x 5 min Z4 @ 3 min spin)	Off
F	Or #25 opt	Rest Day/Slide Day	Rest Day/Slide Day
S	Off	60 min Z2 (at 30 min, insert 25 min Z4)	Off
S	Off	Optional: 0–30 min Z1 (100+ RPM)	45 min Z1 to Z2
Totals: 5:00 hr	1:30+ hr	2:00+ hr	1:30 hr
Week 6	Swim	Bike	Run
M	#27 opt	Rest Day/Slide Day	Rest Day/Slide Day
T	Off	Off	30 min Z2 (at 10 min, insert 15 min Z4)
W	#28	Trans: 15 min Z2 (QC)	15 min Z2
R	Off	45 min Z2 (at 10 min, insert 5 x 2.5 min Z4 Hill Repeats @ spin back down)	Off
F	Or #27 opt	Rest Day/Slide Day	Rest Day/Slide Day
S	Off	60 min Z2 (at 25 min, insert 30 min Z4)	Off
S	Off	Optional: 0–30 min Z1 (100+ RPM)	45 min Z1 to Z2
Totals: 5:00 hr	1:30+ hr	2:00+ hr	1:30 hr

"JUST FINISH" PROGRAM
SPRINT DISTANCE TRIATHLON

Week 7	Swim	Bike	Run
M	#29 opt	Rest Day/Slide Day	Rest Day/Slide Day
T	Off	Off	30 min Z2 (at 10 min, insert 2 x 6 min Z4 @ 3 min jog)
W	#30	Trans: 15 min Z2 (QC)	15 min Z2
R	Off	45 min Z2 (at 10 min, insert 2 x 7.5 min Z4 @ 3.5 min spin)	Off
F	Or #29 opt	Rest Day/Slide Day	Rest Day/Slide Day
S	Off	60 min Z1 to Z2	Off
S	Off	Optional: 0–30 min Z1 (100+ RPM)	45 min Z1 to Z2
Totals: 5:00 hr	1:30+ hr	2:00+ hr	1:30 hr
Week 8	**Swim**	**Bike**	**Run**
M	Off	Rest Day/Slide Day	Rest Day/Slide Day
T	Off	Off	30 min Z1 to Z2 (at 10 min, insert 5 x 1 min PU @ 1 min jog)
W	1/2 hr easy	Trans: 15 min Z1 to Z2 (QC)	15 min Z1 to Z2
R	Off	30 min Z1 (at 10 min, insert 5 x 1 min PU @ 1 min spin)	Off
F	1/2 hr easy	Rest Day/Slide Day	Rest Day/Slide Day
S	Off	15 min Z1—easy bike safety check	15 min Z1—easy (in a.m.)
S	RACE!!!	RACE!!! (Sprint Distance Triathlon)	RACE!!! (Sprint Distance Triathlon)
Totals: 3:00 hr	1:00+ hr	1:00 hr (+ Race)	1:00 hr (+ Race)

SWIM SESSIONS FOR THE "JUST FINISH" PROGRAM

Our swims sessions will all be approximately 2,000 yards or meters in length, which is a workout distance most athletes can complete within 45 minutes. Our suggestion is that if you need to lengthen the session to last 45 minutes, simply extend the warm-up and/or cooldown portion as needed. If, however, you find you need to shorten the session to make it fit into 45 minutes, reduce the main sets as needed, but keep the warm-up, drills, and cooldown the same.

The eight swim sessions of approximately 2,000 yards/meters that are to be used with the "Just Finish" Programs in this book can be found on page 78 in chapter 6.

HELPFUL TIPS AND GUIDELINES FOR ADJUSTING THE SPRINT DISTANCE TRAINING PROGRAMS

Guidelines for adjusting the training programs for practice races can be found on pages 86–87; guidelines for adjusting training program for missed workouts can be found on page 87; and guidelines for using cross-training methods to help you train through injury can be found on page 88. All three of these sections are in chapter 6.

Now that we have presented our three sprint distance triathlon training programs, we will move on to chapter 8 where we will present three standard distance duathlon training programs.

10-Week Standard Distance Duathlon Training Programs

> *"The very basic core of a man's living spirit is his passion for adventure."*
> —CHRISTOPHER McCANDLESS

This chapter includes three detailed 10-week standard distance duathlon (10 km run, 40 km bike, and 5 km run) training programs. Each program is based on the number of hours an athlete has available to train. The Competitive Program includes an average of 10 and a peak of 12 weekly hours; the Intermediate Program includes an average of 7.5 and a peak of 9 weekly hours; and the "Just Finish" Program includes an average of 5 and a peak of 6 weekly hours. All you need to do is simply select the program that best fits your goals, competitiveness, level of experience, and available training time.

Each program explains exactly what to do each and every day throughout the 10-week period. There are no complicated formulas or overly general workout descriptions. Having worked with hundreds of athletes over the years, we know that this is not what most athletes want. Athletes want clear direction on exactly what they need to do and when. That is what this chapter provides. The programs are designed to be efficient, productive, and enjoyable.

Following is a summary comparison of the three 10-week training programs:

Training Program	Average Hours/Week	Peak Hours/Week	Total Hours (Approx.)
Competitive	10	12	100
Intermediate	7.5	9	75
"Just Finish"	5	6	50

First, consider the time management techniques presented in chapter 1 and the athlete profiles presented throughout this book, then conservatively estimate your weekly training time availability. Once you have completed this analysis, simply select the program that best fits your goals, your experience level, and your available training time.

ABBREVIATIONS FOR TRAINING PROGRAMS

An explanation of the abbreviations used in each of the training programs in this book can be found on pages 60–61 in chapter 6.

Following are our three 10-week training programs and full explanations of each, starting with the 10-week Competitive Program.

COMPETITIVE TRAINING PROGRAM FOR STANDARD DISTANCE DUATHLONS

The Competitive Program is for the experienced athlete who wants to maximize his or her potential and has available time to train for an average of about 10 hours a week, with several peak weeks of about 12 hours. The total combined training time over the 10-week period is approximately 100 hours, so we like to refer to this as the "100-hour duathlon plan."

If you are already in your racing season and in good form, you can begin the program immediately after your last race. The first week is fully aerobic, which will help to complete your recovery and firm up your aerobic base. Then in the second week, we will include easy pickups, on both the cycling and running sides, to prepare you to transition into our higher-intensity sessions.

From there our higher-intensity sessions and duration will build and become more challenging. We start at about 8.5 hours of training in the first week and then gradually build to about 12 hours in the seventh week.

As presented, short course duathlon is completed at a much higher intensity level than long course races, so as expected, standard distance training includes a greater focus on higher-intensity Z4 training. Weeks 3–8 will each have four sessions that will include Z4 training sessions, including two bike sessions and two run sessions. Our quantity of Z4 training will gradually build and peak in weeks 7 and 8 at about 105 minutes combined.

We will have two transition sessions per week, often including a long single transition session with a Z4 Insert on Saturdays and either a fully aerobic double or triple transition session on Wednesdays. As discussed, "brick" sessions are a crucial training element for duathlon success, and this plan is designed to maximize the benefits from these fun and challenging sessions.

Our longest sessions in the ten weeks will be three 3-hour transition sessions in weeks 3–8. Our longest runs of the ten weeks will be two 2.25-hour sessions in weeks 5 and 7 of the program.

This 10-week program includes one Rest Day/Slide Day per week. See the section in chapter 2 explaining the concept of Rest Day/Slide Days and how best to use them for optimal time management.

With nine days to go before our race, we will transition into our crisp taper phase to have us rested, sharp, and race-ready. Our durations will gradually decrease and our intensities will be no higher than Z2 during these last nine days. At this point, the most challenging training has been completed, and it is time to taper wisely and become physically and mentally energized.

If you are not coming off a race or you have not already built up to, or close to, 8.5 hours of training per week before starting the Competitive Program, it is suggested that you do so. Depending on your starting point, complete four to eight weeks of moderate aerobic exercise to be properly prepared to begin the program. If you are starting from scratch, we suggest you start with three easy bike sessions of about 30–45 minutes and three easy run sessions of 30–45 minutes. Then, over the four- to eight-week period, make gradual increases each week until you are comfortably up to, or close to, the 8.5-hour level. Once there, you are ready to begin with the first week of the 10-week program.

COMPETITIVE PROGRAM

The following chart details the 10-week Competitive Program:

COMPETITIVE PROGRAM
STANDARD DISTANCE DUATHLON

Week 1	Bike	Run
M	Rest Day/Slide Day	Rest Day/Slide Day
T	Off	60 min Z2
W	Double Trans: 15 min Z2 RUN (QC) 45 min Z2 BIKE (QC) 15 min Z2 RUN	Run portion in box to left
R	60 min Z2	Off
F	Off	60 min Z2
S	Trans: 1:30 hr Z2 (QC)	15 min Z2
S	1:15 hr Z1 (100+ RPM)	1:15 hr Z1 to Z2
Totals: 8:30 hr	4:30 hr	4:00 hr
Week 2	Bike	Run
M	Rest Day/Slide Day	Rest Day/Slide Day
T	Off	60 min Z2 (at 10 min, insert 5 x 1 min PU @ 1 min jog)
W	Triple Trans: 15 min Z2 RUN (QC) 22.5 min Z2 BIKE (QC) 15 min Z2 RUN (QC) 22.5 min Z2 BIKE	Run portion in box to left
R	1:15 hr Z2 (at 10 min, insert 5 x 1 min PU @ 1 min spin)	Off
F	Off	60 min Z2 (at 45 min, insert 5 min Z4)
S	Trans: 1:45 hr Z2 (at 1:30, insert 5 min Z4) (QC)	30 min Z2
S	1:15 hr Z1 (100+ RPM)	1:30 hr Z1 to Z2
Totals: 9:30 hr	5:00 hr	4:30 hr

COMPETITIVE PROGRAM
STANDARD DISTANCE DUATHLON

Week 3	Bike	Run
M	Rest Day/Slide Day	Rest Day/Slide Day
T	Off	60 min Z2 (at 10 min, insert 8 x 2 min Z4 @ 1 min jog)
W	Double Trans: 15 min Z2 RUN (QC) 45 min Z2 BIKE (QC) 15 min Z2 RUN	Run portion in box to left
R	1:15 hr Z2 (at 10 min, insert 5 x 4 min Z4 @ 2 min spin, then 5 x 2 min Z4 @ 1 min spin)	Off
F	Off	60 min Z2 (at 45 min, insert 7.5 min Z4)
S	Trans: 2:15 hr Z2 (at 2:00, insert 10 min Z4) (QC)	45 min Z2
S	1:15 hr Z1 (100+ RPM)	1:45 hr Z1 to Z2
Totals: 10:30 hr	5:30 hr	5:00 hr
Week 4	Bike	Run
M	Rest Day/Slide Day	Rest Day/Slide Day
T	Off	60 min Z2 (at 10 min, insert 7 x 3 min Z4 @ 1.5 min jog)
W	Triple Trans: 15 min Z2 RUN (QC) 30 min Z2 BIKE (QC) 15 min Z2 RUN (QC) 30 min Z2 BIKE	Run portion in box to left
R	1:15 hr Z2 (at 10 min, insert 15 x 2 min Z4 Hill Repeats @ spin back down)	Off
F	Off	60 min Z2 (at 45 min, insert 10 min Z4)
S	Trans: 2:15 hr Z2 (at 1:55, insert 15 min Z4) (QC)	45 min Z2
S	1:15 hr Z1 (100+ RPM)	2:00 hr Z1 to Z2
Totals: 11:00 hr	5:45 hr	5:15 hr

COMPETITIVE PROGRAM
STANDARD DISTANCE DUATHLON

Week 5	Bike	Run
M	Rest Day/Slide Day	Rest Day/Slide Day
T	Off	60 min Z2 (at 10 min, insert 6 x 4.5 min Z4 @ 2 min jog)
W	Double Trans: 15 min Z2 RUN (QC) 60 min Z2 BIKE (QC) 15 min Z2 RUN	Run portion in box to left
R	1:30 hr Z2 (at 10 min, insert 4 x 5 min Z4 @ 3 min spin, then 5 x 2 min Z4 @ 1 min spin)	Off
F	Off	60 min Z2 (at 40 min, insert 12.5 min Z4)
S	Trans: 2:15 hr Z2 (at 1:50, insert 20 min Z4) (QC)	45 min Z2
S	1:15 hr Z1 (100+ RPM)	2:15 hr Z1 to Z2
Totals: 11:30 hr	6:00 hr	5:30 hr
Week 6	Bike	Run
M	Rest Day/Slide Day	Rest Day/Slide Day
T	Off	1:15 hr Z2 (at 10 min, insert 5 x 6 min Z4 @ 3 min jog)
W	Triple Trans: 15 min Z2 RUN (QC) 30 min Z2 BIKE (QC) 15 min Z2 RUN (QC) 30 min Z2 BIKE	Run portion in box to left
R	1:30 hr Z2 (at 10 min, insert 12 x 2.5 min Z4 Hill Repeats @ spin back down)	Off
F	Off	1:15 hr Z2 (at 55 min, insert 15 min Z4)
S	Trans: 2:15 hr Z2 (at 1:50, insert 25 min Z4) (QC)	45 min Z2
S	1:15 hr Z1 (100+ RPM)	1:45 hr Z1 to Z2
Totals: 11:30 hr	6:00 hr	5:30 hr

COMPETITIVE PROGRAM
STANDARD DISTANCE DUATHLON

Week 7	Bike	Run
M	Rest Day/Slide Day	Rest Day/Slide Day
T	Off	1:15 hr Z2 (at 10 min, insert 4 x 7.5 min Z4 @ 3.5 min jog)
W	Double Trans: 15 min Z2 RUN (QC) 60 min Z2 BIKE (QC) 15 min Z2 RUN	Run portion in box to left
R	1:30 hr Z2 (at 10 min, insert 2 x 7.5 min Z4 @ 3.5 min spin, then 3 x 5 min Z4 @ 3 min spin)	Off
F	Off	1:15 hr Z2 (at 55 min, insert 15 min Z4)
S	Trans: 2:15 hr Z2 (at 1:40, insert 30 min Z4) (QC)	45 min Z2
S	1:15 hr Z1 (100+ RPM)	2:15 hr Z1 to Z2
Totals: 12:00 hr	6:00 hr	6:00 hr
Week 8	**Bike**	**Run**
M	Rest Day/Slide Day	Rest Day/Slide Day
T	Off	1:15 hr Z2 (at 10 min, insert 6 x 3 min Z4 @ 1.5 min jog, then 6 x 2 min Z4 @ 1 min jog)
W	Triple Trans: 15 min Z2 RUN (QC) 30 min Z2 BIKE (QC) 15 min Z2 RUN (QC) 30 min Z2 BIKE	Run portion in box to left
R	1:30 hr Z2 (at 10 min, insert 10 x 3 min Z4 Hill Repeats @ spin back down)	Off
F	Off	1:15 hr Z2 (at 55 min, insert 15 min Z4)
S	Trans: 2:15 hr Z2 (at 1:40, insert 30 min Z4) (QC)	45 min Z2
S	1:15 hr Z1 (100+ RPM)	1:45 hr Z1 to Z2
Totals: 11:30 hr	6:00 hr	5:30 hr

COMPETITIVE PROGRAM
STANDARD DISTANCE DUATHLON

Week 9	Bike	Run
M	Rest Day/Slide Day	Rest Day/Slide Day
T	Off	1:15 hr Z2 (at 10 min, insert 4 x 4.5 min Z4 @ 2 min jog, then 6 x 2 min Z4 @ 1 min jog)
W	Double Trans: 15 min Z2 RUN (QC) 60 min Z2 BIKE (QC) 15 min Z2 RUN	Run portion in box to left
R	1:30 hr Z2 (at 10 min, insert 1 x 10 min Z4 @ 5 min spin, then 5 x 4 min Z4 @ 2 min spin)	Off
F	Off	1:15 hr Z2 (at 60 min, insert 10 min Z4)
S	Trans: 1:30 hr Z2 (QC)	30 min Z2
S	60 min Z1 (100+ RPM)	60 min Z1 to Z2
Totals: 9:30 hr	5:00 hr	4:30 hr
Week 10	Bike	Run
M	Rest Day/Slide Day	Rest Day/Slide Day
T	Off	45 min Z1 to Z2 (at 10 min, insert 5 x 1 min PU @ 1 min jog)
W	Trans: 45 min Z1 to Z2 (QC)	15 min Z1 to Z2
R	60 min Z1 (at 10 min, insert 5 x 1 min PU @ 1 min spin)	Off
F	Off	40 min Z1 (at 10 min, insert 5 x 1 min PU @ 1 min jog)
S	15 min Z1—easy bike safety check	20 min Z1—easy (in a.m.)
S	RACE!!! (Standard Distance Duathlon)	RACE!!! (Standard Distance Duathlon)
Totals: 4:00 hr	2:00 hr (+ Race)	2:00 hr (+ Race)

The second of our three 10-week training programs for the standard distance duathlon is the Intermediate Program.

INTERMEDIATE TRAINING PROGRAM FOR STANDARD DISTANCE DUATHLONS

The Intermediate Program is for the athlete who fits best between the Competitive Program and the "Just Finish" Program, both in terms of goals and competitiveness, and has available time to train for an average of about 7.5 hours a week, with several peak weeks of about 9 hours. The total combined training time over the 10-week period is approximately 75 hours, so we like to refer to this as the "75-hour duathlon plan."

If you are already in your racing season and in good form, you can begin the program immediately after your race. The first week is fully aerobic, which will help to complete your recovery and firm up your aerobic base. Then in the second week, we will include easy pickups, on both the cycling and running sides, to prepare you to transition into our higher-intensity sessions.

From there our higher-intensity sessions and duration will build and become more challenging. We start at about 6.25 hours of training in the first week and then gradually build each week to about 9 hours in the sixth week.

As presented, short course duathlon is completed at a much higher intensity level than long course races, so as expected, standard distance training includes a greater focus on higher-intensity Z4 training. Weeks 3–8 will each have three sessions that will include Z4 training sessions, including two bike sessions and one run session. Our quantity of Z4 training will gradually build and peak in week 8 at close to 80 minutes combined.

We will have two transition sessions per week, usually including a long single transition session with a Z4 Insert on Saturdays and either a fully aerobic double or triple transition session on Wednesdays. As discussed, "brick" sessions are a crucial training element for duathlon success, and this plan is designed to maximize the benefits from these fun and challenging sessions.

Our longest sessions in the ten weeks will be three 2.5-hour transition sessions in weeks 4–8 of the program. Our longest runs of the twelve weeks will be 1.5-hour sessions and will occur in weeks 2–8.

This 10-week program includes two Rest Day/Slide Days per week. See the section in chapter 2 explaining the concept of Rest Day/Slide days and how to use them for optimal time management.

With nine days to go before our race, we will transition into our crisp taper phase to have us rested, sharp, and race-ready. Our durations will gradually decrease and our intensities will be no higher than Z2 during these last nine days. At this point, the most challenging training has been completed, and it is time to taper wisely and become physically and mentally energized.

If you are not coming off a race or you have not already built up to, or close to, 6.25 hours of training per week before starting the Intermediate Program, it is suggested that you do so. Depending on your starting point, complete four to eight weeks of moderate aerobic exercise to be properly prepared to begin the program. If you are starting from scratch, we suggest you start with three easy bike sessions of about 30 minutes and three easy run sessions of 15–30 minutes. Then, over the four- to eight-week period, make gradual increases each week until you are comfortably up to, or close to, the 6.25 hour level. Once there, you are ready to begin with the first week of the 10-week program.

INTERMEDIATE PROGRAM

The following chart details the 10-week Intermediate Program:

INTERMEDIATE PROGRAM
STANDARD DISTANCE DUATHLON

Week 1	Bike	Run
M	Rest Day/Slide Day	Rest Day/Slide Day
T	Off	60 min Z2
W	Double Trans: 15 min Z2 RUN (QC) 30 min Z2 BIKE (QC) 15 min Z2 RUN	Run portion in box to left
R	60 min Z2	Off
F	Rest Day/Slide Day	Rest Day/Slide Day
S	Trans: 1:15 hr Z2 (QC)	15 min Z2
S	30 min Z1 (100+ RPM)	1:15 hr Z1 to Z2
Totals: 6:15 hr	3:15 hr	3:00 hr
Week 2	**Bike**	**Run**
M	Rest Day/Slide Day	Rest Day/Slide Day
T	Off	60 min Z2 (at 10 min, insert 5 x 1 min PU @ 1 min jog)
W	Triple Trans: 15 min Z2 RUN (QC) 22.5 min Z2 BIKE (QC) 15 min Z2 RUN (QC) 22.5 min Z2 BIKE	Run portion in box to left
R	60 min Z2 (at 10 min, insert 5 x 1 min PU @ 1 min spin)	Off
F	Rest Day/Slide Day	Rest Day/Slide Day
S	Trans: 1:15 hr Z2 (at 1:00, insert 5 min Z4) (QC)	30 min Z2
S	30 min Z1 (100+ RPM)	1:30 hr Z1 to Z2
Totals: 7:00 hr	3:30 hr	3:30 hr

INTERMEDIATE PROGRAM
STANDARD DISTANCE DUATHLON

Week 3	Bike	Run
M	Rest Day/Slide Day	Rest Day/Slide Day
T	Off	60 min Z2 (at 45 min, insert 5 min Z4)
W	Double Trans: 15 min Z2 RUN (QC) 45 min Z2 BIKE (QC) 15 min Z2 RUN	Run portion in box to left
R	60 min Z2 (at 10 min, insert 4 x 4 min Z4 @ 2 min spin, then 4 x 2 min Z4 @ 1 min spin)	Off
F	Rest Day/Slide Day	Rest Day/Slide Day
S	Trans: 1:30 hr Z2 (at 1:15, insert 10 min Z4) (QC)	45 min Z2
S	30 min Z1 (100+ RPM)	1:30 hr Z1 to Z2
Totals: 7:30 hr	3:45 hr	3:45 hr
Week 4	Bike	Run
M	Rest Day/Slide Day	Rest Day/Slide Day
T	Off	1:15 hr Z2 (at 10 min, insert 7 x 3 min Z4 @ 1.5 min jog)
W	Triple Trans: 15 min Z2 RUN (QC) 22.5 min Z2 BIKE (QC) 15 min Z2 RUN (QC) 22.5 min Z2 BIKE	Run portion in box to left
R	60 min Z2 (at 10 min, insert 12 x 2 min Z4 Hill Repeats @ spin back down)	Off
F	Rest Day/Slide Day	Rest Day/Slide Day
S	Trans: 1:45 hr Z2 (at 1:25, insert 15 min Z4) (QC)	45 min Z2
S	30 min Z1 (100+ RPM)	1:30 hr Z1 to Z2
Totals: 8:00 hr	4:00 hr	4:00 hr

INTERMEDIATE PROGRAM
STANDARD DISTANCE DUATHLON

Week 5	Bike	Run
M	Rest Day/Slide Day	Rest Day/Slide Day
T	Off	1:15 hr Z2 (at 60 min, insert 10 min Z4)
W	Double Trans: 15 min Z2 RUN (QC) 45 min Z2 BIKE (QC) 15 min Z2 RUN	Run portion in box to left
R	1:15 hr Z2 (at 10 min, insert 3 x 5 min Z4 @ 3 min spin, then 5 x 2 min Z4 @ 1 min spin)	Off
F	Rest Day/Slide Day	Rest Day/Slide Day
S	Trans: 1:45 hr Z2 (at 1:20, insert 20 min Z4) (QC)	45 min Z2
S	45 min Z1 (100+ RPM)	1:30 hr Z1 to Z2
Totals: 8:30 hr	4:30 hr	4:00 hr
Week 6	Bike	Run
M	Rest Day/Slide Day	Rest Day/Slide Day
T	Off	1:15 hr Z2 (at 10 min, insert 5 x 4.5 min Z4 @ 2 min jog)
W	Triple Trans: 15 min Z2 RUN (QC) 30 min Z2 BIKE (QC) 15 min Z2 RUN (QC) 30 min Z2 BIKE	Run portion in box to left
R	1:15 hr Z2 (at 10 min, insert 10 x 2.5 min Z4 Hill Repeats @ spin back down)	Off
F	Rest Day/Slide Day	Rest Day/Slide Day
S	Trans: 1:45 hr Z2 (at 1:15, insert 25 min Z4) (QC)	45 min Z2
S	1:00 hr Z1 (100+ RPM)	1:30 hr Z1 to Z2
Totals: 9:00 hr	5:00 hr	4:00 hr

INTERMEDIATE PROGRAM
STANDARD DISTANCE DUATHLON

Week 7	Bike	Run
M	Rest Day/Slide Day	Rest Day/Slide Day
T	Off	1:15 hr Z2 (at 55 min, insert 15 min Z4)
W	Double Trans: 15 min Z2 RUN (QC) 60 min Z2 BIKE (QC) 15 min Z2 RUN	Run portion in box to left
R	1:15 hr Z2 (at 10 min, insert 2 x 7.5 min Z4 @ 3.5 min spin, then 2 x 5 min Z4 @ 3 min spin)	Off
F	Rest Day/Slide Day	Rest Day/Slide Day
S	Trans: 1:45 hr Z2 (at 1:10, insert 30 min Z4) (QC)	45 min Z2
S	1:00 hr Z1 (100+ RPM)	1:30 hr Z1 to Z2
Totals: 9:00 hr	5:00 hr	4:00 hr
Week 8	**Bike**	**Run**
M	Rest Day/Slide Day	Rest Day/Slide Day
T	Off	1:15 hr Z2 (at 10 min, insert 4 x 6 min Z4 @ 3 min jog)
W	Triple Trans: 15 min Z2 RUN (QC) 30 min Z2 BIKE (QC) 15 min Z2 RUN (QC) 30 min Z2 BIKE	Run portion in box to left
R	1:15 hr Z2 (at 10 min, insert 8 x 3 min Z4 Hill Repeats @ spin back down)	Off
F	Rest Day/Slide Day	Rest Day/Slide Day
S	Trans: 1:45 hr Z2 (at 1:10, insert 30 min Z4) (QC)	45 min Z2
S	1:00 hr Z1 (100+ RPM)	1:30 hr Z1 to Z2
Totals: 9:00 hr	5:00 hr	4:00 hr

INTERMEDIATE PROGRAM
STANDARD DISTANCE DUATHLON

Week 9	Bike	Run
M	Rest Day/Slide Day	Rest Day/Slide Day
T	Off	1:15 hr Z2 (at 55 min, insert 15 min Z4)
W	Double Trans: 15 min Z2 RUN (QC) 60 min Z2 BIKE (QC) 15 min Z2 RUN	Run portion in box to left
R	1:15 hr Z2 (at 10 min, insert 1 x 10 min Z4 @ 5 min spin, then 4 x 4 min Z4 @ 2 min spin)	Off
F	Rest Day/Slide Day	Rest Day/Slide Day
S	Trans: 1:15 hr Z2 (QC)	30 min Z2
S	1:00 hr Z1 (100+ RPM)	1:15 hr Z1 to Z2
Totals: 8:00 hr	4:30 hr	3:30 hr
Week 10	**Bike**	**Run**
M	Rest Day/Slide Day	Rest Day/Slide Day
T	Off	45 min Z1 to Z2 (at 10 min, insert 5 x 1 min PU @ 1 min jog)
W	Trans: 45 min Z1 to Z2 (QC)	15 min Z1 to Z2
R	60 min Z1 (at 10 min, insert 5 x 1 min PU @ 1 min spin)	Off
F	Rest Day/Slide Day	Rest Day/Slide Day
S	15 min Z1—easy bike safety check	30 min Z1—easy (in a.m.)
S	RACE!!! (Standard Distance Duathlon)	RACE!!! (Standard Distance Duathlon)
Totals: 3:30 hr	2:00 hr (+ Race)	1:30 hr (+ Race)

The final of our three 10-week training programs for the standard distance duathlon is the "Just Finish" Program.

"JUST FINISH" TRAINING PROGRAM FOR STANDARD DISTANCE DUATHLONS

The "Just Finish" program is for the athlete who has limited time available to train, but would like to be able to complete a standard distance duathlon safely, in good health, and in good spirits. The "Just finish" athlete needs to have available time to train for an average of about 5 hours a week, with several peak weeks of about 6 hours. The total combined training time over the 10-week period is approximately 50 hours, so we like to refer to this as the "50-hour duathlon plan."

If you are already in your racing season and in good form, you can begin the program immediately after your race. The first week is fully aerobic, which will help to complete your recovery and firm up your aerobic base. Then in the second week, we will include easy pickups, on both the cycling and running sides, to prepare you to transition into our higher-intensity sessions.

From there our higher-intensity sessions and duration will build and become more challenging. We start at about 4 hours of training in the first week and then gradually build to about 6 hours in the fifth week.

As presented, short course duathlon is completed at a much higher intensity level than long course races, so as expected, standard distance training includes a greater focus on higher-intensity Z4 training. Weeks 3–8 will each have three sessions that will include Z4 training sessions, including two bike sessions and one run session. Our quantity of Z4 training will gradually build and peak in week 8 at about 66 minutes combined.

We will have two transition sessions per week, usually including a long single transition session with a Z4 Insert on Saturdays and either a fully aerobic double or triple transition session on Wednesdays. As discussed, "brick" sessions are a crucial training element for duathlon success, and this plan is designed to maximize the benefits from these fun and challenging sessions.

Our longest sessions in the ten weeks will be 2-hour transition sessions in weeks 5–8 of the program. Our longest runs of the ten weeks will be 1-hour sessions and will occur in weeks 3–8.

This 10-week program includes two Rest Day/Slide Days per week. See the section in chapter 2 explaining the concept of Rest Day/Slide Days and how to use them for optimal time management. This program also includes optional high-RPM cycling technique sessions.

With nine days to go before our race, we will transition into our crisp taper phase to have us rested, sharp, and race-ready. Our durations will gradually decrease and our intensities will be no higher than Z2 during these last nine days. At this point, the most challenging training has been completed, and it is time to taper wisely and become physically and mentally energized.

In chapter 14 we present a specific racing strategy for "Just Finish" athletes, which we suggest you consider.

If you are not coming off a race or you have not already built up to, or close to, 4 hours of training per week before starting the "Just Finish" Program, it is suggested that you do so. Depending on your starting point, complete four to eight weeks of moderate aerobic exercise to be properly prepared to begin the program. If you are starting from scratch, we suggest you start with two easy bike sessions of about 15–30 minutes and two easy run sessions of 15–30 minutes. Then, over the four- to eight-week period, make gradual increases each week until you are comfortably up to, or close to, the 4-hour level. Once there, you are ready to begin with the first week of the 10-week program.

"JUST FINISH" PROGRAM

The following chart details the 10-week "Just Finish" Program:

"JUST FINISH" PROGRAM
STANDARD DISTANCE DUATHLON

Week 1	Bike	Run
M	Rest Day/Slide Day	Rest Day/Slide Day
T	Off	30 min Z2
W	Double Trans: 15 min Z2 RUN (QC) 30 min Z2 BIKE (QC) 15 min Z2 RUN	Run portion in box to left
R	45 min Z2	Off
F	Rest Day/Slide Day	Rest Day/Slide Day
S	Trans: 45 min Z2 (QC)	15 min Z2
S	Optional: 30 min Z1 (100+ RPM)	45 min Z1 to Z2
Totals: 4:00 hr	2:00+ hr	2:00 hr
Week 2	**Bike**	**Run**
M	Rest Day/Slide Day	Rest Day/Slide Day
T	Off	45 min Z2 (at 10 min, insert 5 x 1 min PU @ 1 min jog)
W	Triple Trans: 15 min Z2 RUN (QC) 15 min Z2 BIKE (QC) 15 min Z2 RUN (QC) 15 min Z2 BIKE	Run portion in box to left
R	45 min Z2 (at 10 min, insert 5 x 1 min PU @ 1 min spin)	Off
F	Rest Day/Slide Day	Rest Day/Slide Day
S	Trans: 1:00 hr Z2 (at 45 min, insert 5 min Z4) (QC)	15 min Z2
S	Optional: 30 min Z1 (100+ RPM)	45 min Z1 to Z2
Totals: 4:30 hr	2:15+ hr	2:15 hr

"JUST FINISH" PROGRAM
STANDARD DISTANCE DUATHLON

Week 3	Bike	Run
M	Rest Day/Slide Day	Rest Day/Slide Day
T	Off	45 min Z2 (at 30 min, insert 5 min Z4)
W	Double Trans: 15 min Z2 RUN (QC) 30 min Z2 BIKE (QC) 15 min Z2 RUN	Run portion in box to left
R	45 min Z2 (at 10 min, insert 3 x 4 min Z4 @ 2 min spin, then 3 x 2 min Z4 @ 1 min spin)	Off
F	Rest Day/Slide Day	Rest Day/Slide Day
S	Trans: 1:15 hr Z2 (at 1:00, insert 10 min Z4) (QC)	15 min Z2
S	Optional: 30 min Z1 (100+ RPM)	60 min Z1 to Z2
Totals: 5:00 hr	2:30+ hr	2:30 hr
Week 4	**Bike**	**Run**
M	Rest Day/Slide Day	Rest Day/Slide Day
T	Off	60 min Z2 (at 10 min, insert 7 x 3 min Z4 @ 1.5 min jog)
W	Triple Trans: 15 min Z2 RUN (QC) 15 min Z2 BIKE (QC) 15 min Z2 RUN (QC) 15 min Z2 BIKE	Run portion in box to left
R	60 min Z2 (at 10 min, insert 8 x 2 min Z4 Hill Repeats @ spin back down)	Off
F	Rest Day/Slide Day	Rest Day/Slide Day
S	Trans: 1:15 hr Z2 (at 55 min, insert 15 min Z4) (QC)	15 min Z2
S	Optional: 30 min Z1 (100+ RPM)	60 min Z1 to Z2
Totals: 5:30 hr	2:45+ hr	2:45 hr

"JUST FINISH" PROGRAM
STANDARD DISTANCE DUATHLON

Week 5	Bike	Run
M	Rest Day/Slide Day	Rest Day/Slide Day
T	Off	60 min Z2 (at 45 min, insert 10 min Z4)
W	Double Trans: 15 min Z2 RUN (QC) 30 min Z2 BIKE (QC) 15 min Z2 RUN	Run portion in box to left
R	60 min Z2 (at 10 min, insert 2 x 5 min Z4 @ 3 min spin, then 4 x 2 min Z4 @ 1 min spin)	Off
F	Rest Day/Slide Day	Rest Day/Slide Day
S	Trans: 1:30 hr Z2 (at 1:05, insert 20 min Z4) (QC)	30 min Z2
S	Optional: 30 min Z1 (100+ RPM)	60 min Z1 to Z2
Totals: 6:00 hr	3:00+ hr	3:00 hr
Week 6	**Bike**	**Run**
M	Rest Day/Slide Day	Rest Day/Slide Day
T	Off	60 min Z2 (at 10 min, insert 4 x 4.5 min Z4 @ 2 min jog)
W	Triple Trans: 15 min Z2 RUN (QC) 15 min Z2 BIKE (QC) 15 min Z2 RUN (QC) 15 min Z2 BIKE	Run portion in box to left
R	60 min Z2 (at 10 min, insert 7 x 2.5 min Z4 Hill Repeats @ spin back down)	Off
F	Rest Day/Slide Day	Rest Day/Slide Day
S	Trans: 1:30 hr Z2 (at 1:00, insert 25 min Z4) (QC)	30 min Z2
S	Optional: 30 min Z1 (100+ RPM)	60 min Z1 to Z2
Totals: 6:00 hr	3:00+ hr	3:00 hr

"JUST FINISH" PROGRAM
STANDARD DISTANCE DUATHLON

Week 7	Bike	Run
M	Rest Day/Slide Day	Rest Day/Slide Day
T	Off	60 min Z2 (at 40 min, insert 15 min Z4)
W	Double Trans: 15 min Z2 RUN (QC) 30 min Z2 BIKE (QC) 15 min Z2 RUN	Run portion in box to left
R	60 min Z2 (at 10 min, insert 1 x 7.5 min Z4 @ 3.5 min spin, then 2 x 5 min Z4 @ 3 min spin)	Off
F	Rest Day/Slide Day	Rest Day/Slide Day
S	Trans: 1:30 hr Z2 (at 55 min, insert 30 min Z4) (QC)	30 min Z2
S	Optional: 30 min Z1 (100+ RPM)	60 min Z1 to Z2
Totals: 6:00 hr	3:00+ hr	3:00 hr
Week 8	**Bike**	**Run**
M	Rest Day/Slide Day	Rest Day/Slide Day
T	Off	60 min Z2 (at 10 min, insert 3 x 6 min Z4 @ 3 min jog)
W	Triple Trans: 15 min Z2 RUN (QC) 15 min Z2 BIKE (QC) 15 min Z2 RUN (QC) 15 min Z2 BIKE	Run portion in box to left
R	60 min Z2 (at 10 min, insert 6 x 3 min Z4 Hill Repeats @ spin back down)	Off
F	Rest Day/Slide Day	Rest Day/Slide Day
S	Trans: 1:30 hr Z2 (at 55 min, insert 30 min Z4) (QC)	30 min Z2
S	Optional: 30 min Z1 (100+ RPM)	60 min Z1 to Z2
Totals: 6:00 hr	3:00+ hr	3:00 hr

"JUST FINISH" PROGRAM
STANDARD DISTANCE DUATHLON

Week 9	Bike	Run
M	Rest Day/Slide Day	Rest Day/Slide Day
T	Off	60 min Z2 (at 40 min, insert 15 min Z4)
W	Double Trans: 15 min Z2 RUN (QC) 30 min Z2 BIKE (QC) 15 min Z2 RUN	Run portion in box to left
R	60 min Z2 (at 10 min, insert 1 x 10 min Z4 @ 5 min spin, then 2 x 4 min Z4 @ 2 min spin)	Off
F	Rest Day/Slide Day	Rest Day/Slide Day
S	Trans: 60 min Z2 (QC)	15 min Z2
S	Off	45 min Z1 to Z2
Totals: 5:00 hr	2:30 hr	2:30 hr
Week 10	**Bike**	**Run**
M	Rest Day/Slide Day	Rest Day/Slide Day
T	Off	45 min Z1 to Z2 (at 10 min, insert 5 x 1 min PU @ 1 min jog)
W	Trans: 45 min Z1 to Z2 (QC)	15 min Z1 to Z2
R	30 min Z1 (at 10 min, insert 5 x 1 min PU @ 1 min spin)	Off
F	Rest Day/Slide Day	Rest Day/Slide Day
S	15 min Z1—easy bike safety check	30 min Z1—easy (in a.m.)
S	RACE!!! (Standard Distance Duathlon)	RACE!!! (Standard Distance Duathlon)
Totals: 3:00 hr	1:30 hr (+ Race)	1:30 hr (+ Race)

HELPFUL TIPS AND GUIDELINES FOR ADJUSTING THE STANDARD DISTANCE DUATHLON TRAINING PROGRAMS

Guidelines for adjusting the training programs for practice races can be found on pages 86–87; guidelines for adjusting training program for missed workouts can be found on page 87; and guidelines for using cross-training methods to help you train through injury can be found on page 88. All three of these sections are in chapter 6.

Now that we have presented our three standard distance duathlon training programs, we will move on to chapter 9, where we will present three sprint distance duathlon training programs.

» 6-Week Sprint Distance Duathlon Training Programs

A failure isn't a failure if it prepares you for success tomorrow. —LOLO JONES

This chapter includes three detailed 6-week sprint distance duathlon (5 km run, 20 km bike, and 2.5 km run) training programs. Each program is based on the number of hours an athlete has available to train. The Competitive Program includes an average of 8.5 and a peak of 10 weekly hours; the Intermediate Program includes an average of 6.5 and a peak of 8 weekly hours; and the "Just Finish" Program includes an average of 5 and a peak of 6 weekly hours. All you need to do is simply select the program that best fits your goals, competitiveness, level of experience, and available training time.

Each program explains exactly what to do each and every day throughout the 6-week period. There are no complicated formulas or overly general workout descriptions. Having worked with hundreds of athletes over the years, we know that this is not what most athletes want. Athletes want clear direction on what they need to do and when. That is exactly what this chapter provides. The programs are designed to be efficient, productive, and enjoyable.

Following is a summary comparison of the three 6-week training programs:

Training Program	Average Hours/Week	Peak Hours/Week	Total Hours (Approx.)
Competitive	8.5	10	50
Intermediate	6.5	8	40
"Just Finish"	5	6	30

First, consider the time management techniques presented in chapter 1 and the athlete profiles presented throughout this book, then conservatively estimate your weekly training time availability. Once you have completed this analysis, simply select the program that best fits your goals, your experience level, and your available training time.

ABBREVIATIONS FOR TRAINING PROGRAMS

An explanation of the abbreviations used in each of the training programs in this book can be found on pages 60–61 in chapter 6.

Following are our three 6-week training programs and full explanations of each, starting with the 6-week Competitive Program.

COMPETITIVE TRAINING PROGRAM FOR SPRINT DISTANCE DUATHLONS

The Competitive Program is for the experienced athlete who wants to maximize his or her potential and has available time to train for an average of about 8.5 hours a week, with three peak weeks of about 10 hours. The total combined training time over the 6-week period is approximately 50 hours, so we like to refer to this as the "50-hour sprint duathlon plan."

If you are already in your racing season and in good form, you can begin the program immediately after your last race. The first week will include easy pickups, on both the cycling and running sides, to prepare you to transition into our higher-intensity sessions.

From there our higher-intensity sessions and duration will build and become more challenging. We start at about 8 hours of training in the first week and then gradually build to about 10 hours in the third week.

As presented, short course duathlon is completed at a much higher intensity level than long course races, so as expected, sprint distance training includes a greater focus on higher-intensity Z4 training. Weeks 2–4 will each have four sessions that will include Z4 training sessions, including two bike sessions and two run sessions. Our quantity of Z4 training will gradually build and peak in week 4 at over 100 minutes combined.

We will have two transition sessions per week, usually including a long single transition session with a Z4 Insert on Saturdays and either a fully aerobic double or triple transition session on Wednesdays. As discussed, "brick" sessions are a crucial training element for duathlon success, and this plan is designed to maximize the benefits from these fun and challenging sessions.

Our longest sessions in the six weeks will be two 2.5-hour transition sessions in weeks 3 and 4. Our longest runs of the six weeks will be 1.25-hour sessions in weeks 2–5 of the program.

This 6-week program includes one Rest Day/Slide Day per week. See the section in chapter 2 explaining the concept of Rest Day/Slide Days and how best to use them for optimal time management.

With nine days to go before our race, we will transition into our crisp taper phase to have us rested, sharp, and race-ready. Our durations will gradually decrease and our intensities will be no higher than Z2 during these last nine days. At this point, the most challenging training has been completed, and it is time to taper wisely and become physically and mentally energized.

If you are not coming off a race or you have not already built up to, or close to, 8 hours of training per week before starting the Competitive Program, it is suggested that you do so. Depending on your starting point, complete four to eight weeks of moderate aerobic exercise to be properly prepared to begin the program. If you are starting from scratch, we suggest you start with three easy bike sessions of about 30–45 minutes and three easy run sessions of 30–45 minutes. Then, over the four- to eight-week period, make gradual increases each week until you are comfortably up to, or close to, the 8-hour level. Once there, you are ready to begin with the first week of the 6-week program.

COMPETITIVE PROGRAM

The following chart details the 6-week Competitive Program:

COMPETITIVE PROGRAM
SPRINT DISTANCE DUATHLON

Week 1	Bike	Run
M	Rest Day/Slide Day	Rest Day/Slide Day
T	Off	60 min Z2
W	Double Trans: 15 min Z2 RUN (QC) 45 min Z2 BIKE (QC) 15 min Z2 RUN	Run portion in box to left
R	60 min Z2	Off
F	Off	60 min Z2 (at 10 min, insert 5 x 1 min PU @ 1 min jog)
S	Trans: 1:15 hr Z2 (at 1:00, insert 5 x 1 min PU @ 1 min spin) (QC)	30 min Z2
S	60 min Z1 (100+ RPM)	60 min Z1 to Z2
Totals: 8:00 hr	4:00 hr	4:00 hr
Week 2	Bike	Run
M	Rest Day/Slide Day	Rest Day/Slide Day
T	Off	60 min Z2 (at 10 min, insert 8 x 2 min Z4 @ 1 min jog)
W	Triple Trans: 15 min Z2 RUN (QC) 22.5 min Z2 BIKE (QC) 15 min Z2 RUN (QC) 22.5 min Z2 BIKE	Run portion in box to left
R	1:15 hr Z2 (at 10 min, insert 5 x 4 min Z4 @ 2 min spin, then 5 x 2 min Z4 @ 1 min spin)	Off
F	Off	60 min Z2 (at 45 min, insert 5 min Z4)
S	Trans: 1:30 hr Z2 (at 1:15, insert 10 min Z4) (QC)	45 min Z2
S	1:00 hr Z1 (100+ RPM)	1:15 hr Z1 to Z2
Totals: 9:00 hr	4:30 hr	4:30 hr

COMPETITIVE PROGRAM
SPRINT DISTANCE DUATHLON

Week 3	Bike	Run
M	Rest Day/Slide Day	Rest Day/Slide Day
T	Off	1:15 hr Z2 (at 10 min, insert 7 x 3 min Z4 @ 1.5 min jog)
W	Double Trans: 15 min Z2 RUN (QC) 45 min Z2 BIKE (QC) 15 min Z2 RUN	Run portion in box to left
R	1:15 hr Z2 (at 10 min, insert 15 x 2 min Z4 Hill Repeats @ spin back down)	Off
F	Off	1:15 hr Z2 (at 60 min, insert 10 min Z4)
S	Trans: 1:45 hr Z2 (at 1:20, insert 20 min Z4) (QC)	45 min Z2
S	1:15 hr Z1 (100+ RPM)	1:15 hr Z1 to Z2
Totals: 10:00 hr	5:00 hr	5:00 hr
Week 4	Bike	Run
M	Rest Day/Slide Day	Rest Day/Slide Day
T	Off	1:15 hr Z2 (at 10 min, insert 6 x 4.5 min Z4 @ 2 min jog)
W	Triple Trans: 15 min Z2 RUN (QC) 22.5 min Z2 BIKE (QC) 15 min Z2 RUN (QC) 22.5 min Z2 BIKE	Run portion in box to left
R	1:15 hr Z2 (at 10 min, insert 2 x 7.5 min Z4 @ 3.5 min spin, then 3 x 5 min Z4 @ 3 min spin)	Off
F	Off	1:15 hr Z2 (at 55 min, insert 15 min Z4)
S	Trans: 1:45 hr Z2 (at 1:10, insert 30 min Z4) (QC)	45 min Z2
S	1:15 hr Z1 (100+ RPM)	1:15 hr Z1 to Z2
Totals: 10:00 hr	5:00 hr	5:00 hr

COMPETITIVE PROGRAM
SPRINT DISTANCE DUATHLON

Week 5	Bike	Run
M	Rest Day/Slide Day	Rest Day/Slide Day
T	Off	1:15 hr Z2 (at 10 min, insert 5 x 6 min Z4 @ 3 min jog
W	Double Trans: 15 min Z2 RUN (QC) 45 min Z2 BIKE (QC) 15 min Z2 RUN	Run portion in box to left
R	1:15 hr Z2 (at 10 min, insert 12 x 2.5 min Z4 Hill Repeats @ spin back down)	Off
F	Off	1:15 hr Z2 (at 55 min, insert 15 min Z4)
S	Trans: 1:30 hr Z2 (QC)	30 min Z2
S	60 min Z1 (100+ RPM)	60 min Z1 to Z2
Totals: 9:00 hr	4:30 hr	4:30 hr
Week 6	Bike	Run
M	Rest Day/Slide Day	Rest Day/Slide Day
T	Off	45 min Z1 to Z2 (at 10 min, insert 5 x 1 min PU @ 1 min jog)
W	Trans: 45 min Z1 to Z2 (QC)	15 min Z1 to Z2
R	60 min Z1 (at 10 min, insert 5 x 1 min PU @ 1 min spin)	Off
F	Off	40 min Z1 (at 10 min, insert 5 x 1 min PU @ 1 min jog)
S	15 min Z1—easy bike safety check	20 min Z1—easy (in a.m.)
S	RACE!!! (Sprint Distance Duathlon)	RACE!!! (Sprint Distance Duathlon)
Totals: 4:00 hr	2:00 hr (+ Race)	2:00 hr (+ Race)

The second of our three 6-week training programs for the sprint distance duathlon is the Intermediate Program.

INTERMEDIATE TRAINING PROGRAM FOR SPRINT DISTANCE DUATHLONS

The Intermediate Program is for the athlete who fits best between the Competitive Program and the "Just Finish" Program, both in terms of goals and competitiveness, and has available time to train for an average of about 6.5 hours a week, with several peak weeks of about 8 hours. The total combined training time over the 6-week period is approximately 40 hours, so we like to refer to this as the "40-hour sprint duathlon plan."

If you are already in your racing season and in good form, you can begin the program immediately after your race. The first and second weeks will include easy pickups, on both the cycling and running sides, to prepare you to transition into our higher-intensity sessions.

From there our higher-intensity sessions and duration will build and become more challenging. We start at about 6 hours of training in the first week, and then gradually build each week to about 8 hours in the third week.

As presented, short course duathlon is completed at a much higher intensity level than long course races, so as expected, sprint distance training includes a greater focus on higher-intensity Z4 training. Weeks 3 and 4 will each have three sessions that will include Z4 training sessions, including two bike sessions and one run session. Our quantity of Z4 training will gradually build and peak in week 4 at close to 80 minutes combined.

We will have two transition sessions per week, usually including a long single transition session with a Z4 Insert on Saturdays and either a fully aerobic double or triple transition session on Wednesdays. As discussed, "brick" sessions are a crucial training element for duathlon success, and this plan is designed to maximize the benefits from these fun and challenging sessions.

Our longest sessions in the six weeks will be three 2-hour transition sessions in weeks 2–4 of the program. Our longest runs of the six weeks will be 1.25-hour sessions and will occur in weeks 2–4.

This 6-week program includes two Rest Day/Slide Days per week. See the section in chapter 2 explaining the concept of Rest day/Slide days and how to use them for optimal time management.

With nine days to go before our race, we will transition into our crisp taper phase to have us rested, sharp, and race-ready. Our durations will gradually decrease and our intensities will be no higher than Z2 during these last nine days. At this point, the most challenging training has been completed, and it is time to taper wisely and become physically and mentally energized.

If you are not coming off a race or you have not already built up to, or close to, 6 hours of training per week before starting the Intermediate Program, it is suggested that you do so. Depending on your starting point, complete four to eight weeks of moderate aerobic exercise to be properly prepared to begin the program. If you are starting from scratch, we suggest you start with three easy bike sessions of about 30 minutes and three easy run sessions of 15–30 minutes. Then, over the four- to eight-week period, make gradual increases each week until you are comfortably up to, or close to, the 6-hour level. Once there, you are ready to begin with the first week of the 6-week program.

INTERMEDIATE PROGRAM

The following chart details the 6-week Intermediate Program:

INTERMEDIATE PROGRAM
SPRINT DISTANCE DUATHLON

Week 1	Bike	Run
M	Rest Day/Slide Day	Rest Day/Slide Day
T	Off	60 min Z2
W	Double Trans: 15 min Z2 RUN (QC) 30 min Z2 BIKE (QC) 15 min Z2 RUN	Run portion in box to left
R	60 min Z2	Off
F	Rest Day/Slide Day	Rest Day/Slide Day
S	Trans: 60 min Z2 (at 10 min, insert 5 x 1 min PU @ 1 min spin) (QC)	30 min Z2
S	30 min Z1 (100+ RPM)	60 min Z1 to Z2
Totals: 6:00 hr	3:00 hr	3:00 hr
Week 2	**Bike**	**Run**
M	Rest Day/Slide Day	Rest Day/Slide Day
T	Off	60 min Z2 (at 10 min, insert 5 x 1 min easy PU @ 1 min jog)
W	Triple Trans: 15 min Z2 RUN (QC) 15 min Z2 BIKE (QC) 15 min Z2 RUN (QC) 15 min Z2 BIKE	Run portion in box to left
R	60 min Z2 (at 10 min, insert 4 x 4 min Z4 @ 2 min spin, then 4 x 2 min Z4 @ 1 min spin)	Off
F	Rest Day/Slide Day	Rest Day/Slide Day
S	Trans: 1:15 hr Z2 (at 1:00, insert 10 min Z4) (QC)	45 min Z2
S	45 min Z1 (100+ RPM)	1:15 hr Z1 to Z2
Totals: 7:00 hr	3:30 hr	3:30 hr

INTERMEDIATE PROGRAM
SPRINT DISTANCE DUATHLON

Week 3	Bike	Run
M	Rest Day/Slide Day	Rest Day/Slide Day
T	Off	1:15 hr Z2 (at 10 min, insert 7 x 3 min Z4 @ 1.5 min jog)
W	Double Trans: 15 min Z2 RUN (QC) 45 min Z2 BIKE (QC) 15 min Z2 RUN	Run portion in box to left
R	1:15 hr Z2 (at 10 min, insert 12 x 2 min Z4 Hill Repeats @ spin back down)	Off
F	Rest Day/Slide Day	Rest Day/Slide Day
S	Trans: 1:15 hr Z2 (at 50 min, insert 20 min Z4) (QC)	45 min Z2
S	1:00 hr Z1 (100+ RPM)	1:15 hr Z1 to Z2
Totals: 8:00 hr	4:15 hr	3:45 hr
Week 4	Bike	Run
M	Rest Day/Slide Day	Rest Day/Slide Day
T	Off	1:15 hr Z2 (at 10 min, insert 6 x 4.5 min Z4 @ 2 min jog)
W	Triple Trans: 15 min Z2 RUN (QC) 22.5 min Z2 BIKE (QC) 15 min Z2 RUN (QC) 22.5 min Z2 BIKE	Run portion in box to left
R	1:15 hr Z2 (at 10 min, insert 2 x 7.5 min Z4 @ 3.5 min spin, then 2 x 5 min Z4 @ 3 min spin)	Off
F	Rest Day/Slide Day	Rest Day/Slide Day
S	Trans: 1:15 hr Z2 (at 40 min, insert 30 min Z4) (QC)	45 min Z2
S	1:00 hr Z1 (100+ RPM)	1:15 hr Z1 to Z2
Totals: 8:00 hr	4:15 hr	3:45 hr

INTERMEDIATE PROGRAM
SPRINT DISTANCE DUATHLON

Week 5	Bike	Run
M	Rest Day/Slide Day	Rest Day/Slide Day
T	Off	1:15 hr Z2 (at 10 min, insert 5 x 6 min Z4 @ 3 min jog)
W	Double Trans: 15 min Z2 RUN (QC) 45 min Z2 BIKE (QC) 15 min Z2 RUN	Run portion in box to left
R	1:15 hr Z2 (at 10 min, insert 12 x 2.5 min Z4 Hill Repeats @ spin back down)	Off
F	Rest Day/Slide Day	Rest Day/Slide Day
S	Trans: 1:15 hr Z2 (QC)	15 min Z2
S	45 min Z1 (100+ RPM)	60 min Z1 to Z2
Totals: 7:00 hr	4:00 hr	3:00 hr
Week 6	Bike	Run
M	Rest Day/Slide Day	Rest Day/Slide Day
T	Off	45 min Z1 to Z2 (at 10 min, insert 5 x 1 min PU @ 1 min jog)
W	Trans: 45 min Z1 to Z2 (QC)	15 min Z1 to Z2
R	60 min Z1 (at 10 min, insert 5 x 1 min PU @ 1 min spin)	Off
F	Rest Day/Slide Day	Rest Day/Slide Day
S	15 min Z1—easy bike safety check	30 min Z1—easy (in a.m.)
S	RACE!!! (Sprint Distance Duathlon)	RACE!!! (Sprint Distance Duathlon)
Totals: 3:30 hr	2:00 hr (+ Race)	1:30 hr (+ Race)

The final of our three 6-week training programs for the sprint distance duathlon is the "Just Finish" Program.

"JUST FINISH" TRAINING PROGRAM FOR SPRINT DISTANCE DUATHLONS

The "Just Finish" program is for the athlete who has limited time available to train, but would like to be able to complete a sprint distance duathlon safely, in good health, and in good spirits. The "Just Finish" athlete needs to have available time to train for an average of about 5 hours a week, with several peak weeks of about 6 hours. The total combined training time over the 6-week period is approximately 30 hours, so we like to refer to this as the "30-hour sprint duathlon plan."

If you are already in your racing season and in good form, you can begin the program immediately after your race. The first and second weeks will include easy pickups, on both the cycling and running sides, to prepare you to transition into our higher-intensity sessions.

From there our higher-intensity sessions and duration will build and become more challenging. We start at about 4 hours of training in the first week, and then gradually build to about 6 hours in the third week.

As presented, short course triathlon is completed at a much higher intensity level than long course races, so as expected, sprint distance training includes a greater focus on higher-intensity Z4 training. Weeks 3 and 4 will each have three sessions that will include Z4 training sessions, including two bike sessions and one run session. Our quantity of Z4 training will gradually build and peak in week 4 at over 60 minutes combined.

We will have two transition sessions per week, usually including a long single transition session with a Z4 Insert on Saturdays and either a fully aerobic double or triple transition session on Wednesdays. As discussed, "brick" sessions are a crucial training element for duathlon success, and this plan is designed to maximize the benefits from these fun and challenging sessions.

Our longest sessions in the six weeks will be 2-hour transition sessions in weeks 3–4 of the program. Our longest runs of the six weeks will be 1-hour sessions and will occur in weeks 3 and 4.

This 6-week program includes two Rest Day/Slide Days per week. See the section in chapter 2 explaining the concept of Rest Day/Slide Days and how to use them for optimal time management. This program also includes optional high-RPM cycling technique sessions.

With nine days to go before our race, we will transition into our crisp taper phase to have us rested, sharp, and race-ready. Our durations will gradually decrease and our intensities will be no higher than Z2 during these last nine days. At this point, the most challenging training has been completed, and it is time to taper wisely and become physically and mentally energized.

In chapter 14 we present a specific racing strategy for "Just Finish" athletes, which we suggest you consider.

If you are not coming off a race or you have not already built up to, or close to, 4 hours of training per week before starting the "Just Finish" Program, it is suggested that you do so. Depending on your starting point, complete four to eight weeks of moderate aerobic exercise to be properly prepared to begin the program. If you are starting from scratch, we suggest you start with two easy bike sessions of about 15–30 minutes and two easy run sessions of 15–30 minutes. Then, over the four- to eight-week period, make gradual increases each week until you are comfortably up to, or close to, the 4-hour level. Once there, you are ready to begin with the first week of the 6-week program.

"JUST FINISH" PROGRAM

The following chart details the 6-week "Just Finish" Program:

"JUST FINISH" PROGRAM
SPRINT DISTANCE DUATHLON

Week 1	Bike	Run
M	Rest Day/Slide Day	Rest Day/Slide Day
T	Off	30 min Z2
W	Double Trans: 15 min Z2 RUN (QC) 30 min Z2 BIKE (QC) 15 min Z2 RUN	Run portion in box to left
R	45 min Z2	Off
F	Rest Day/Slide Day	Rest Day/Slide Day
S	Trans: 45 min Z2 (at 30 min, insert 5 x 1 min PU @ 1 min spin) (QC)	15 min Z2
S	Optional: 0–30 min Z1 (100+ RPM)	45 min Z1 to Z2
Totals: 4:00 hr	2:00+ hr	2:00 hr
Week 2	Bike	Run
M	Rest Day/Slide Day	Rest Day/Slide Day
T	Off	45 min Z2 (at 10 min, insert 5 x 1 min easy PU @ 1 min jog)
W	Triple Trans: 15 min Z2 RUN (QC) 15 min Z2 BIKE (QC) 15 min Z2 RUN (QC) 15 min Z2 BIKE	Run portion in box to left
R	60 min Z2 (at 10 min, insert 3 x 4 min Z4 @ 2 min spin, then 3 x 2 min Z4 @ 1 min spin)	Off
F	Rest Day/Slide Day	Rest Day/Slide Day
S	Trans: 60 min Z2 (at 45 min, insert 10 min Z4) (QC)	30 min Z2
S	Optional: 0–30 min Z1 (100+ RPM)	45 min Z1 to Z2
Totals: 5:00 hr	2:30+ hr	2:30 hr

"JUST FINISH" PROGRAM
SPRINT DISTANCE DUATHLON

Week 3	Bike	Run
M	Rest Day/Slide Day	Rest Day/Slide Day
T	Off	45 min Z2 (at 10 min, insert 5 x 3 min Z4 @ 1.5 min jog)
W	Double Trans: 15 min Z2 RUN (QC) 45 min Z2 BIKE (QC) 15 min Z2 RUN	Run portion in box to left
R	60 min Z2 (at 10 min, insert 8 x 2 min Z4 Hill Repeats @ spin back down)	Off
F	Rest Day/Slide Day	Rest Day/Slide Day
S	Trans: 1:15 hr Z2 (at 50 min, insert 20 min Z4) (QC)	45 min Z2
S	Optional: 0–30 min Z1 (100+ RPM)	60 min Z1 to Z2
Totals: 6:00 hr	3:00+ hr	3:00 hr
Week 4	**Bike**	**Run**
M	Rest Day/Slide Day	Rest Day/Slide Day
T	Off	45 min Z2 (at 10 min, insert 4 x 4.5 min Z4 @ 2 min jog)
W	Triple Trans: 15 min Z2 RUN (QC) 22.5 min Z2 BIKE (QC) 15 min Z2 RUN (QC) 22.5 min Z2 BIKE	Run portion in box to left
R	60 min Z2 (at 10 min, insert 2 x 7.5 min Z4 @ 3.5 min spin)	Off
F	Rest Day/Slide Day	Rest Day/Slide Day
S	Trans: 1:15 hr Z2 (at 40 min, insert 30 min Z4) (QC)	45 min Z2
S	Optional: 0–30 min Z1 (100+ RPM)	60 min Z1 to Z2
Totals: 6:00 hr	3:00+ hr	3:00 hr

"JUST FINISH" PROGRAM
SPRINT DISTANCE DUATHLON

Week 5	Bike	Run
M	Rest Day/Slide Day	Rest Day/Slide Day
T	Off	45 min Z2 (at 10 min, insert 3 x 6 min Z4 @ 3 min jog)
W	Double Trans: 15 min Z2 RUN (QC) 45 min Z2 BIKE (QC) 15 min Z2 RUN	Run portion in box to left
R	60 min Z2 (at 10 min, insert 7 x 2.5 min Z4 Hill Repeats @ spin back down)	Off
F	Rest Day/Slide Day	Rest Day/Slide Day
S	Trans: 60 min Z2 (QC)	15 min Z2
S	Optional: 0–30 min Z1 (100+ RPM)	45 min Z1 to Z2
Totals: 5:00 hr	2:45+ hr	2:15 hr
Week 6	Bike	Run
M	Rest Day/Slide Day	Rest Day/Slide Day
T	Off	45 min Z1 to Z2 (at 10 min, insert 5 x 1 min PU @ 1 min jog)
W	Trans: 45 min Z1 to Z2 (QC)	15 min Z1 to Z2
R	60 min Z1 (at 10 min, insert 5 x 1 min PU @ 1 min spin)	Off
F	Rest Day/Slide Day	Rest Day/Slide Day
S	15 min Z1—easy bike safety check	30 min Z1—easy (in a.m.)
S	RACE!!! (Sprint Distance Duathlon)	RACE!!! (Sprint Distance Duathlon)
Totals: 3:30 hr	2:00 hr (+ Race)	1:30 hr (+ Race)

HELPFUL TIPS AND GUIDELINES FOR ADJUSTING THE SPRINT DISTANCE DUATHLON TRAINING PROGRAMS

Guidelines for adjusting the training programs for practice races can be found on pages 86–87; guidelines for adjusting training program for missed workouts can be found on page 87; and guidelines for using cross-training methods to help you train through injury can be found on page 88. All three of these sections are in chapter 6.

Now that we have presented our twelve triathlon and duathlon training programs, we will move on to chapter 10 where we will present and discuss functional strength and core training, warm-up programs, and flexibility programs.

» Functional Strength and Core, Warm-Up, and Flexibility Programs

Things work out best for those who make the best of how things work out.

—JOHN WOODEN

The great thing about doing short course racing is that it allows you to add an element of strength and core training to your daily training routine, along with a proper warm-up and flexibility routine. In long course racing these elements are often neglected or get pushed out of your training regimen due mostly to lack of time.

As you are learning from reading this book, a large component of training for short course racing involves higher-intensity training. This means the body must be strong enough and powerful enough to endure the impact of speed work. Speed work takes the body out of its normal range of motion and stresses our joints and tendons. Strength training plays an integral part in supporting this higher-intensity training, allowing you to develop the necessary muscle strength and power, and to do so without injury.

The best time to begin building that base core and functional strength training is in the off-season. When you are ready to begin your higher-intensity training, you can move to our pre-season core and functional strength program, and finally to our in-season maintenance program when your racing season begins. You can tie these phases in with our training programs in chapters 6–9 and 16.

We recommend starting with two days a week of about 30 minutes each of core and strength training in the off-season or anytime you are not racing. For our pre-season and maintenance phase, we also recommend two days a week. These sessions will range from about 15–30 minutes each and are best done immediately after any higher-intensity cardio session. This allows for plenty of recovery before the next higher-intensity workout or strength training.

We also encourage all our athletes to use our dynamic warm-up and flexibility programs before and after all workouts. These programs prepare the athlete for exercise and help with recovery and preparation for the next day's workout. No matter your age, the body needs time to warm up and cool down properly from a workout. These simple programs will help to do that and keep you injury free.

Let's start with our recommended dynamic warm-up program. This program takes as little as 10 minutes to do, or you can extend it to 15 minutes depending on your own personal needs. As most of you have probably experienced, it is more difficult to prepare your body for a morning workout than for a late afternoon or evening workout. But as our body's core temperature rises, the transition to exercise becomes easier. This is the basis for doing a dynamic warm-up—to raise our core body temperature and to ready our joints and tendons for exercise.

DYNAMIC WARM-UP: THE TARGETED TEN

1. BACK STRETCHES

Lie on your back on the floor with legs straight. With both hands pull one knee to your chest and hold for a count of 30 seconds. Repeat with the other leg for a count of 30 seconds. Then bring both knees to your chest and hold for another count of 30 seconds.

2. PRESS-UPS

Roll onto your stomach and lie flat, keeping your legs stretched out and elbows bent with hands on the floor just outside your shoulders. Inhale through your nose and then exhale as you raise your head and torso off the floor while extending your lower back. Keep your glutes relaxed and let your belly fall toward the floor while keeping your hips on the ground. Return flat to the floor and repeat for a total of ten repetitions.

3. CHILD'S POSE

From the press-up position, bend at the hips and sit back on your heels with your head down and your arms stretched out in front of you. Hold the stretch for 30 seconds.

4. DOWNWARD DOG WITH CALF STRETCH

From child's pose, curl your toes under and straighten your legs while lifting your rear end toward the ceiling. Take one foot and place it on the heel of the opposite foot. Rise onto the toes and then lower the heel of the bottom foot back to the floor for ten repetitions. Switch legs and repeat for ten repetitions.

5. REVERSE LUNGES WITH ARM REACH

From a standing position, take a step back with your left leg, bending both legs while simultaneously raising your left arm in an arching position over your head and allowing your right arm to swing behind you with a slight rotation of your torso. Repeat this movement with the opposite leg and continue to alternate legs for a total of ten repetitions.

6. SIDE STEP SQUAT

From a standing position with feet together, take a step to your left and with straight arms touch the floor with your fingertips while sitting back into a squat position. Then return to a standing position, simultaneously raising your arms straight over your head and bringing your right leg next to your left leg. Repeat by stepping to the right and continue this alternating side-to-side movement with legs and arms for ten repetitions.

7. LEG SWINGS

In a standing position holding on to a wall or fixed surface, if necessary, swing your leg front to back like you are kicking a soccer ball for ten repetitions. Repeat for ten repetitions with the opposite leg.

8. HIP STRETCH

From a pushup position, bring your right leg to the outside of your right hand, drop your hips, and sink into the stretch. Then return the leg to the start position and repeat with the left leg. Continue to alternate sides for a total of ten repetitions.

9. SCORPION

From the hip stretch, lie flat on your stomach with your arms stretched out to the sides. Roll to your left, lifting your right hip off the floor while raising your right heel up and behind your body toward your left hand. Return to the start position and repeat with your left leg. Continue to alternate sides for a total of ten repetitions.

10. LEG CROSSOVERS

Roll onto your back with arms stretched out to the sides and legs extended, and bring your right foot across your body toward your left hand. Return to the start position and repeat with your left foot. Continue to alternate sides for a total of ten repetitions.

This simple warm-up routine will help prepare and ready your body for a cardio workout, as well as a core and strength training program.

Now that we are properly warmed up, let's begin with our core and strength training programs. We'll start with our off-season core and strength training program.

In the off-season we want to build a base of core and functional strength training before we progress to a pre-season power routine. Before you begin a strength routine, however, make sure you take care of any chronic-type injuries that you are experiencing. Work with a physical therapist to evaluate and help you correct any muscle imbalances or weaknesses. Some basic corrective-type exercises can and should be incorporated into your routine before you begin this program. You will also want to ensure you have a good understanding of how to activate and engage your abdominals, especially your lower abdominals (transverse abdominus), before beginning this program.

SUGGESTED EQUIPMENT

- **Stability ball/Swiss ball**—round inflated ball in various sizes to fit your height (e.g., 35cm, 45cm, 65cm, 75cm, etc.)

- **Medicine ball**—round weighted ball with a rubberized coating available in various weights from 1 to 15 or 20 pounds

- **Dumbbells**—weighted bars in various coatings such as plastic or metal and weights from 1 pound to 50-plus pounds

- **Stretch cord**—latex cord with rubber or plastic handles on each end

- **Kettle bell**—a bell-shaped metal or hard plastic weighted ball with a handle at the top

- **Step**—a plastic elevated platform with multiple risers to adjust height

- **Plyometric box**—made of wood or steel at varying heights

Aside from securing all the necessary equipment, we recommend you read through the exercises thoroughly so you understand the proper technique before embarking on this program.

OFF-SEASON STRENGTH PROGRAM

We'll begin our off-season strength program with two days of strength training. We recommend you incorporate your strength training routine after a higher-intensity cardio workout during the week or after one of your longer weekend sessions. We'll begin by doing four to five sets of three to five repetitions using a weight that is difficult to finish for that number of repetitions.

We will use this format of sets and repetitions for the twelve exercises to be performed over two days. We recommend doing them in a circuit fashion by completing one set of three exercises, then repeating for a total of four to five sets. Then move to the next three exercises and perform them in the same fashion.

If you are new to strength training or have not done any strength training in over a year, then you will want to reduce the number of sets to three and increase the repetitions to eight to ten using a lighter weight. Do this for a period of at least three to four weeks before you move into the increased four- to five-set range and three- to five-repetition range with heavier weights.

OFF-SEASON: STRENGTH AND CORE TRAINING PHASE

Six Exercises: Day 1

1. BULGARIAN SPLIT/SQUATS

Start in a standing position with your arms raised over your head. Take a large step forward with your left leg while bending your back leg into a lunge position. Push off your left leg and return to a standing position while your arms remain raised. Repeat with your right leg and continue to alternate legs for 4–5 sets and 3–5 repetitions on each leg.

Progression #1: Starting in the standing position with a dumbbell in each hand, take a step forward with your right foot, bending both legs. While remaining in the lunge position, raise and lower your body toward the floor by straightening and then bending at your knees into a split/squat lunge position. Repeat for a total of 3–5 repetitions before switching to the other leg. Complete 4–5 sets of 3–5 repetitions on each leg.

Progression #2: Same as Progression 1, except place the back leg on an elevated chair or bench while performing the split/squat lunge. Complete 4–5 sets of 3–5 repetitions on each leg.

2. PULLOVERS OVER STABILITY BALL OR BENCH

Start by sitting on a stability ball holding one dumbbell with both hands. Walk out from the ball with both feet, bringing your back and shoulders to the top of the ball, while raising the dumbbell overhead with arms slightly bent. Keeping the arms in that position, inhale and begin the exercise by lowering the dumbbell from your shoulders toward the floor. Then exhale and raise the dumbbell back to the start position. Be sure to keep a straight bridge from your knees to your shoulders and avoid allowing your hips to sag. Perform 4–5 sets of 3–5 repetitions.

Progression #1: Same as above, except hold a dumbbell in each hand. Perform 4–5 sets of 3–5 repetitions.

Progression #2: Same as the original exercise, except hold a weight plate with both hands. Perform 4–5 sets of 3–5 repetitions.

3. SQUAT/CURL/PRESS

Start in a standing position with your feet facing forward about shoulder-width apart, while holding a dumbbell in each hand with a pronated grip. With all your weight on your heels, inhale as you squat back by flexing at the knee and sticking your butt back as you lower toward the floor. Keep your head and chest up, and your eyes looking forward. As you return to the standing position, simultaneously perform a reverse curl, keeping the pronated grip with both arms, and then continue into a press with both arms overhead and palms facing forward. Perform 4–5 sets of 3–5 repetitions.

Progression #1: Same as above, except do a one-arm curl and press. Perform 4–5 sets of 3–5 repetitions with each arm.

Progression # 2: Same as Progression 1, except do only a one-leg squat and a one-arm curl and press. Perform 4–5 sets of 3–5 repetitions on each leg and arm.

4. PUSHUPS

Start in a pushup position with your arms straight and hands under your shoulders. Keeping your back straight, inhale and then begin to lower your body toward the floor, leading with your chest. Exhale and press back up into the start position. Perform 4–5 sets of 5–6 repetitions.

Progression #1: One-leg raised pushups: Begin in a pushup position on the floor. Raise one leg off the floor and perform a one-leg pushup for half the repetitions before switching legs and performing the other half of the repetitions. Perform 4–5 sets of 5–6 repetitions.

5. LATERAL LUNGES WITH REACH DOWN

Start in a standing position holding a dumbbell in each hand. Begin by taking a step to the side, bending the knee of that leg while keeping the stationary leg straight. As you bend into the lunge position, reach down with the dumbbells, bringing them as close to the floor as possible. You can bring one dumbbell to the outside of the leg, while keeping the other dumbbell on the inside of the leg. Repeat with that leg before switching to the other side. Perform 4–5 sets of 3–5 repetitions on each side.

Progression #1: Same as above, except perform the exercise while holding a dumbbell only in the opposite hand of the lunging leg. Repeat on one side before switching to the other leg. Perform 4–5 sets of 3–5 repetitions on each side.

Progression #2: Same as the original exercise, except perform a transverse lunge while holding a dumbbell in each hand. Instead of stepping to the side, with your left leg step back to the 8 o'clock position and with your right leg step back to 4 o'clock. Repeat on one side before switching to the other side. Perform 4–5 sets of 3–5 repetitions on each side.

6. FOREARM PLANKS

Lie flat on your stomach resting on your forearms. Begin the exercise by raising your body into a straight line and holding in that position. Perform 4–5 sets of 30–60 seconds.

Progression #1: Same as above, except raise one leg and hold. Continue by alternating legs. Perform 4–5 sets of 30 seconds on each leg.

Progression #2: Starting in a plank position on your forearms, begin by straightening one arm and then the other so you end up in a straight arm plank position. Then return one arm at a time to the forearm position. Continue this alternating continuous movement starting with the opposite arm each time and perform 4–5 sets for 30–60 seconds.

Six Exercises: Day 2

1. LATERAL STEP-UPS

Start by standing laterally next to a box, bench, or step about 1 foot high. Starting with the leg next to the step, raise the leg onto the box, bench, or step and then raise the other leg off the floor, lifting the knee above hip height; hold for 1–3 seconds. Lower the outside leg and return to the side of the step with both legs. Turn to the other side and repeat on that side. Perform 4–5 sets of 3–5 repetitions on each leg.

Progression #1: Same as above, except hold a weight in the hand farthest from the step and perform the desired number of repetitions on that side. Turn to the other side, switch the weight to the other hand and repeat on that side. Perform 4–5 sets of 3–5 repetitions on each leg.

Progression #2: Same as Progression 1, except hold a dumbbell in each hand. Perform 4–5 sets of 3–5 repetitions on each side.

2. PEC FLYS OVER STABILITY BALL WITH DUMBBELLS

Start by sitting on a stability ball with a dumbbell in each hand. Walk your feet out from the ball as you lie back onto the ball, with your shoulders and head keeping your body in a bridge position. Raise both dumbbells straight up toward the ceiling over your chest. Inhale and begin the exercise by lowering the dumbbells to your sides just below shoulder height, keeping yours arms slightly bent. Exhale as you raise the dumbbells toward the ceiling and together by squeezing your chest muscles. Perform 4–5 sets of 3–5 repetitions.

Progression #1: Alternating Arm Pec Flys: Same as above, except inhale and lower only one arm out to the side, then exhale and return that arm to the start position. Then lower the opposite arm out to the side and return to the start position. Continue to alternate sides. Perform 4–5 sets of 3–5 repetitions on each arm.

Progression #2: Same as Progression #1, except perform all the repetitions with one arm before switching to the other arm. Perform 4–5 sets of 3–5 repetitions on each arm.

3. THRUSTER SQUAT AND PRESS

Start in a standing position with feet about shoulder-width apart, holding a dumbbell in each hand with palms facing each other at your shoulders. Begin by performing a deep squat with quads parallel to the ground, then press back to the start position while simultaneously pressing the dumbbells over your head. Perform 4–5 sets of 3–5 repetitions.

Progression #1: Thruster Clean and Press: Same as above, except start with the dumbbells at your side in a prone grip, and in one motion as you come out of the squat, raise both dumbbells to your shoulders and then overhead. Perform 4–5 sets of 3–5 repetitions.

Progression #2: One-Arm Thruster Clean and Press: Same as Progression #1, except perform the exercise with a dumbbell in one hand only before switching to the other hand. Perform 4–5 sets of 3–5 repetitions with each arm.

4. DECLINE PUSHUPS WITH FEET ON STEP

Start in a pushup position with your feet elevated on a step or bench. Lower your torso, leading with your chest, to the floor and then press back up. Perform 4–5 sets of 5–6 repetitions.

Progression #1: Same as above, except cross one leg over the other leg for half the repetitions before switching legs. Perform 4–5 sets of 4–6 repetitions.

Progression #2: Same as the original exercise, except raise one leg as high as you can while performing the pushup. Perform 4–5 sets of 3–5 repetitions on each leg.

5. BENT OVER DUMBBELL ROWS

Start with a dumbbell in each hand with palms facing each other and arms straight. Bend your knees slightly and bring your torso forward by bending at the waist. As you bend make sure to keep your back straight until it is almost parallel to the floor, and make sure that you keep your head up. Begin by pulling the dumbbell up toward your lower ribs and hips until your elbows bend past 90 degrees. Hold for one second before returning your arms to the start position.

Progression #1: Same as above, except alternate arms while performing the row. Perform 4–5 sets of 3–5 repetitions on each arm.

Progression #2: Same as the original exercise, but lower into a one-leg squat and then raise the dumbbells as you extend out of the squat. Perform 4–5 sets of 3–5 repetitions on each leg.

6. SIDE PLANKS WITH ARM RAISED

Start by lying on the floor on your side with your legs stacked and the top arm raised straight up toward the ceiling, while keeping your hip on the floor and resting your torso on your elbow and forearm. Begin the exercise by raising your hip off the floor until your body is in a straight line, and continue to raise and lower your hip to the floor. Perform 4–5 sets of 3–5 repetitions on each side.

Progression #1: Same as above, except with a lightweight dumbbell in the arm that is extended straight up toward the ceiling.

Progression #2: With dumbbell rotation: Lie on your left side with your feet stacked and a dumbbell in your right hand resting on the floor in front of you. Raise your hips off the floor, keeping your body in alignment. Then raise the dumbbell off the floor in an arcing motion toward the ceiling and repeat this movement for the desired number of repetitions while the hip remains off the floor. Perform 4–5 sets of 3–5 repetitions on each side.

These twelve exercises completed over two days will help you to build a solid foundation to move to the next phase of our strength training, which is the power phase. This strength phase can last up to six weeks before you move into our pre-season power phase.

PRE-SEASON: POWER PHASE

In our pre-season power phase, we'll perform three to five sets of six to eight repetitions for each of the ten exercises over a two-day period. We'll again want to find a weight that is difficult to complete the desired number of repetitions.

» 5 Exercises: Day 1

1. WALKING LUNGES WITH DUMBBELLS

Stand straight up with a dumbbell in each hand. Begin the exercise by taking a step with your left foot and bending your back leg into a lunge position. Then push off your left foot and step forward with your right leg and bend into a lunge position. Keep repeating this forward movement with alternating legs. Perform 3–5 sets of 6–8 steps total.

2. AX CHOPS LOW TO HIGH WITH CABLE OR STRETCH CORD

Standing parallel to a machine with a cable or affixed stretch cord, reach down and into a squat position while grabbing hold of the cable or cord with both hands. Begin by pulling the cable or cord with both arms up and across your body from a low position to a high position as you extend out of the squat. Return the cable or cord to your side while returning to the start position; repeat for the desired number of repetitions. Then switch sides and perform the same number of repetitions. Perform 3–5 sets of 6–8 repetitions on each side.

Progression #1: Same as above, except perform a one-leg squat, pulling the cable or cord across your body from a low to a high position as you extend back up. Perform 3–5 sets of 6–8 repetitions on each side.

3. BOX JUMPS

Start by standing in an athletic position, with your feet shoulder-width apart, at a comfortable distance from the box or step. When you're ready to jump, drop quickly into a quarter squat, then extend your hips, swing your arms, and push your feet through the floor to propel yourself onto the box or step. Step off the box and repeat for the desired number of repetitions. Perform 3–5 sets of 4–6 repetitions.

Progression #1: Same as above, except land on one foot only. Perform 3–5 sets of 6–8 repetitions with each leg.

4. PUSHUPS WITH CLAP

Start by kneeling in a front of an elevated step and placing your hands on the step or bench. Begin by extending into a pushup position with your legs straight. Then continue the exercise by lowering your torso toward the step or bench and immediately pushing back up as fast and strongly as you can, so your hands leave the step and you can rapidly clap your hands together before placing them back in the original position. Perform 3–5 sets of 6–8 repetitions.

Progression #1: Same as above, except perform the pushup with your hands on the floor. This makes the exercise more difficult by having to push up more of your body weight. Perform 3–5 sets of 6–8 repetitions.

5. CRUNCHES WITH MEDICINE BALL THROWS

Start by lying on the floor in front of a wall with knees bent and holding a medicine ball over your head on the floor. Begin by raising the medicine ball and your torso as you throw the medicine ball high against the wall in front of you. Or ideally, if you have a friend available, you can throw the ball and have him or her pass it back to you before you extend back down to the floor. Perform 3–5 sets of 6–8 repetitions.

Progression #1: Same as above, except perform the crunch over a stability ball with the medicine ball extended behind you but still throwing the ball against a wall or to a friend.

»5 Exercises: Day 2

1. SQUAT AND PULL

Stand facing a cable or affixed stretch cord and grab hold of it with arms extended in front of you in a standing position. Begin by performing a squat with arms extended in front of you; as you extend your legs and hips back up, pull the cable or stretch cord toward your chest with both hands. Perform 3–5 sets of 6–8 repetitions.

Progression #1: Same as above, except perform a one-leg squat and then pull the cable or stretch cord toward your chest with both hands as you extend out of the squat.

2. ALTERNATING ARM CHEST PRESS OVER STABILITY BALL

Start by sitting on a stability ball with a dumbbell in each hand. Walk your feet out from the ball so your shoulders and head rest on top of the ball with your arms bent and the dumbbells at your chest. Press one arm toward the ceiling and then, as you return to the start position, press the other arm toward the ceiling. Repeat in a fluid and quick manner, alternating arms throughout. Perform 3–5 sets of 6–8 repetitions with each arm.

Progression #1: Same as above, except using one arm only, perform a chest press across your body as you simultaneously rotate onto your opposite shoulder with the opposite arm extended out to the side. This should be a fluid and quick movement. Switch the weight to the opposite hand and repeat on the other side for the desired number of repetitions. Perform 3–5 sets of 6–8 repetitions with each arm.

3. REVERSE LUNGES WITH DUMBBELLS

Begin in a standing position with feet together and a dumbbell in each hand. Begin the exercise by stepping back with one leg and bending both legs into a lunge position. Push off the back foot and return to a standing position. Repeat, alternating legs with each repetition. Perform 3–5 sets of 6–8 repetitions with each leg.

Progression #1: With or without dumbbells, begin in a lunge position with one foot forward and the other foot back. Lower to the floor and then jump up as you switch leg positions, bringing the back leg forward and the forward leg back. Stay low to the ground as you continuously and fluidly switch legs. Perform 3–5 sets of 6–8 total repetitions.

4. KETTLE BELL SWINGS

Stand with your legs about hip-width apart and knees slightly bent, holding the kettle bell between them and allowing it to swing slightly behind your legs. Propel your hips forward and, with straight arms, bring the kettle bell straight out in front of you and parallel to the ground. Be sure to keep your eyes on the kettle bell at all times and point it straight out in front of you or slightly forward. Lower the kettle bell back down from that position and repeat. Perform 3–5 sets of 6–8 repetitions.

Progression #1: Same as above, except with a lighter-weight kettle bell in only one hand. Perform 3–5 sets of 6–8 repetitions with each hand.

5. PLANKS WITH ONE-ARM ROW

Start in a plank position with each hand positioned on a dumbbell. With your abdominals engaged, with one hand perform a row by pulling your elbow back. Perform all the repetitions with that arm and then switch and perform the same number of repetitions with the other arm. Perform 3–5 sets of 6–8 repetitions with each arm.

Progression #1: Same as above, except alternate arms. Perform 3–5 sets of 6–8 repetitions with each arm.

Similar to the strength phase, the power phase should be done for no more than six weeks before moving into the in-season maintenance phase, or back to the strength phase if your racing plans have changed. These ten exercises will help you to develop power on top of the strength you have already developed, and will prepare you for your race season.

IN-SEASON MAINTENANCE

This phase of our strength training will run through our entire racing season. Most of the exercises are done using your own body weight or lighter weights. We will be performing only three sets of eight to twelve repetitions for each of the eight exercises to be completed over two days. The wider range of repetitions will allow you to start with fewer repetitions and increase them as the exercises get easier. You can also vary the speed and intensity of these exercises if you begin to plateau after staying with the program for longer than six weeks.

» *4 Exercises: Day 1*

1. REVERSE LUNGES WITH ROW

Start in a standing position with a dumbbell in each hand. Begin by stepping back into a lunge position, bending both legs and slightly leaning forward, and then simultaneously pulling your elbows back in a rowing motion. Push off your lead leg and return to a standing position, while returning your arms to your sides. Continue to repeat this movement, alternating each leg. Perform 3 sets of 8–12 total repetitions.

Progression #1: Same as above, except with only one dumbbell in the same hand as the reverse lunging leg. Then switch hands and perform on the other side. Perform 3 sets of 8–12 repetitions on each side.

2. TRAVELING PUSHUPS

Start in a plank position with your arms straight and hands about shoulder-width apart. Perform the first pushup by lowering your torso, leading with your chest toward the floor, and then pushing back up to the start position. Take your right hand and move it next to your left hand, then shift your left hand about a foot to the left. Perform another pushup and then repeat the traveling movement to the same side. Repeat this movement back in the opposite direction for another two pushups and continue this alternating side-to-side traveling pattern. Perform 3 sets of 8–12 repetitions.

3. ONE-LEG HIP EXTENSIONS

Lie flat on the floor with your arms at your sides and your knees bent. Raise and straighten one leg off the floor, keeping both knees in alignment. Then extend your hips toward the ceiling while still keeping the knee of the raised leg and the other knee in alignment. Repeat the desired number of repetitions with that leg raised before switching legs and repeating the desired repetitions with the other leg. Perform 3 sets of 8–12 repetitions on each leg.

Progression #1: Same as above, except alternate legs while keeping hips extended. Perform 3 sets of 8–12 total repetitions.

4. BACK EXTENSIONS

Lie facedown on the floor with your legs straight and arms stretched out in front of you. Raise both arms and legs off the floor and hold for a 3-second count before lowering back to the floor. Perform 3 sets of 8–12 repetitions.

Progression #1: Back Extensions over Stability Ball: Start by lying facedown over a stability ball with your feet spread and touching the floor. Bend over the ball at your waist with your arms at your sides, palms facing up, and your head hanging toward the floor. Start the exercise by raising your head and torso off the ball by flexing your back and rotating your hands so your palms face down. Hold for a 3-second count and then return to the start position. Perform 3 sets of 8–12 repetitions.

Progression #2: Superman on Floor: Same as the original exercise, except while holding your arms and legs off the floor, flutter them for a count of 30–60 seconds. Perform 3 sets of 30–60 seconds.

» 4 Exercises: Day 2

1. SINGLE-LEG STEP-UPS

Start in a standing position with feet together facing a step or box. Raise one foot onto the step while raising the other leg high with a bent knee. Then return to the floor with the high raised leg first, then the other leg. Repeat for the desired number of repetitions before switching to the opposite leg. Perform 3 sets of 8–12 repetitions.

2. REVERSE DELT FLYS ON ONE LEG

Start by standing on one leg with a dumbbell in each hand. Bend forward at the hips into a stork position with your arms extended straight toward the floor. Raise both arms to the sides, keeping them slightly bent, to about shoulder height. Hold for 1 second and then return to the start position. Perform the desired number of repetitions on that leg before switching to the other leg. Perform 3 sets of 8–12 repetitions total.

Progression #1: Same as above, except lower into a one-leg squat and then perform the fly movement as you extend back up. Perform 3 sets of 4–6 repetitions on each leg.

3. SIDE LUNGES WITH CURL

Start in a standing position with feet together and a dumbbell in each hand, palms forward. Take a step to your left, bending your knee and pushing your hips back while keeping the right leg straight. Then, using your biceps, curl the weights toward your biceps before pushing off the left leg and returning to the start position. Continue the exercise, alternating the lunge from side to side. Perform 3 sets of 8–12 total repetitions.

Progression #1: Same as above, except hold only one dumbbell in the left arm and, as you step to the left, curl with the left arm. Repeat that movement for the desired number of repetitions. Then switch the dumbbell to your right hand and lunge with the right leg and curl with the right arm. Perform 3 sets of 8–12 repetitions on each side.

4. RUSSIAN TWIST OVER STABILITY BALL

Start by sitting on a stability ball holding a medicine ball in both hands. Walk your feet out from the ball while lying back onto your shoulders. Keep your hips extended in a bridge position, while extending your arms straight up toward the ceiling with the medicine ball. Begin the exercise by rotating your torso and shoulders while bringing the medicine ball out to the side and toward the floor. Then, in a fluid movement, return to the start position and rotate to the other side. Perform 3 sets of 8–12 total repetitions.

Progression #1: Same as above, except use a single weight plate.

If done regularly and consistently, these eight simple exercises will help you to maintain overall strength throughout your racing season. If you do find yourself injured or notice any areas of instability, seek the help of a good trainer or physical therapist to develop and incorporate some corrective exercises.

A great way to complete a workout of any intensity, including strength training, is to do a brief but thorough flexibility routine immediately following the workout. These eight exercises will help you to maintain good flexibility and will help your muscles to recover and ready them for the next day's workout. You can take as little as 10 minutes, or extend the hold times, especially for the stretches affecting your areas of tightness.

» *Flexibility Routine*

1. STANDING HAMSTRING STRETCH

Begin by raising one leg onto a chair, bench, or step. While keeping the leg straight, bend forward at the waist until you feel a stretch in your hamstring. Hold this stretch for 30 seconds. Then drop the foot of the extended leg outward and again hold for 30 seconds. Lastly, turn that foot inward and hold for 30 seconds before repeating the sequence with the other leg.

2. KNEELING QUAD STRETCH

Start in a lunge position with the back knee on the floor. Reach back and pull the rear foot back while the other the foot remains in front of you on the floor with a bent knee. Hold the stretch for 30 seconds before switching legs.

3. HIP FLEXOR AND PSOAS STRETCH

Start in a wide-stance lunge position with your left leg back (knee remaining off the floor) and right leg forward, while you raise your left arm straight up toward the ceiling. Hold that stretch for 30 seconds, then extend the same arm slightly over your head and hold for another 30 seconds. Repeat the two stretches with the right leg back and right arm raised.

4. SHOULDER, NECK, BACK, AND GLUTE STRETCH

Lie on your back with your knees bent and arms straight at your sides. Extend your hips into a bridge position and then clasp your hands together underneath you while pulling your shoulders back into the floor. Hold for 30 seconds.

5. TORSO ROTATION ON THE FLOOR

Lie on your back with your knees bent and arms straight out to the sides. Keeping your knees together, raise them off the floor about an inch and twist at your waist as you bring both knees together toward the floor. Hold that stretch for 30 seconds, then rotate your knees to the opposite side and hold for another 30 seconds.

6. PIRIFORMIS STRETCH

Lying on your back, cross your right leg with a bent knee over your left knee and clasp your hands behind the left leg. Pull both legs toward your chest and hold the stretch for 30 seconds. Switch leg positions and hold for another 30 seconds.

7. ADDUCTOR STRETCH

Sit on the floor and bring the soles of your feet together in front of you with your knees bent. Gently press your knees toward the floor while keeping your back straight, feeling a stretch in your groin area. You can also perform this stretch with your back against a wall. Hold the stretch for 30 seconds.

8. CALF STRETCH

Stand with both feet on a step. Begin by bringing one foot to the edge of the step and dropping your heel toward the floor. Hold that stretch for 30 seconds before switching feet and holding for another 30 seconds.

As with any strength and core training, warm-up, and flexibility programs, you will only benefit if you actually do them and incorporate them into your weekly training regimen on a regular basis. We recommend incorporating the strength training programs into your routine year-round (corresponding to your racing season), except during the week before a race.

We recommend doing the warm-up and flexibility routines before and after, respectively, any cardio or strength training routine to help ready you for the workout and prepare you for the next day's workout.

Okay, what are you waiting for? Go strength train, warm-up, and stretch!

» *Mastering Transitions for Short Course Triathlon and Duathlon*

If you are not willing to risk the unusual, you will have to settle for the ordinary.

—JIM ROHN

One of the most overlooked opportunities in triathlon and duathlon is mastering transitions. It is often referred to as the third or fourth sport, yet most athletes rarely practice their transitions or give them much thought until race day.

In this chapter, we will take you through the various aspects of transitions in both triathlon and duathlon. This includes the three main areas of focus: knowing the race course transitions, practicing your transitions in training, and doing a dry run of the transitions. We provide you with a helpful race day checklist to make sure you pack all the necessary equipment. We'll review some of the mounting and dismounting techniques of cycling, as well as our "tops down and bottoms up" approach to changing gear from one sport to the next.

Let's review what and how many transitions exist in triathlon and duathlon. Regardless of the distance, short or long course, triathlons and duathlons have two transition phases. The first one is referred to as "T1," and this occurs when the athlete transitions from swimming to cycling in triathlon, or from running to cycling in duathlon. The second transition is known as "T2," and this occurs when the athlete transitions from cycling to running.

As simple as this may sound, these transitions are some of the most challenging portions of any triathlon or duathlon. They are especially important for faster-paced short course racing, as they can greatly affect your overall performance and placing. A lot can go wrong during transitions, and the inexperienced athlete can spoil his or her entire race due to a host of easy-to-make "rookie mistakes." While there may be opportunities during a long course race to make up for transition mistakes, unfortunately this is not the case in short course, where races can be won or lost in the transitions.

Alice Hector, elite age group triathlete
James Mitchell Photography

However, the positive aspect of transitions is that you can master them with just a little bit of practice and learn how to take a significant amount of time off your race.

There are three main areas of focus when dealing with transitions:

- First, know and understand the transition layout of the race you are planning to do and be prepared with the necessary equipment for each transition.

- Second, practice this type of transition in your training on a weekly basis.

- And third, do a dry run of the actual transition area(s) when you get to the race the day before and/or the morning of the race.

If you accomplish these three things prior to the race, your transitions will go very smoothly.

Let's review these three aspects in more detail so we can go into our race confident about our transitions.

KNOW THE RACE COURSE TRANSITIONS

Once you have selected your race, you will want to go to the race website where you can usually find the athlete guide and course maps laying out both transitions (T1 and T2). If you are unable to gather the information from the website, email the race director for the details of the transitions. You will often find race directors are more than happy to provide this information.

The most common setup for triathlon and duathlon transitions is to have T1 and T2 in the same location. This is pretty typical for most races as logistically it is the easiest to manage.

However, there may be races, more often triathlons than duathlons, where you will have two separate transition areas for T1 and T2. For triathlons, this can mean that T1 will be near, or at, the start and finish of the swim, but T2 is located in a different area. This may require you to drop your run bag off at T2 the day before the race, or set it up at T2 the morning of the race before heading to the swim start. Or it may require you to give your run bag to the race organizers who will deliver it to T2.

There are many variations of transitions, so do your homework. Proper planning will go a long way to reduce your stress level on race morning and allow for a much more pleasant race experience.

Once you know and understand the transitions for your race, then plan what equipment you will need for each transition, including what you will need before the race begins. By doing so, you will have all the transition gear needed, from start to finish, including both T1 and T2, and you can easily pack the items and have them ready for the race. Below is a race day checklist of equipment you may need.

RACE DAY CHECKLIST/EQUIPMENT

SWIM GEAR	T1: BIKE GEAR	T2: RUN GEAR
☐ Two pairs of goggles	☐ Bike	☐ Running shoes with lace locks or speed laces
☐ Defogger for goggles	☐ Bike shoes	☐ Socks (if wearing them)
☐ Wetsuit	☐ Socks (if wearing them)	☐ Cap/visor
☐ Body Glide/PAM®	☐ Bento-type box filled with race nutrition (e.g., energy gels, etc.)	☐ Sunglasses (if different from bike sunglasses)
☐ Running shoes, if needed	☐ Helmet	☐ Sunblock
☐ Sunblock	☐ Sunglasses	☐ Race belt (if number is not affixed to your tri-suit)
☐ Pre-race fueling and hydration	☐ Race belt (if number is not affixed to your bike or tri-suit)	☐ Energy gels or other nutrition
	☐ Bike bottles (1–2) or other hydration system filled with energy drink on your bike	☐ Energy drink or water bottle
	☐ Energy gels or other nutrition	

TIP: *If you will not be wearing socks on the bike or run, sprinkle some baby powder in both your bike and running shoes to making getting them on easier.*

PRACTICE YOUR TRANSITIONS IN TRAINING

Once you understand the transition setup at your race and the equipment you will need, then you will want to practice your transitions in training—and practice them some more!

You can do this many ways, but we have had success with the tops down and bottoms up approach. This approach provides a consistent sequence of removing and then replacing your gear in an orderly and easy to remember fashion. Many of our athletes have had great success with this methodology.

›› *Tops Down/Bottoms Up Approach [T1—Swim to Bike or Run to Bike] without a Wetsuit for Triathlon*

You can practice this in one of your training sessions. For triathletes, do this on one of your swim days, and for duathletes, during one of your transition sessions. Bring your bike gear and set it up in an area near the pool, open water, or wherever you will finish your run.

Lay out your bike shoes, socks, shirt (if necessary), race belt (if necessary), helmet, and sunglasses on a towel in an area where you can practice your transition, just as you would expect to in the race.

» Tops Down

Either standing up or sitting down, follow the order below:

Triathletes

1. Remove your cap and goggles and place them on your towel.

Duathletes

1. Remove your running cap or visor if you are wearing one.

2. Remove your running shoes and carefully place them on top of your running cap or visor.

» Bottoms Up

Triathletes/Duathletes

1. Put on your socks (if wearing them or not already on for duathletes).

2. Bike shoes (if not clipped in to your bike already).

3. Race shirt (if not already wearing one or a one-piece tri-suit).

4. Place your nutrition in your back pocket (if not already in your gear box on your bike).

5. Put on your race belt (if you are using one).

6. Sunglasses.

7. Helmet—and be sure to buckle it!

We call this the tops down/bottoms up approach. In a race, once this is complete, you are ready to run or walk your bike to the bike exit and mount it when you get to the mounting line.

» *Mounting Your Bike in T1*

For beginner or novice triathletes or duathletes, you will probably want to put your bike shoes on in T1 and then run in them while holding onto the bike seat with your right hand and swinging your left arm, until you get to the mounting line. Once at the mounting line, you will clip in with your dominant foot first, then your other foot, and begin pedaling.

TIP: *Make sure your bike is in the proper gearing for you to mount it and easily begin pedaling.*

For more elite athletes, you may want to practice a "flying" mount. To do this, you will have your bike shoes already clipped into the pedals and affixed to the bike with an elastic band around the heel, and the frame of the bike in T1. The elastic band will hold your bike shoes in place while running through the transition area and break as you mount your bike and begin pedaling.

You will want to practice this mounting style in training. You will begin running as you hold onto the bike seat with your right hand and your left arm swings. Once you get to the mounting line, grab the handlebars with both hands and using your momentum, sort of hurdle your right leg over the rear tire and saddle. Then slide into place onto the saddle while placing both of your feet on top of your bike shoes and begin pedaling. As you build up your momentum, you can coast while putting one foot then the other into your bike shoes. A one-strap bike shoe is recommended to make for a quicker and easier transition. This is a difficult transition to do and requires a lot of practice.

You can practice with your racing shoes on first until you get comfortable with the flying mount. Once you are comfortable with that, then practice again with just socks or bare feet so you can practice putting one foot at a time into your bike shoes.

For short course racing, a lot of athletes will forgo wearing socks to save time in the transition. But again, you need to practice in training with bare feet so you are comfortable in the race. Even with practice you will probably experience blisters and chafing so be prepared for sore feet after the race.

» *Tops Down/Bottoms Up Approach [T1—Swim to Bike] with a Wetsuit*

This transition applies to triathletes only and is the same as above, except in this scenario you are wearing a wetsuit in the swim and have to take it off before putting on your cycling gear. If not practiced, removing your wetsuit quickly can be a difficult task. We recommend you practice this quite a bit in training until you are really comfortable removing it quickly.

» *Tops Down*

Once you exit the pool or water, and you are in a standing position either on the edge of the water or on land, you want to follow the steps below:

1. Unzip the back of your wetsuit with one hand by grabbing the pull string and pulling it straight down.

2. Remove your goggles and cap with one hand and hold them in that hand.

3. With the other hand, begin to pull the opposite side of your wetsuit down off your shoulder, while pulling your arm through it. As you do this, allow the cap and goggles to get pulled into the sleeve that you are pulling off and leave them there. They will remain there for safe keeping until you finish the race.

4. Repeat with the other shoulder and arm and pull the wetsuit down to your waist. You can do all of this while you are running to your towel, or in the actual race, to the bike transition area.

5. At your towel or bike, pull the wetsuit down to your ankles.

6. Take one foot and place it on some portion of the pulled down wetsuit and hold it with that foot while you pull up with your other leg and pull your foot out of the wetsuit. You may need to use your thumb and forefinger to get the wetsuit over your heel. Then do the same thing with the other leg.

7. Leave the wetsuit in your transition area or throw the wetsuit over your shoulder and run to the transition area.

Once you have completed these steps, go back to the "without a wetsuit" approach described above and follow the seven steps for triathletes.

TIP: *If there is a long transition from the water exit to T1, it is best to remove your wetsuit upon exiting the water. This is because your wetsuit will dry as you run to T1, making it much more difficult to remove once you get there.*

>> *Tops Down/Bottoms Up Approach (T2—Bike to Run)*

During one of your bike-to-run brick training sessions, you will want to practice your transitions from bike to run. Before you begin your bike session, using all of the equipment you plan to use in the race, set up your run gear on a towel near where you will return from your bike ride so you can practice your bike-to-run transition.

A simple setup with minimal gear is having your running shoes on top of your running cap or visor and race belt (if you are using one). If you are using lace locks make sure your laces are loosened. Lace locks are a time-saving device that allows you to tighten and loosen your running shoes without tying and untying your laces. And finally, you may want to leave an energy gel or bottle of hydration in each running shoe if you plan to drink or eat it in transition, or if you plan to carry it with you for some portion of the run.

For duathletes, in a race situation, the setup of your T2 is completed when you make your first transition from running to cycling. It is important that after removing your cap or visor, you place your running shoes on top of it so it stays in place and is ready for you when you transition from biking to running in T2. If you are haphazard about taking off your running gear in T1 and placing it in the proper setup for T2, you may end up increasing your transition time.

>> *Dismounting Your Bike as You Approach T2*

Before you begin your T2 transition, you will want to practice dismounting your bike. For more experienced athletes, as you approach T2, you will want to take your feet out of your bike shoes and place them on top of your bike shoes as you continue to pedal toward the transition area. At the dismount line, holding the handlebars with both hands, you will want to swing your right leg over the saddle and rear bike wheel, placing it on the ground first and then take your left foot off your bike shoe and begin running to your bike rack. This may sound pretty simple and it is; however, you will want to practice this technique in training so you can do it flawlessly in the race.

For beginners or novices, if you are not comfortable with this approach, you may want to stop at the dismount line and simply unclip your bike shoes from the pedals. Then run while wearing your bike shoes to the transition area.

Once you have dismounted from your bike, you are ready to begin the second transition with our tops down/bottoms up approach as follows:

» Tops Down

1. Rack your bike.

2. Remove your helmet and place on the towel.

3. Remove your bike shoes (if not clipped to the bike).

This is the tops down portion of the transition and removes all of your cycling gear. Then, move to the bottoms up portion of the transition as follows:

» Bottoms Up

1. Put on your socks (if you plan to wear socks).

2. Put on your running shoes.

3. Put on your cap or visor (if you plan to wear one).

4. Grab your energy gel or bottle (if you plan to carry them with you).

5. Run to the transition exit.

This is the bottoms up portion of the transition. Now you are ready to begin your fast run!

Tip: During the transitions, you may want to take advantage of the situation and have some extra fluids available or take an energy gel or other fueling before heading out on the bike or run.

Transitions sound simple and, if practiced, they are simple. However, you need to practice both your T1 and T2 transitions to master them. This will allow you to be on auto-pilot during the race and not have to think about what you are going to do because it will be ingrained from your training. We suggest practicing once a week for 15 minutes with your actual race gear and maybe more in your taper week.

DRY RUN OF TRANSITIONS

Now that you have arrived at the race, either the day before or the morning of the race, you will want to do a "dry run" of the transition areas for both T1 and T2. For triathletes, start from the swim exit to your bike rack, then from your bike rack to the bike exit for T1, and then the bike return entrance and run exit for T2. For duathletes, this is a bit simpler as you will only need to find the transition entrance that you will approach as you return from your first run, and then the bike return entrance and run exit for T2.

For triathletes, start by walking from the swim exit to the bike transition entrance, and for duathletes, begin at the bike transition entrance. Once you get to the transition entrance, you will want to count the number of bike racks from where you enter to where your bike is or will be located. Familiarize yourself with the location of the racks so you can find your bike easily when you get out of the water, or back from the first run on race morning.

If T1 and T2 are in the same place, you will want to locate where you will return to the transition area from the bike course. From the bike return entrance, walk to your bike rack. Again, count the number of bike racks to your bike. From there, you will want to walk to the run exit. Obviously, the day of the race, the transitions will be a bit more chaotic once all the bikes and athletes are in and around the transition area coming and going.

Here are a few good mental tips to use during the race. As you are nearing the shore to exit the water, in your mind start to run through the steps in T1—from taking off your swim cap and goggles to mounting your bicycle. For duathletes, as you approach T1 from your first run, do the same thing. This will get you focused on the task ahead while putting the swim or first run behind you.

You want to do the same thing as you are nearing the bike finish. Again, begin to run through in your mind the steps, from dismounting your bike to putting on your running shoes and heading out on the run.

We know most athletes realize the value in practicing their transitions and the benefit to their overall racing performance, but it is something often neglected. A quote we love to use with our athletes is, "Fail to plan and you plan to fail." This could not be truer for transitions in a triathlon or duathlon. Such a simple task can become a disaster if you haven't given it the proper attention and practice in training.

Save yourself the extra time and maximize your race potential by having a well-thought-out and practiced transition plan. Make sure you practice your transitions and improve your transition technique before you move on to perfecting your technique in the other two or three disciplines.

Marienne Hill-Treadway has a challenging career as a chief supply chain officer and a busy family life with a husband and three dogs. Amazingly, Marienne has found the time over the past eight years to be an accomplished triathlete as well.

As with many successful athletes, Marienne's first race was a sprint triathlon, and that's all it took. She was hooked. Marienne has since competed in mostly short course races, but she has ventured into long course and other races as well. She has even competed in cycling competitions like Gran Fondo-New York.

Although she makes it look easy, it surely hasn't been. Marienne has encountered more than her share of challenges along the way—most notably a medical issue with her foot that she struggled with for two years. It took a lot of time and doctor visits to actually diagnose the issue, which turned out to be cysts embedded in her plantar fibroma. But thanks to her persistence and positive attitude, Marienne triumphed over this challenge, just as she seems to triumph over any and all challenges she is confronted with.

As with all successful triathletes, Marienne is a time management expert. In addition to utilizing some of the "Big Five" time management tips presented in chapter 1, Marienne has several other great ones of her own:

"Family Meetings": When Marienne is entering her peak training phase prior to a major race, she utilizes the technique we refer to as "family meetings." These can apply to your actual family, your work family, and your family of friends. Marienne lets them all know ahead of time what she is doing and the time commitment it will take. This helps to set everyone's expectations of her and also tends to garner their support for her goal.

Schedule Training as an Appointment: Marienne schedules her training right on her daily calendar just like any other appointment. This helps to ensure that her workout does not get "squeezed out" by some other activity.

It's Okay to Say "No Thank-You": Marienne knows that you can't overcrowd your schedule if you want to achieve your goals. She gives herself permission to simply say "no thank-you" to nonessential invitations that will interfere with her training. Your true friends will absolutely understand and want to be supportive in the achievement of your goals.

Watch for Marienne Hill-Treadway as she continues to build her performances and achieve her goals!

» Perfecting Technique

We see things not as they are, but as we are.
—H. M. TOMLINSON

In a sport like triathlon or duathlon, technique is often overlooked, and the "more is better" concept is invoked. Although building your strength and endurance are key components in your training for a triathlon or duathlon, another key element is perfecting technique in the two or three disciplines.

This chapter focuses on helping you to understand proper technique in all three sports and providing you with the tools to determine potential weaknesses and ways to improve those weaknesses.

In our experience, the one discipline for triathletes where lacking technique will greatly affect your performance is swimming. As we mentioned earlier, swimming is much more technique oriented than cycling and running. Another reason we suggest this is because swimming is the first of the three disciplines of the race, and what happens here will more than likely affect the rest of your race, as some of you may have experienced.

If you lack good technique in swimming, or have a panic attack, or exceed your desired effort level, you will see the results in your performance and potentially risk spoiling your entire race.

We recommend to our coached athletes to view triathlon and duathlon as "one sport" instead of two or three separate disciplines. Experienced runners may not be able to maximize their running ability if they have wasted a great deal of effort in the swim or bike. Each discipline is tied to the other. What you do in the swim will affect the bike and the run, and similarly the run and bike for duathlon.

With that in mind, let's go through the three disciplines with a focus on technique, starting with swimming.

SWIM TECHNIQUE

Let's start with the basic concept of swimming. Swimming freestyle, or "the crawl," as is done in triathlon is generally about finding your balance in the water, having the ability to maintain that balance, and then gaining the efficiency in your catch and pull and recovery to maximize your effort.

Inexperienced swimmers have to start with the basics and build from there. Collegiate-level and serious high school–level swimmers have forgotten or don't even realize how they swim so well. Hours and hours in the pool, from the time they were five years old, has taught them to become efficient and hydrodynamic in the water. For them, the recovery and catch and pull are areas to focus on, as well as swimming in open water.

Even for the experienced pool swimmer, swimming in open water is a different beast and requires some minor changes in stroke, but also some basic facts about swimming straight, handling currents, and sighting.

FOUR COMMON FLAWS OF SWIMMERS

The most common flaws we see in swimming are: (1) incorrect body position and rotation, (2) improper breathing, (3) inefficient recovery and entry, and (4) inefficient catch and pull. If you can correct the first two, it is much easier to work on the last two. Let's review these common technique mistakes and ways to correct them.

Equipment Needed: kickboard, swim fins, pull buoy, and paddles

Recommended Drill Sets: The drills presented within this chapter should be substituted for the drill sets provided in the swim workouts presented in chapters 6–9 and chapter 16.

»» *1. Body Position and Rotation*

We like to put these two together because body position affects rotation and rotation affects body position. Someone who is new to the sport of swimming oftentimes is not able to float in the water on his or her back or stomach. This is a problem. If you can't float in the water, it is really difficult to swim freestyle efficiently.

To correct this, start by practicing floating on your back. Lie on your back with your ears submerged in the water, chin up, chest up, hips up, and arms out to the sides. You can also place your hands behind your head to help get your elbows back in the water. It is OK if your knees are slightly bent and your feet sag in the water. You will want to learn to float on your stomach as well, as this is the starting position for freestyle. Inhale and hold your breath, push off the wall, and place your face and body flat into the water with your arms spread out and your legs extended behind you. Once you can master floating, you can begin to work on the correct body position for freestyle.

The correct body position is when you are able to balance on your armpit with one arm extended and your torso rotated through your hips, while keeping your head in alignment with your spine as your body remains at the surface of the water. In the freestyle stroke, you are either in this position on one side or moving toward it on the other side. Oftentimes, beginner swimmers will only rotate to their breathing side and not their non-breathing side.

The rotation through your torso and hips is a constant and fluid movement, whether you are breathing or not. The constant rotation is necessary not only for hydrodynamics but also to avoid impingement of your shoulder during recovery. If your torso is rotated, as opposed to flat, it is much easier on your shoulder for your arm to recover.

CORRECTIVE BODY POSITION AND ROTATION DRILLS

Here are some drills to help you obtain correct body position and rotation in the water:

Push Off Wall and Float Drill

Begin by taking a breath and holding it while you push off the wall. Place your head and arms extended in front of you in the water, with one hand on top of the other, while squeezing your arms to your ears. Point your hands in a downward slope in the water, while keeping your head down (slight chin tuck) and your legs extended behind you. Pull in your belly and stretch through your arms, shoulders, and torso. Your balance point in this drill is the center of your chest at your sternum. Try to float for as long as you can before your legs start to sink. Once you sink, repeat the drill, for a total of five or so times. This should help you understand proper balance in the water.

Kick on Side with Head Down

You may want to use fins for this drill because you will not be using your arms to stroke.

Begin by pushing off the wall, with one arm extended in front of you with your armpit flat to the floor of the pool and your other arm resting relaxed at your side. Place your head in the water and almost submerged, with your lead arm pointing at a downward slope and your feet extended behind you. Your torso from your chest to your hips should be rotated so your belly button is facing toward the side of the pool, while your armpit remains flat to the bottom of the pool. With a gentle kick, continue down the lane in this position, only turning your head upward when you need to breath. On the return length, switch arms.

Kick on Side with Head Down and Stroking with One Arm

You may want to use fins for this drill to start and then remove them as you get better at the drill.

This drill starts out the same as the above drill, except you are going to keep one arm extended and allow the other arm to stroke. You can time your breathing with the stroke during this drill so that you are breathing every other stroke. The goal is to learn to rotate whether you are breathing or not.

Begin the stroke with your top arm at your side and your torso and hips rotated toward the side of the pool. As you recover the top arm, rotate your hips and torso in the opposite direction as your hand enters the water. Then perform the catch and pull while rotating your torso and hips back in the direction of the side of the pool, and finally, rest your arm at your side for at least 3 seconds before repeating with another stroke.

The lead arm should not have changed position throughout this drill. Your lead hand should have the palm facing down and pointed slightly downward in the water. It should extend directly from your shoulder, where your left arm would be extended at 11 o'clock and your right arm at 1 o'clock. As you rotate while stroking, this hand can move to the center (12 o'clock) but not beyond. Be sure you are not pulling your lead arm across in front of you.

Pull Buoy at Your Ankles (Advanced)

This is a difficult drill but will help teach you to maintain a proper and fluid body rotation during freestyle. If you have any lower back issues or a weak core, you may want to avoid this drill.

Start by placing a pull buoy between your ankles. (Yes, we said ankles.) Then push off the wall with your arms wide so you can find your balance without having the pull buoy flip you over, and begin swimming freestyle. Try to take three or four strokes before attempting to take your first breath, to allow you to find your balance and get a good rhythm going. A couple of other pointers to help you perform this drill: (1) be sure to keep your head in alignment with your spine, (2) keep your arms wider in front when you start until you understand your balance point in the water, (3) try to breathe every third stroke, which will help you to improve your breathing on both sides, and (4) be sure you are rotating side to side even if it is uncomfortable to do so.

» 2. Breathing

One of the most difficult things to learn in freestyle stroke is proper breathing. It's instinctive for humans to want to lift their head out of the water to breath. However, the most efficient, though counterintuitive, way of breathing is to keep your head in the water while just turning your head.

Another common mistake new swimmers make is holding their breath while their face is in the water and then trying to exhale and inhale when taking a breath. This causes swimmers to turn their head too far out of the water, or even to lift their head out of the water. When you lift your head, your back end is going to sink in the water, causing your legs to create a lot of resistance as they drag behind you, or, worse yet, causing you to do a large or uneven kick to counterbalance yourself in the water.

The way you should breathe in swimming freestyle is by exhaling slowly while your face is in the water and only inhaling when you turn your head to breathe. A good physical cue to keep your head in the water while you are breathing is to pull your chin toward your chest as you turn to breathe. This will help you to keep one goggle in the water and only allow the top goggle to come out of the water with your mouth.

You will want to practice breathing on both sides to help balance out your stroke and also to give you the flexibility to breathe when you need to. Also, some races will have a clockwise swim and others a counterclockwise swim, and currents in open water will vary. If you are able to breathe on both sides, you will better equipped to handle most any race situation.

CORRECTIVE BREATHING DRILLS

Here are some drills to help you breathe properly in the water:

One-Arm Stroke with a Kickboard

You may want to use fins for this drill to start and then remove them as you get more comfortable with this drill.

Place your face in the water, looking at the bottom of the pool directly underneath you, with only one hand on the kickboard. You will want to kick a bit to get some momentum as you push off the wall and begin stroking with the arm that is not on the kickboard. The focus of this drill is to practice breathing to one side down the lane, and then return breathing on the other side. You want to make sure you are turning your head just enough so that only one goggle comes out of the water, and you are pulling your eyes downward and looking slightly back and to the side. This will help to keep your head in the water. Be sure you are rotating your torso and hips to the breathing side, as you learned in the body position and rotation drills.

Freestyle with a Kickboard

You may also want to initially use fins for this drill and remove them as you perfect your breathing technique.

In this drill, we are going to start with both hands on the kickboard and practice breathing to both sides by breathing every third stroke. Push off the wall with your face in the water, looking directly underneath you at the bottom of the pool, and begin kicking. Begin stroking and take a breath to one side or the other, then on the third stroke breathe to the opposite side. Your stroking hand should return back to the kickboard. This may feel a little awkward, but it will help you to obtain proper head position and also keep your arm extended while you breathe—a key element when learning to breathe. Always keep the lead arm extended while you are breathing. Try to maintain a fluid torso and a side-to-side hip rotation, to make breathing easier throughout this drill.

The key to swimming freestyle is mastering your breathing so you can focus on developing the other parts of the stroke that generate power and ultimately speed.

» *3. Recovery and Entry*

Another common flaw we see in some swimmers is their lack of a relaxed recovery leading to an improper entry of their hand. The recovery begins when your hand exits the water at your thigh and continues until it enters the water beyond your head. An efficient and relaxed recovery is led by your elbow with a relaxed hand. As soon as your hand exits the water at your thigh, you want to relax your hand and begin the recovery with your elbow leading it. You want the recovery close and in alignment with your body, extending just beyond your head before your hand enters the water directly in front of your shoulder. A good way to practice a relaxed recovery is by keeping your fingers slightly spread apart.

CORRECTIVE RECOVERY AND ENTRY DRILLS

Here are some drills to help you improve your recovery and entry in the water:

One-Arm Elbow Raise with a Kickboard

You will want to use your fins for this drill because you will need some momentum from your kick.

Start by pushing off the wall with one hand on the kickboard and your torso and hips rotated to the side, with the other arm relaxed at your side. Begin the drill by gently kicking as you raise your elbow toward the ceiling, with your fingers spread apart and hand relaxed directly under your elbow. Only bring your elbow up to the point where it is perpendicular to the water and pointed at the ceiling before returning it back to your side. Repeat this all the way down the lane, then switch arms on the return length. This drill will help you to learn to lead the recovery with your elbow, not your hand.

One-Arm Fingertip Drag with a Kickboard

You can use swim fins for this drill to start, but also attempt this drill without them.

We will be focusing on a relaxed recovery and proper entry with this drill. Start with one arm on the kickboard and the other arm relaxed at your thigh with your torso and hips rotated to the side. Begin by placing your face in the water and gently kicking. With the hand at your side, begin the recovery by pointing your elbow toward the ceiling but maintaining contact with your fingertips to the water. Keeping your fingers spread apart, drag your fingertips close to your body until your hand extends beyond your head. Then drop your hand into the water underneath the kickboard and extend your arm fully before you finish the stroke and return your hand to your thigh. Repeat this all the way down the lane, then switch arms on the return length.

Two-Stroke Drill

You can again use fins to do this drill, but try it without them too. This is a great drill to put it all together to practice your relaxed recovery and entry.

Begin by pushing off the wall with both arms extended in front of you and your head facing down. Start with either arm, taking a full stroke with that arm and then repeating the stroke again with the same arm. You want to do this drill slowly and deliberately so you can maintain a relaxed hand and continue to lead the recovery with your elbow. After taking two strokes with one arm, switch arms and take two strokes with the other, again with the same focus. Remember to rotate through your torso and hips with each stroke to properly execute this drill.

» 4. Catch and Pull

This is the most difficult part of the freestyle stroke and should only be focused on once you have corrected the first three common flaws. A lot of new swimmers will push their arm straight down to the bottom of the pool before bending their elbow to create the catch and pull. And oftentimes, looking for extra power, they will extend their hand beyond their thigh and behind them while their hand exits the water before they begin the recovery. The catch and pull ends at your thigh, and any motion beyond that is wasted motion if you are not beginning the recovery.

The catch and pull in freestyle begins with the arm that is extended in the water in front of you. The first movement of the catch is when your elbow bends as your body rotates through your torso and hips to create "the catch." As your torso and hips continue to rotate, you "pull" that hand through the water and finish the stroke by accelerating the movement of your hand until it reaches your thigh. This portion of the stroke is what creates the power in swimming, along with a strong kick.

CORRECTIVE CATCH AND PULL DRILLS

Here are some drills to help you correct your catch and pull technique in the water:

One-Arm Catch Drill with a Kickboard

You may want to use fins for this drill, as we won't be doing a complete stroke and you'll need the momentum.

Place your face in the water, looking at the bottom of the pool directly underneath you, with one hand on the kickboard and the other arm extended underneath the kickboard and pointed slightly downward in the water. Start by attempting to bend your arm only at the elbow of the extended arm, creating a paddle with your hand by bringing your thumb to your forefinger as your hand extends toward the bottom of the pool. Your arm from your elbow down to your fingertips should be perpendicular to the floor of the pool with your palm facing back. The lower your hand is in the water, the easier it is to perform the catch. However, the higher your hand is in the water, the more water you will be able to catch. This requires a lot of flexibility in your shoulders.

This movement is sort of like a windshield wiper movement from your hand to your elbow as you keep repeating this bending movement down the lane. The movement is only from the extended arm position to the bent elbow position. Then switch arms for the return length. Remember to rotate through your torso and hips as you perform the catch.

One-Arm Pull Drill with a Kickboard

You may want to use fins for this drill, as we won't be doing a complete stroke and you'll need the momentum.

This drill starts where the last drill left off, which is when your arm from your elbow to your fingertips is perpendicular to the floor of the pool. Begin there and pull your hand toward your thigh as your body finishes rotating through your torso and hips. Then, keeping your hand in the water, bring it back to the starting position and repeat this movement with that same arm down the lane; switch arms for the return length. Remember to rotate through your torso and hips as you perform the pull.

Catch-up Drill with Paddles (Advanced)

This drill is best for swimmers who have good body position and a relaxed recovery. With a paddle on each hand, push off the wall with your head down but eyes looking at both arms extended in front of you and pointed slightly downward in the water. Start with one arm and bend at your elbow as you rotate through your torso and hips. Watch the palm of your hand until it goes out of view underneath you. Then extend that arm as if you are doing a triceps extension to bring your hand to your thigh. To complete the stroke, recover and bring the hand back in front of you. Repeat that same movement with your opposite hand. Always start with both hands in front of you to maintain good balance. You want to avoid pushing really hard with the paddles, but instead work on perfecting the movement of bending the elbow and extending the triceps.

Incorporate these drills into your swim workouts as presented in chapter 6 in the form of drill sets to help you to perfect your swimming technique and become a more confident and proficient swimmer. The best swimmers in the world continually work to improve their technique, and so should you!

» AN IRONFIT MOMENT:
Open Water Training and Racing Tips

As you may have experienced, swimming in open water is an entirely different beast than swimming in a pool. The elements of currents, salt water versus fresh water, temperature, the inability to see the bottom, the lack of lanes lines, and many bodies fighting for the same space make the opening segment of a triathlon the most difficult. Even the most experienced swimmers or triathletes will tell you they have had their share of uncomfortable experiences in open water, and the only way to overcome this is to understand good technique and practice it.

Here are a few tips to help you execute a better open water swim in a triathlon:

15-Second Wait: If you are new to triathlon, line up in the back of your wave and wait 15 seconds before starting after the gun goes off. This will help you to avoid getting swum over or kicked or punched and give you that extra space to get into a nice rhythm of swimming. Please also consider the "Just Finish" strategies in chapter 14.

Count the Buoys: Study the swim course so you know the direction you will be swimming and how many buoys to each turnaround point.

Head Position: You will want to hold your head a bit higher in the water than in the pool to allow for easier breathing. If you are wearing a wetsuit, it will allow you to float higher in the water without any extra effort.

Breathe More Often: You should breathe every two strokes in a race, as your heart rate will be elevated and you will need air more often. Try to breathe toward the buoys or swim markers so you are sure you are staying on course. It's fine if you have to rotate farther onto your side to get a good breath. This is sometimes necessary if the water is too rough and you can't get air by just turning your head. Again, wearing a wetsuit will help maintain good position to do this.

Alligator Sighting: Use the alligator method of sighting to make sure you are swimming in a straight line. Start by taking a breath, then as you turn your head back keep your eyes above the water level (not your mouth) and take a couple of strokes with your head in this position as you sight for the next buoy. After you take a couple or a few strokes, turn your head and breathe. If you can't see the next buoy after two to four strokes, or if you are unsure if you are on course, then do a couple of breaststrokes, lifting your head out of the water until you are able to find the next buoy.

Know the Currents: Understand which way the current is going and if you will need to compensate for it. For instance, if it is a counterclockwise swim and the current is going from left to right, it is going to push you away from the buoys. You may have to angle yourself slightly to the left so you compensate for that extra push to the right from the current. Watch the swim waves that go off before you to get a better understanding of the current and how it is affecting the swimmers.

Befriend the Enemy: As we like to tell our athletes, if you don't like open water swimming you need to do it more. Practice, practice, practice. There is no substitute for practicing your swim in open water with or without your wetsuit.

If after practicing all these techniques you are still struggling, it may be helpful to find a triathlon or swim coach who can help you to perfect your swimming technique, be it in the pool or open water.

CYCLING TECHNIQUE

If you are new to the sport of duathlon or triathlon, learning good cycling technique will go a long way. After all, you will likely spend the greatest amount of time on the bike.

Although the bicycle has been around since the early 1800s, it hasn't changed all that much, which is good news. As complicated as it may seem, once you get to know the basics it's relatively easy to get comfortable maintaining your bike.

With the help of any good bike shop, you can learn the basics of cycling, from general bike handling skills and safety to changing a flat tire. And more often than not, bike shop owners are very happy to help a new rider get into the sport.

Let's start with the basic riding skills and techniques necessary for cycling. We break them up for you into five categories: "quick" stopping, efficient gearing and cadence, climbing, descending, and cornering.

A key piece of equipment that you will *always* need to wear when riding is a helmet. Before you practice any of these cycling techniques, be sure you are wearing a good helmet and it is buckled under your chin.

» *"Quick Stopping"*

Most athletes have been in a situation where they must stop very quickly due to a car turning in front of them, or an animal running across the road, or any number of other reasons. Without this skill, cycling can be very dangerous.

A beginner cyclist may use both brakes to stop, which may work for a slow or gradual stop, but not a quick hard stop. Using both brakes to stop can either cause fishtailing of the rear tire or a "going over the top" crash. If you just use the rear brake, it takes twice as long to stop as with the front brake alone. With that said, reliance on the rear brake is unsafe for most faster cyclists.

A skilled cyclist will use the front brake 95 percent of the time to stop, because this is the fastest way to stop any bike. When firmly applying the front brake only, however, the rear wheel will lift off the ground and can no longer help you to stop.

To prevent this, a good technique involves moving back on your saddle as far as you can comfortably go, to keep your center of gravity as far back as possible. This technique applies whether you are using the front, rear, or both brakes. It is important to use your arms to brace yourself securely during hard braking, to prevent fishtailing and "going over the top" of your handlebars.

You will want to practice quick, safe stopping in a safe area like a parking lot or other empty space. Start by applying both brakes at once, but putting most of the effort into the front brake. You should keep pedaling as you brake, so that your legs will tell you immediately when the rear wheel starts to skid. It is best to squeeze the brake levers as opposed to grabbing them, so you can get a better sense of when the rear wheel starts to skid. Keep practicing harder and harder stops to learn the feel of stopping fast up to the point where the rear wheel feels ready to lift off the ground. This will greatly improve your stopping skills.

Another good technique to practice is releasing the brakes to recover control. You want this to become an automatic reflex, and to do so you have to practice it quite a bit. Starting at a very low speed, apply the brakes hard enough that the rear wheel skids or just begins to lift. When it does, you will want to immediately release the brakes. Continue to practice this with a harder and harder stop to improve your recovery skills.

» *Efficient Gearing and Cadence*

A common question from the beginner cyclist is, "What should my cadence be?" Good question! For most riders your ideal cadence, or pedal speed, is that which allows you to put out your maximum amount of power efficiently over a sustained period of time. Your ideal cadence is maintained by shifting gears based on the terrain. For purposes of this discussion, a higher or harder gear means more resistance against the pedals, and a lower or easier gear means less resistance against the pedals.

To maximize your cadence on a hill or incline, you will shift to a lower gear, and on a descent or decline, you will shift to a higher gear. As you approach an incline, you want to shift to a lower gear in anticipation, as opposed to waiting until you are halfway up the hill when you have lost all momentum. By then it's too late. You are usually in too high of a gear and can no longer pedal at the desired cadence.

A good starting point is to use gearing that allows for 90–94 revolutions per minute (RPMs) on the trainer or a fairly flat to rolling section of a ride. A lot of new riders will use a very low cadence and push hard on the pedals, thinking that pushing harder is better. However, this leads to burning out your quads and is not an effort that can be sustained for any length of time. A better approach to maximizing output is to increase your cadence in a lower gear so you can sustain it for a longer period of time.

TIP: *While all athletes are unique, we find that many of our successful coached athletes are most efficient using an RPM in the low 90s for Zone 2 heart rate and low 80s for Zone 4 heart rate.*

For beginner riders, it is best to get comfortable shifting gears by practicing on a bike trainer. As you shift through the gearing, using the two front chainrings along with the rear sprockets, actually watch the movement of the chain. This will help you to understand the left and right shifters and what gearing they control. The left controls the derailleur for the two front chainrings, and the right shifter controls the derailleur for the rear sprockets.

» Climbing

Now that you understand gearing and cadence, we can talk about climbing. For the most part, climbing a hill requires being in the proper gear and understanding when to stay seated and when to stand. This is easier said than done, as most new riders have a difficult time standing and climbing.

As you approach a hill, shift to a lower gear to try and maintain your cadence for as long as you can while climbing the hill. To build power in training, try to stay seated for the entire climb to develop those climbing-specific muscles. Maintain a loose grip on the handlebars, engage your core, glutes, and hamstrings, and sit back a bit farther on the saddle. Try to maintain the seated position for as long as you can, as this is the most efficient position for climbing. Avoid any unnecessary rocking of your body side to side.

However, for a longer climb, to give yourself some relief or to power briefly over the top of a hill, you may want to stand. To stand while climbing, shift to a higher gear before you stand. The reason for this is that you will put out more power while standing because your entire body weight will be on the pedals. Then grab the handlebars at or near the brake hoods, while keeping your elbows bent and arms and hands soft, as you rock the bike slightly side to side while pulling up on one handlebar and pushing down on the opposite pedal. Be sure to keep the front and rear wheel in alignment and the bike straight when doing this side-to-side motion.

» Descending

Once you have crested a hill, continue to pedal as you begin the descent. You want to avoid coasting and losing momentum. On a very steep downhill you may just want to stop pedaling and keep your feet at the 3 and 9 o'clock positions to avoid anything coming up from the road and hitting your feet. To maintain an aerodynamic position if you don't have aero bars, you may want to get into your drops with your knees tucked in to maximize your speed on the downhill. Throughout the downhill, while keeping your arms and knees bent, you also want to maintain a loose grip on the handlebars with relaxed shoulders. To increase stability, focus on keeping your weight on the back wheel.

If you are new to cycling and are not comfortable descending, you still want to be sure to keep your feet in the 3 and 9 o'clock positions, but also have your hands on the brake hoods and out of the aero bars so you can react quickly if necessary. A good way to slow down besides feathering your brakes is by sitting up or lifting your head a bit to increase your wind resistance.

Always make sure you are looking a good distance ahead, so you have plenty of time to react to a pothole or other object in the road.

» Cornering

The technique of turning or cornering in cycling is something that is used more often than you realize. From the simple curve in the road to a sharp, unexpected turn, this is a skill that you should learn and understand. It will not only make you more comfortable on the road, but will allow you to maximize your speed through a turn.

Cornering starts with the basic idea of shifting the center of gravity on the bicycle to force a change in your direction. Start by braking before you get into the turn and looking in the direction you want to go. If at all possible, you want to cut the tightest line to the apex by going into the turn wide and coming out wide. This isn't always possible on the roads, and you don't want to cross the solid yellow centerline. Your weight should be pressed down on your outer leg and your hands should be in your drops for maximum weight on the front tire. For sharp turns, you should stop pedaling with the outer leg at 6 o'clock and the inner leg at 12 o'clock to avoid hitting the ground with your pedal.

A good way to practice corning is to set up some cones in an empty parking lot and practice wide and tight turns in both directions.

The more you practice these techniques in cycling, the better you will become at quick stopping, efficient gearing and cadence, stronger climbing, and skillful descending and cornering. Always be safe when riding, wear a helmet, and never assume a driver sees you until you make eye contact.

» Cycling Drills

1. Pyramid One-Leg Spinning

A good way to practice efficient spinning and thus efficient cadence is to perform one-leg spinning. While keeping one foot clipped in and the other foot out (or still clipped in but only using one foot), practice spinning revolutions with only one foot. A format we like to recommend to our athletes is to start by doing a pyramid of spinning, beginning with 15 seconds on one leg then the other, and repeating for 30 seconds, 45 seconds, and 60 seconds, before reversing and going back down the pyramid (45, 30, 15 seconds). You will recognize very quickly which leg is the stronger or more efficient in pedaling, and it will help you to work on the weaker leg. You will notice which ankle has more or less flexion too, and you can work on correcting that.

You can incorporate this drill at the beginning, middle, or end of any cycling session as well as during your high-cadence recovery workout as described below and presented in our training schedules in chapters 6–9.

2. High Cadence RPMs

As you have seen, we find this drill so helpful, we made it one of the essential training workouts described in chapter 2, and it is a scheduled workout in the training programs in chapters 6–9. To perform a high-cadence workout, you want to sit flat on the saddle and bring your inner thighs and legs close to the saddle and top tube. While keeping your hips steady, use your glutes, hamstrings, inner thighs, and quads to generate power to spin the pedals at a relatively high cadence of about 100–105 revolutions per minute while keeping your upper body nice and steady.

If this is a technique that you find difficult or an area you find you are weak in, we encourage you to incorporate some extra 30- or 60-second high-cadence RPMs in your warm-up and cooldown portions of your other cycling workouts as well.

RUNNING TECHNIQUE

The beauty of running is that most of us have done it since we were children. First you learn to crawl, then you walk, then you run. This, you think, would give us all an advantage. However, as natural as running is for some of us, it is not that way for everyone. In this section, we'll describe proper running technique and provide you with the tools to help you improve your technique.

Good technique in running begins with good posture. If you lean too far forward or too far back with your upper body, you will affect what is happening in your lower body. You may shorten your stride length or reduce your knee lift as a result.

Good posture is maintaining an upright, what we call "running tall," position. This position should have your ear over your shoulder, your shoulder over your hip and your hip over your knee. Your shoulders should be relaxed and your arms bent at a 90-degree angle. You want to keep your hands with a relaxed but closed fist and your thumb resting on your forefinger.

Here are a few good techniques to help you to develop a relaxed and efficient running form.

➤➤ *"Two Strings" Visualization*

A visualization we like to use is running like a marionette with our "two strings" concept. You want to begin in a standing position with your arms relaxed at your sides and looking straight ahead. Envision a string coming out of the top of your head pulling you straight up while your shoulders remain relaxed, and envision another string coming out of your chest pulling you straight forward. Your arms should be relaxed and bent at your elbows at your sides, with your forearms parallel to the ground. As you begin running, swing your arms like a pendulum from your shoulders while keeping your arms at a 90-degree angle.

You can practice this positioning by standing in front of a mirror in a staggered stance as you rise up on your toes and swing your arms from front to back while maintaining the "two strings" visualization. Switch legs and practice with the opposite leg forward as well.

➤➤ *Bounceless Running*

Oftentimes we see runners wasting a lot of energy creating a straight up and down movement while running as opposed to a forward movement. You'll know if you are one of these runners because everything in the distance is bouncing up and down in front of you.

A good technique to remediate this problem—in conjunction with the two strings approach—is to engage your lower abs by pulling in your belly, which will naturally push out your chest as you achieve a neutral pelvic position. Then begin to take your first strides while maintaining that position. You will experience much less bouncing and more forward momentum, as your hips remain level. This is a good drill to practice on a treadmill in front of a mirror, focusing on keeping your hips level and moving from the tops of your legs down.

➤➤ *Hill Running*

Running hills for many athletes can be a challenge, and while most athletes realize this, they will at all costs avoid practicing hills in training. Although we do not incorporate hill repeats in our training programs, we do provide ways to incorporate them for healthy or more experienced athletes. We recommend that you incorporate varied terrain in your long runs to help you acclimate to hills.

Although, as mentioned above, we recommend "running tall," hill climbing is an exception. Here you want to lean slightly forward, shortening your stride as you pick a point about 20 feet in front of you to focus on. Climb to that point and then look ahead another 20 feet and so on until you reach the top.

» Running Drills

1. High Knee Lifts

The high knee lift drill will help you to develop strength and endurance in the hip flexors while stretching the hip extensors.

Phase 1: Start by standing straight up with your arms bent but relaxed at your sides and feet about 5–6 inches apart. While remaining in place, raise one knee up to hip height and then lower it back down, landing on the ball of your foot. Then repeat with the other leg. Repeat this motion for 30–60 seconds.

Phase 2: Same as above, except add forward and backward movement with both arms. Repeat this motion for 30–60 seconds.

Phase 3: Same as Phase 2, except do the exercise faster as though you are running in place. Be sure to land on the balls of your feet while keeping your hips level and high. Repeat this motion for 30–60 seconds.

2. Butt Kickers

This drill will help to strengthen and develop power in your hamstrings, which can be a weak area for many triathletes and duathletes.

Phase 1: Start in a standing position with your arms bent in a relaxed position. While remaining in place, simply bring your heel to your butt and then lower it back to the ground; alternate legs. Be sure to keep the heel-kicking knee and the knee of the straight leg even and land on the ball of your foot. Repeat this drill for 30–60 seconds.

Phase 2: Same as above, except add the arm movement and perform the drill faster while remaining in place. Repeat this drill for 30–60 seconds.

Phase 3: Same as Phase 2, except move in a forward motion for 30–60 seconds.

3. Lateral Leg Crossovers

The lateral leg crossover helps with hip mobility and calf and ankle strength, as well as balance and coordination.

Start with your feet about shoulder-width apart and your shoulders squared off. Begin by taking your right leg and bringing it behind your left leg, and then move your left leg to the side as you cross your right leg in front. Keep repeating this sequence to one side. Keep your shoulders straight and only twist at your hips while landing on the balls of your feet. After about twenty crossovers, come back the opposite direction with the left leg leading, crossing over in front and then behind. Repeat this exercise about three or four times back and forth.

We have given you a lot of tools to help you improve your form and technique in all three disciplines. Most athletes continue to focus on improving their strengths and avoid working on their weaknesses. We understand this—working on your weaknesses can be frustrating, as the progress can be slow. However, a little technique work will go a long way to help you improve in the sport. As we tell our athletes, we want to turn our weaknesses into strengths and our strengths into weapons.

Pick one or even two areas of weakness, incorporate some of our suggested drills in your training, and take your swimming, cycling, and running to the next level. Let's work on turning our weaknesses into strengths!

» IRONFIT SUCCESS STORY:
Fred Marashi

Fred Marashi is a retired chemist/regulatory adviser. He is married and has one child who is now grown and off on her own. Fred has also been an accomplished runner for over twelve years and a successful triathlete for over seven years.

As with most triathletes, Fred's first triathlon was a sprint distance race. When a friend suggested it, Fred had to Google "triathlon" to see exactly what it was. Fred had been running marathons for a few years at that time, but triathlon was something new altogether.

Not only did Fred successfully finish his first sprint triathlon, but he enjoyed it so much, he went right to work on improving his skills and training. Now, several years later, he is an accomplished triathlete with success in all race distances. Fred consistently wins or places near the top of his age group.

Although he makes it look easy, it surely hasn't been. Fred has encountered more than his share of challenges. After years of focusing on his career, family, and other responsibilities, Fred's physical health suffered due to a generally unhealthy

(continued on next page)

(continued from previous page)

lifestyle. As Fred puts it, "In 2001, I woke up to the ugly truth of being overweight and always having the feeling of indigestion. I realized that I needed to do something about it." Fortunately, Fred's determination, positive approach, and resolve first led him to road racing, then to triathlon, and, in the process, to the healthy endurance sports lifestyle.

Amazingly, after many years in the sport, Fred continues to improve his performances. After recently establishing yet another personal record, Fred said, "If anything, the sport has once again demonstrated to me that with the right training anything is possible. What I have seen in my own training and conditioning in the recent past is a true testament to that statement."

As with all successful triathletes, Fred is a time management expert. In addition to utilizing some of the "Big Five" time management tips presented in chapter 1, he has developed several more of his own.

Now that he is retired, his time is more flexible. Thanks to a very supportive spouse, he is able to get in all his training and do the other "little things" necessary to get his sleep, eat smart, and generally live a healthy lifestyle conducive to athletic success.

Back when he worked full time, however, Fred used to combine two of the "Big Five" time management tips from chapter 1 in a very effective way—namely, "early bird" workouts and lunchtime training. Fred would wake up at 3:30 a.m. many days each week so that he could not only get his bike or run session in, but also finish them early so he could arrive at work early as well. Because of his early work arrival, his manager was flexible in allowing him to take a slightly longer lunchtime so that he could get his swim in as well. Having an understanding on this approach in advance with both his wife and his manager resulted in highly efficient time management. This in turn resulted in some amazing racing results. His supportive wife and manager surely shared in those accomplishments. As Fred puts it, "With my manager and my wife being on board, it was a victory for everyone."

Watch for Fred Marashi as he continues to build his performances and achieve his goals!

Short Course Equipment

You are never too old to set another goal or dream a new dream. —C. S. LEWIS

The sport of triathlon and duathlon are not only a great way to test your overall fitness and ability in several sports, but also a great way to test your wallet! As some of you have probably experienced, one of the biggest hurdles is the cost—from all the equipment needed to the race entry fees.

But don't pack it in just yet. There are many opportunities to purchase reasonably priced and used equipment to get you started. If you just do a search on the Web of "used triathlon or duathlon gear," or email your local triathlon or duathlon club, you'll surely find better-priced equipment. From our experience, you may even find other athletes generous enough to lend you their used equipment.

With that said, we'll break down the equipment you need in training and racing for each discipline and help you to navigate the "must haves" versus the "nice to haves."

We'll start first with swimming gear, then move to the common sports in triathlon and duathlon of cycling and running, outlining the specific race gear needed for each sport.

SWIMMING EQUIPMENT

For most men and women, it's fairly easy to secure a swim suit, cap, and goggles at your local swim or triathlon shop with a little help from a sales clerk, or if you are confident enough you can order these items online.

To find the proper fit for goggles, it is best to try them on. A proper fit for goggles can be determined by pressing the goggles on your face around your eyes. If they stay on with just a little pressure and without use of the strap around your head, then they should be a good fit. The seal around your eyes is important so as not to allow water to enter while swimming.

Goggles come in varying sizes, including smaller frames to fit smaller faces and women specifically. It may take one or two tries to get the right fit, so keep trying. Also, goggles only last for three to four months depending on how much you swim. You want to always have a second pair with you in case they break, and be prepared to replace them when the seal no longer works.

There are specific open water swimming goggles that look more like a dive mask to allow for better peripheral vision. However, we recommend using regular pool goggles in the pool as you are learning good technique, especially breathing, and only using the mask-type goggles in open water, if at all.

In addition to the necessary basics of swimming, you may also want to pick up a few "pool toys" to use in training. What we mean by "toys" are training aides to help various aspects of your swim technique. Most pools will have some, if not all, of these pool toys available for you to use. Before you purchase them yourself, ask at your local pool and save yourself the money if you can.

The first is a pull buoy, which is a flotation device made of foam that you hold between your thighs or ankles. This device will keep your hips and legs elevated at the surface so you don't have to kick. This will help you to develop better arm, shoulder, and back strength, and simulate proper body position in the water.

Another practice device, which is a "nice to have" but not a "need to have," are swim paddles. Paddles are typically made of a hard plastic and vary in size. We recommend you stick with a medium-to-small hand-size paddle as opposed to an oversized one to avoid potential shoulder injuries. This device will also help to develop better arm, shoulder, and back strength and a better feel for the water.

The last pool toy is a kickboard. The kickboard is utilized in many of our drills to help you with the various aspects of swimming, from proper body position and breathing to a more efficient kick.

You'll see that some of our swim drills presented in chapter 12, as well as some of the swim workouts referenced in chapters 6–9, utilize some of these "pool toys."

SWIM RACE EQUIPMENT

Besides goggles and a cap (which most races provide), the major purchase is a wetsuit. Wetsuits are permitted in races based on the water temperature. A wetsuit is best suited for triathletes who will more than likely be swimming in colder-water races.

If you will be racing in a wetsuit legal race, we encourage you to get one or rent one for the race. A wetsuit can really give an advantage to a beginner swimmer, and it also acts like a flotation device for safety purposes.

The wetsuit is one of those pieces of equipment that we recommend you try on before purchasing. Many triathlon shops will even rent a wetsuit for you to use in a race or just in training. This is ideal as you can really get a better idea of the fit and size that you require before you make the investment. If not, then it's best to take your measurements and call the wetsuit company directly. They can often advise you as to the proper size and help you secure the proper wetsuit.

Wetsuits are available in a pretty large price range—you can literally buy speed. The maximum allowed thickness of a wetsuit according to most triathlon governing bodies is 5mm. This allows for the most buoyancy in the water and is what we would recommend getting. Do your homework as to what would work best for you before you make the investment.

For races that are not wetsuit legal, you may want to consider using a skin suit to reduce drag in the water. This is something you wear over your tri-suit. They are worn fairly tight, so be sure to practice with it in training so you are comfortable swimming with it in a race.

An important piece of equipment you'll need for the swim and the remainder of the race is a racing suit in place of your swimsuit. Both triathletes and duathletes use similar racing suits called tri-suits. They come in one or two pieces, fit fairly tight for aerodynamics, and have a smaller cycling pad in the shorts. For shorter races, the one-piece racing suit is best suited as it is more aerodynamic. However, if you are new to the sport and bathroom issues are a concern, a two-piece race suit can save the day.

We mention race number and race belt here because if you are not using a race belt, it means you have pinned your race number to your tri-suit and will be wearing it from start to finish. However, if you prefer, you can also wear a race belt with your number pinned to it. The race belt is part of your cycling and running race equipment.

CYCLING EQUIPMENT

The fun part of cycling is getting a new bike, if you are so lucky. For many athletes, you may start out with an old bike you have lying around in the garage or a borrowed bike from a friend, which is probably a good thing. For one, after you do your first triathlon or duathlon, you'll realize you have so much room for improvement just by getting a bike that doesn't weigh a ton and one on which you can actually reach the pedals.

But for those of you who are going to take the plunge and get a new bike, we have a few tips to help you navigate the cycling world. You'll find that most bike shops carry several brands of bicycles, and thus will try to sell you one of those brands. Both triathletes and duathletes will use either a road bike or a triathlon bike. However, if you have some experience and are upgrading and know the brand you want, find a shop that sells that brand.

The most common question we get from athletes is whether they should get a triathlon bike with aero bars or stick with a road bike. For the experienced triathlete or duathlete who plans to race in the sport for many years, we recommend getting a triathlon bike. If you are new to the sport and have never seriously cycled, you probably should get a road bike to learn proper cycling technique, and only upgrade at some point in the future when you have some experience under your belt.

The road bike is better suited for a new cyclist and easier to manage in terms of positioning on the bike and ease of riding. The aggressive positioning of a triathlon bike is usually better suited for someone with some cycling and multisport experience.

What will drive up the cost of a bicycle is the material of the bicycle frame. Typically, the lighter the bike, the more expensive. Most athletes will opt for a lighter-frame bicycle that is usually made of carbon fiber or some type of carbon composite, as opposed to the less expensive, heavier steel frame.

In addition to the frame of a bicycle, there are also its components. The level of componentry will also drive the cost of a bike. Without listing all the components, they consist generally of chainrings, cassettes, derailleurs, brakes, and cranks. There are many levels of components, which vary greatly in cost. Unless you are buying a frame and having your bicycle built for you, most bicycles will have a preset componentry package that is used to build the bicycle and is figured into the final price.

The other must haves for cycling are a helmet, pedals (usually clipless ones), bottle cages, and a flat tire repair kit that includes spare tubes, CO_2 cartridges, and levers. You may be able to purchase a complete bicycle package that comes with a bike saddle and pedals, but more often than not, you will need to purchase these items separately. When purchasing a triathlon bike, it will more often than not come with a bike saddle and aero bars as well.

You will also want to purchase a cyclometer for your bike. This is a computer-like device mounted to your handlebars that reflects your total time, speed, distance, and sometimes heart rate. There are varying types of computers for your bike, from the simple to the complex, like a Garmin Edge with all the bells and whistles including navigation, altimeter, average heart rate, and so forth. This is a personal preference, so consider the features you will actually use and get what works best for you.

We can pretty much guarantee that when you go to buy your new bike, the bike shop will more than likely try to sell you a "power meter." Buyer beware! Power meters can cost an extra $1,000–$2,000. It is something you can always add to your bike in the future. Unless you plan to train using "watts" (see the sidebar in chapter 5), a power meter is not a necessary component of cycling, especially for the newbie triathlete or duathlete.

The cost to benefit for most athletes is not justified. As the price of power meters begin to drop, it may become a regular component on a bike, but for now, unless you are an elite athlete or someone who trains with watts, it is not necessary.

The most important component of securing a bicycle is that it is the correct size for you and that you get fitted properly on it. Find a reputable bike shop that has an experienced bike fitter. You can get the most expensive bike in the world, but if it doesn't fit you properly, you'll never maximize your potential on that bike.

Another big component of your cycling success is making sure you are fueling and hydrating properly on the bike. To do this, you'll need to carry water bottles and fueling. In training it is easy to stash your fueling items in the back of your cycling jersey while carrying two bike bottles in cages on the down tube, seat tube, or a rear seatpost-mounted double bottle cage. You may also have a "bento"-type box affixed to your top tube to carry your energy gels or fueling. These are things you will use in training and racing.

If you have a triathlon bike, you probably have only one bottle cage on the down tube or seat tube, but more than likely have an aero hydration system affixed to your aero bars. This is a very useful hydration system and we highly recommend it. There are several brands of aero hydration systems, so find the one that fits your bike and works best for you.

CYCLING RACE EQUIPMENT

To get your bike ready for a race, you'll want to have all the gear mentioned above, but you may want to swap out a few things or add some extra things as well.

For starters, the more elite athletes will use an aerodynamic helmet to race. This is a helmet that reduces wind resistance with its aerodynamic shape. This can be a bit of a costly investment, but for elite athletes it is probably worth the cost in terms of the aerodynamics and potential time savings.

Additionally, you may want to swap out your training wheels for some deep rim or disc wheels. These are also a costly investment but for the elite athlete, again, a must have. Most races will allow deep rim wheels and a solid disc wheel, but be sure to check the race website before heading off to the race.

There are varying rim depths aside from a solid disc wheel, and you can use different widths on the front and rear wheels. These types of wheels tend to be a bit more unstable in windy conditions than a non-disc wheel. However, they can definitely buy time for a faster rider. A deep rim or solid disc wheel will give you better aerodynamics and overall time savings in a race. This is especially true for a faster rider, because the faster you are on the bike, the more speed you'll gain with deep rim or disc wheels.

RUNNING EQUIPMENT

Ah, the simplicity of running! The beauty of running is that the only equipment you really need are your running shoes. Additionally, many athletes will don a cap or visor and a bit of sunblock before heading out on a long run. For training you might possibly wear a fuel belt or carry a handheld bottle to secure your fueling and hydration along the way.

There are a lot of running shoes out there, and, as you know, proper fit is important for running. For the overpronator, the supinator, and the orthotic-wearing athlete, this can be a bit confusing. If you wear orthotics, however, selecting a running shoe is much simpler. Your imbalances are corrected by the orthotics, so all you need is a neutral running shoe in your size.

For non-orthotic wearers who are overpronators or supinators, you will want to try to find a running shoe that compensates for these issues. First you want to work on correcting your running form using the techniques in chapter 12, and then seek out the proper running shoes for you. You will want to avoid overcorrecting, but some correction may be helpful.

Most running stores will allow you to take a test run and see how they feel. Take advantage of this and give a few pairs a try before settling on the one that works best for you.

We recommend getting two pairs of running shoes and alternating them on your runs. This allows you to always have a pair available in good condition, or if one gets wet when training you will have a dry pair to use the following day.

You will want to track the mileage on your running shoes so you know when to replace them. A good rule of thumb is about 300–500 miles, but this can vary greatly with each athlete. A heavier runner or an inefficient runner may wear out his or her running shoes faster than a lighter or more efficient runner. Start with about 300 miles and see how your running shoes wear. If you start to see breakdown or feel breakdown in them while running, then replace them at 300 miles. If not, then check again in a month, and be prepared to replace them after 400 or 500 miles or when noticeable breakdown begins to occur.

RUN RACE EQUIPMENT

In a race, you will probably want to swap out your training running shoes for lightweight training shoes or, for elite athletes, racing flats. You'll want to use either lace locks or stretch laces in your running shoes to make for easier transitions. This is especially important for duathlon because you'll be taking off and putting on your running shoes during the race.

For the average triathlete or duathlete, a good lightweight running shoe will suffice to race in. For the elite athlete who runs 7-minute miles or faster, you may want to experiment with racing flats. Racing flats are a minimalist running shoe, fairly lightweight, and without a whole lot of support or cushioning. If you are planning to use a racing flat in the race, you'll want to run with them in a few of your moderate distance runs to make sure they are broken in and will work well for you.

>> IRONFIT SUCCESS STORY:
Jackie Day

Jackie Day is married, has a challenging career as a physical therapist, and is an experienced road racer at all distances from 5K to marathon. Recently, however, Jackie added "triathlete" to her list of accomplishments.

After many successful years as a road racer, Jackie came to us for coaching as she prepared for her first year of triathlons. They included the Grizzly Triathlon (sprint distance), the Onion Man (standard distance), and ultimately the Coeur d'Alene Ironman 70.3. Not surprisingly, everything went very well, and Jackie's first year in triathlon was an amazing success.

Although she makes it look easy, it surely hasn't been. Years ago Jackie suffered a stress fracture in her pelvis and was sidelined for six months. Thanks to her persistence and positive attitude, Jackie not only made a successful comeback, but came back better than ever. It's rare to find a successful endurance athlete who has not had to overcome adversity, and Jackie is no exception.

As with all successful triathletes, Jackie is a time management expert. In addition to utilizing some of the "Big Five" time management tips presented in chapter 1, Jackie has several other great tips, two of which are the following:

Create a Weekly Planner: Jackie creates a weekly planner each week consisting of her daily workouts and all her other appointments and commitments, as well as those of the people in her life.

Turn Off Social Media Notifications: When it's time to focus on training, Jackie turns off all social media notifications. As Jackie says, "This may seem silly, but it really has saved me a lot of wasteful time."

Watch for Jackie Day as she continues to build her performances and achieve her goals!

»*Sprint and Standard Distance Race Strategies*

Motivation is when your dreams put on work clothes. —BENJAMIN FRANKLIN

A great training plan alone will not guarantee that an athlete achieves his or her goals. In fact, many athletes who arrive at the starting line physically prepared to achieve their goals fail to do so because of a flawed strategy on race day. Mistakes in effort level, fueling and hydration, and pre-race planning are among the many common culprits for subpar performances.

In this chapter we will present the following strategies and approaches for before and during your race to help maximize your chances to achieve your goals:

- "90/95/100" Perceived Effort Racing Strategy

- The "Just Finish" Racing Strategy

- Race Fueling and Hydration Strategy

- Pre-Race Logistics Approach

We will begin with our "90/95/100" Perceived Effort Racing Strategy.

"90/95/100" PERCEIVED EFFORT RACING STRATEGY

One of the challenges of maximizing your performance in a short course triathlon or duathlon is knowing the effort level or pace you should target. If you push too hard early on in the race, you are likely to tire and fade later on. If you go too easy early in the race, you are likely to find at the conclusion of the race that you had "too much left in the tank" and missed an opportunity to go faster. Both situations result in suboptimal results, disappointment, and frustration.

What makes it even more complicated is that short course races are optimally run within a very narrow range of heart rates—basically from 85–100 percent of maximum heart rate (MHR). Yet even with a heart rate monitor, most short course athletes find heart rate to be an unreliable guide in races when you are challenged by hills, wind, and the "heat of the battle."

Because of this, many years ago we developed a perceived effort approach to racing, which, through many years of battle-testing, evolved into our "90-95-100" (percent) perceived effort strategy. While we also apply this approach to other distances, it fits short course racing especially well and has proven to be the best strategy for maximizing sprint and standard distance performance.

Here is how to apply the "90-95-100" perceived effort strategy to racing short course triathlons and duathlons:

1. Start by racing the swim portion or first run portion in a duathlon at a 90 percent perceived effort. What this means is that we should think about what effort level we would race this swim distance, or run distance in duathlon, if that were all we were doing. We should mentally feel like we are backing off that level by 10 percent.

2. Then race the bike portion at a 95 percent perceived effort. What this means is that we should think about what effort level we would race this bike distance if we were going to stop after the bike and not do the run portion. We should mentally feel like we are backing off that level by 5 percent.

3. Finally, race the run portion, or second run portion in duathlon, at an even 100 percent perceived effort of whatever strength and energy you have at the start of the run. In other words, race at the maximum level of effort you feel you can maintain straight through to the finish line. While running, continue to reassess and make adjustments as you go. Perhaps you will get halfway through the run and feel that you have more energy than expected. If so, increase your level of effort to one that you now feel you can maintain to the finish.

Likewise, if you feel you have less energy than you expected at some point in the race, make that adjustment as well.

We have used the "90-95-100" perceived effort strategy with many of our coached athletes at all levels over the years, and most find it helps to put them at the exact right level of effort at the exact right time, and maximizes their overall racing performance. We hope you will give it a try as well.

THE "JUST FINISH" RACING STRATEGY

While the "90/95/100" perceived effort racing strategy is for athletes who want to optimize their race time, what about athletes whose goal is just finishing? For those athletes we suggest our "Just Finish" racing strategy. This strategy fits perfectly with athletes training with one of the "Just Finish" training programs in chapters 6–9.

It may be surprising to many, but we receive continual positive feedback from athletes all over the world on this approach. Not everybody feels the need to maximize his or her race time. Many take great pride and pleasure in being able to complete a triathlon or duathlon. Some like to enjoy the race experience a little more, talk to the volunteers and spectators, and take in the wonderful experience of endurance sports events. We often joke that these are the smart ones because they spend more time on the course, consume more food and drinks at the aid stations, and in general get the highest rate of return on their race fee investment.

The most important detail to be aware of when planning for a "Just Finish" racing strategy is to know the cut-off times for the event you will be racing. Most races have cut-off times for completing each sport. If you do not reach the cut-off point in time, the race may not allow you to be counted as an official finisher, and they may even ask you to stop racing.

Cut-off times may seem somewhat harsh; after all, the "Just Finish" athletes are every bit as important as the twenty-five-year-old elite athlete who finishes first overall. But when you consider the event's ability to hold volunteers for several hours, insurance requirements, restrictions from municipalities, and other factors, it is totally understandable.

The reality is, however, that while we have never seen it in writing, we have experienced many situations where races provided flexibility to "Just Finish" athletes. Once we were at an event where there was one athlete still out on the run course and the finish line cut-off time was about to expire. Amazingly, just before hitting the cut-off time, there was some kind of mechanical malfunction and the clock froze just short of the expiration time. Just after the final finisher was safely across the finish line, the mechanical issue was sorted out and all was well.

When selecting your race, check the website to learn the specific race cut-off times. If it is not 100 percent clear, contact the race and ask. Make sure that the race you select has times you are comfortable with. Once you have selected your race and know the cut-off times, you are ready to plan your specific "Just Finish" racing strategy.

›› *"Just Finish" Swim Strategy*

The swim course cut-off time is usually the one most "Just Finish" athletes are concerned with. Many don't come from a swimming background and find this cut-off to be the biggest challenge.

As an example, let's take a look at the swim cut-off times for one of our favorite races, the Columbia Triathlon in Maryland. This an excellent race, with great management and a beautiful setting. It is also usually wetsuit legal, which is a good feature for "Just Finish" athletes, as wetsuits help your buoyancy and usually result in faster swim times.

According to the website, the swim cut-off is 55 minutes from the time the last swim wave begins. This race has multiple swim waves based on age groups that are spaced out by several minutes. Yet the cut-off is based off the start time of the last wave, which means that you have 55 minutes if you begin in the final wave, but even more than that if you are in one of the earlier waves. You can, of course, check the website or ask race management when your age group is scheduled to start to better pinpoint how much time you will have.

Let's take the worst-case scenario: that you are in the final wave and have 55 minutes to complete the 0.93-mile swim course. There are about 1,637 yards in 0.93 mile. What we encourage "Just Finish" athletes to do is not think about the swim as being 0.93 mile long. Instead, think of it as being about 16.5 times 100 yards at your local pool. Fifty-five minutes equates to about 3 minutes and 20 seconds per 100 yards. Test this pace in training, so you can be sure that you are ready.

The buoys for triathlons in general are often set up about 100 yards apart, so they may even help you with your plan. Count them before the race, do the math, and then estimate the distance between buoys. Our strategy will be to swim to each buoy, stop there for 10 seconds to rest, and then swim to the next buoy. In the above example, where there are sixteen buoys, we are going to swim from one to the next and tread water for 10 seconds or so at each. One of the great benefits of a wetsuit is that it allows you to just stop and rest in the water, without having to exert much energy to stay afloat.

Swim Tip: *Some races will allow you to wear a wetsuit for safety even if it is a non-wetsuit swim. While you are not usually eligible for age group awards in this situation, you may still be counted as an official finisher. Check the website or ask the race director of any race you are considering in advance to see what the policy is on wetsuits.*

In the above example, if you can swim the 100 yards between each buoy in about 3 minutes, and you stop for about 10 seconds at each buoy, you will comfortably complete the swim course within the allowed time, even if you are in the last wave.

The keys to this strategy are to select a race that is wetsuit legal, estimate the distance between buoys, know the swim cut-off times, and execute swimming from buoy to buoy with a brief rest in between.

Additional Swim Tip: *Begin at the back of the pack and start out swimming easy. Remember, you are going to stop at the first buoy, so you don't want to block athletes behind you. What many athletes do to really get off to a relaxed and peaceful swim start is simply count about 15 seconds after the starting gun goes off before beginning to swim. It's amazing how frantically most athletes start the swim. You would think it was a 50-meter sprint. By waiting just 15 seconds, the water will clear nicely for you, and the lack of collisions and hysteria will more than make up for the 15 seconds.*

❯❯ "Just Finish" Bike Strategy

To design our "Just Finish" bike strategy, we need to know the bike cut-off time and have an estimation of the time we will complete the swim. We also want to know the number of aid stations on the bike course.

Staying with the example of the Columbia Triathlon, in addition to an aid station at the transition area, the bike course has two aid stations spaced approximately evenly on the 25-mile bike course, making three segments of approximately 8.3 miles each between aid stations.

The cut-off time for the bike course is 11 a.m., regardless of when you start on the bike course. So the first step is to estimate when you will start the bike based on your wave start time, your estimated swim time, and your estimated transition time.

As a conservative example, let's say that you are not in the first wave at 6:45 a.m. and you don't actually start until 25 minutes later. Then, let's assume you complete the 0.93-mile swim in 55 minutes and take 10 minutes in the first transition area. This has you starting the 25-mile bike course at about 8:15 a.m. This means you have 2 hours and 45 minutes to complete the bike course. This equates to an average of 9 miles per hour.

Test this pace in training rides to be sure that you are ready for it. As with the swim, you may want to consider a slightly faster pace and plan for some brief breaks for resting, fueling, and bathroom use. One approach would be to safely stop for a planned 2-minute break at each aid station after each cycling segment of about 8.3 miles. With the brief stops, you will need to cycle slightly faster than the 9 mph calculated above, but it may be well worth it.

»» *"Just Finish" Run Strategy*

Just like with the swim and bike, we will start by estimating our available time before the cut-off time and then calculate how fast we will need to go to make the final cut-off time.

Using the example of the Columbia Triathlon, let's make these calculations. Columbia has a 1 p.m. run cut-off time, and, as we just noted, it has an 11 a.m. bike cut-off time. For purposes of our calculation, let's assume the worst-case scenario that we complete the bike just under the cut-off time and then require 10 minutes in transition to be ready to begin our run. This leaves us with 1 hour and 50 minutes to complete 6.2 miles, which equates to over 17 minutes per mile. This is very encouraging to hear, as this is a pace that can be accomplished with even a crisp walk for most people. And in fact, many "Just Finish" athletes do choose to walk all or most of the run. More common is a walk-run approach where you walk for a set period of time and then run for a set period of time. This can be as simple as a 2-minute walk followed by a 2-minute run, which is actually a very popular approach. This cycle is repeated over and over until completion of the run.

Just like with the bike course, we suggest you take short breaks at each aid station to fuel and hydrate. In the example of Columbia, they have three aid stations on the run course with about 1.5 miles between each. This fits perfectly into this approach.

Additional *"Just Finish" Tips*

- *Keep up your fueling and hydrating to maintain high energy levels. After a while you may not be exactly enjoying the cuisine, but stay focused and stick to your fueling and hydration plan.*

- *Wear well-tested, comfortable running shoes and socks and keep your feet dry. While it may be helpful to pour some cool water on your head on a hot day, try to keep your feet as dry as possible. Wet running shoes can lead to blisters, which, believe us, you don't want!*

- *Attitude is crucial. Stay positive. Smile to the spectators. Thank the volunteers. Keep reminding yourself that this is "your day" and you are in the process of achieving your goals.*

RACE FUELING AND HYDRATION STRATEGY

After the training itself, the biggest factor for triathlon racing success is proper fueling and hydration. Our bodies need sufficient hydration and calories to perform at their best. As coaches we preach this regularly, but we are often surprised at how often athletes neglect it. This is a big "rookie mistake."

In fact, when an athlete has a disappointing performance, the first question we ask is about exact fueling and hydration before and during the race. The athlete usually thinks it was "pretty good," but as soon as we start reviewing it in detail, we both realize that it was insufficient.

It is also important to understand that the longer the race and the warmer the conditions (thus the higher your sweat rate), the more important your hydration and fueling. Unfortunately, many athletes associate the importance of fueling and hydration with long course events, but it is key for short course racing as well. In fact, the higher the intensity of the race, the faster you will burn fuel.

We all have unique needs for fueling and hydration, and it is important for us to determine what they are well before race day. Once we know this information, we want to use it to design the best fueling and hydration plan for us. Finally, we want to test our plan regularly in training.

» Determining Race Hydration Needs

If you wait until you are thirsty, you have probably already waited too long. There is a delayed reaction between when we first start to get behind on our hydration and when we actually feel thirsty.

What we want to do is to determine personal hydration needs and then evenly consume that amount of hydration throughout our race. The easiest way to determine your body's own unique hydration needs is through proper testing in training. We have developed a simple "sweat rate test" that we have successfully used over the years with the athletes we coach.

Our sweat rate test protocol is as follows:

Sweat Rate Test

1. Weigh yourself (without clothing) just prior to beginning your endurance activity (e.g., run, cycle, swim, etc.).

2. Do your endurance activity for 60 minutes at a heart rate equal to 75 percent of your MHR.

3. During the 60 minutes of activity, very evenly consume 16 ounces of water.

4. Weigh yourself (without clothing) immediately after your 60-minute activity has been completed.

5. Complete the following calculations:

   - Weight Before – Weight After = Net Weight Loss
   - Net Weight Loss + 1.0 pound (16 oz. of water consumed) = Hourly Sweat Loss

Note: 1 pound = 16 ounces

Athlete Example: Sweat Rate Test

The following example applies the sweat rate test protocol to Liam, a short course triathlete who finds that he weighs 160 pounds before the test and 159.5 pounds after the test. Following is the calculation:

Weight Before = 160.0 pounds
Weight After = 159.5 pounds
Weight Loss: 160.0 – 159.5 = 0.5 pound (8 ounces)
Hourly Sweat Rate: 0.5 pounds (8 ounces) + 1.0 pound
(16 oz. of water consumed) = 1.5 pounds (24 ounces)

Liam lost 8 ounces, despite replenishing with 16 ounces of fluid. Therefore, he is down a net 24 ounces for the hour. This indicates that under similar conditions (i.e., temperature, heart rate level, and activity), he should replenish his fluids at a rate of about 24 ounces per hour, as it's important to replenish our fluids by as close to 100 percent as possible.

Liam should begin training with this level of hydration per hour and see how it makes him feel. He should also consider testing slightly higher amounts on hotter days, and perhaps slightly lower amounts on cooler days, to adjust for slight changes in sweat rate. Furthermore, he should test for higher amounts for higher-intensity workouts, which will more closely simulate racing conditions. Over time, he will fine-tune these amounts and know exactly what his consumption needs should be on race day.

What about pre-race hydration? Generally we find that you should consume about 50 percent of your race hydration targets during each pre-race hour. Test this out in training and see if this amount makes you feel at your best. Liam plans to wake 3 hours before the race, so he should target about 36 ounces of hydration during this period (i.e., 3 hours x 50 percent x 24 oz. = 36 oz.).

›› Determining Your Race Fueling Needs

When we are talking "fueling," we are talking about calories. While we suggest consuming straight water for racing and training sessions lasting less than 75 minutes, we find that for races and training sessions of 75 minutes or more, athletes need to be replacing calories as well, to maximize performance. We refer to this as the "75-minute guideline," and while it varies slightly from one athlete to another, most athletes fall right around the 75-minute point. If the workout or race will take more than 75 minutes to complete, you should start fueling (i.e., replacing calories) along with hydrating, right from the start.

How much calorie replacement do we need? We find that most athletes should evenly replace between one-third and one-half of their calories utilized while racing. The longer it takes the athlete to complete the race, the closer we should typically be targeting 50 percent calorie replenishment.

For example, if the activity you are doing for over 75 minutes burns calories at a rate of 900 per hour, then you should be replacing your calories at a rate of 300–450 calories per hour (i.e., one-third of 900 equals 300 and one-half of 900 equals 450). Short course triathletes and duathletes should estimate their range and test it in training to determine exactly what calorie amount per hour is optimal for them. Then they should test this range frequently in training. Based on the results, they should further adjust and fine-tune to arrive at the optimal amount for them.

The sources from which you get these calories are also an important consideration. While some athletes prefer solid foods such as energy bars and other items, we find that for short racing, due to the higher intensity, many of the simpler calorie sources like energy gels are much more effective. They quickly provide energy and are easier to carry and manage in a race situation.

Now that we have discussed the various components of a successful fueling and hydration plan, let's put it all together with the example of the optimal race fueling and hydration strategy for Liam:

- **Pre-Race:** Liam consumes about 600 calories and 36 ounces of fluid within the 3 hours before the race. Liam plans to have two energy bars (400 calories combined) with 6 ounces of water and 6 ounces of coffee immediately after waking three hours before his race. He then plans to gradually consume 24 ounces of energy drink (200 calories) over the next couple of hours leading up to race time.

- **Race Hydration:** Liam plans to consume 24 ounces of energy drink per hour during the bike and run portions of the race. Because his estimated completion time for the combined bike and run portions for a standard distance race is about 2 hours, he plans to consume the equivalent of 48 ounces in total (i.e., 2 hours x 24 oz. = 48 oz.).

- **Race Fueling:** Liam plans to consume 450 calories per hour (i.e., 50 percent of his 900 per hour calorie burn) during the bike and run portions of the race. Because his estimated completion time for the combined bike and run portions for a standard distance race is about 2 hours, and he estimates that he will burn 900 calories per hour, he plans to consume the equivalent of 900 calories in total. Because Liam's energy drink has 200 calories for 24 ounces, his 48 ounces of hydration alone will provide him with 400 of the 900 calories he needs. In addition to this, he will consume five energy gels over this 2-hour period, one at the start of the bike and another every 24 minutes thereafter, for an additional 500 calories.

We are frequently asked by athletes if they should take salt or electrolyte supplements to improve their racing performance. Electrolytes are needed by our cells to function properly. Sodium (salt) is an important electrolyte, and it can be lost through exercise and perspiration.

Because of this, many athletes take a variety of salt and electrolyte tablets in the hope of improving their performance. While salt and electrolyte tablets can be beneficial for some athletes, what we tend to find is that many athletes quickly jump to taking salt tablets before first properly addressing their fueling and hydration needs. The majority of athletes can receive the electrolytes they need through a proper fueling and hydration routine. Adding salt tablets on top of this may just be overkill and an added layer of complication.

Having said this, on the other side of the spectrum is the risk of hyponatremia (diluted sodium levels). So proper sodium levels are something all endurance athletes should take seriously and address proactively—especially for those who are "salty sweaters."

Our suggestion for most athletes is to first use all the approaches and suggestions in this book to build your optimal fueling and hydration plan. Consider trying to get all your sodium from your fueling and hydration sources.

For example, some energy drinks have up to 200 milligrams of sodium per 8 ounces, and some energy gels have from 20 to over 100 milligrams per serving. For most athletes, these are the most convenient ways to consume proper sodium intake. Test these options thoroughly in training and see which methods and amounts work best for you. Then, if you would like to experiment with adding salt or electrolyte tablets to the mix, first clear it with your doctor and safely test it in training, starting with very modest, safe levels. Always take salt or electrolyte tablets with water.

Remember, salt and electrolyte tables may help, but they are not a replacement for a proper fueling and hydration routine.

We encourage you to complete these same easy steps to determine your hydration and calorie needs and then testing and fine-tuning the results in training. If you do, you will help to maximize your chances for success on race day.

PRE-RACE LOGISTICS APPROACH

The final few days before your short course race can be a stressful time. You have worked so long and hard, and you have made such an enormous personal investment in this one day. It's totally natural to feel nervous.

Instead of taking steps to make the best of these last days and to reduce pre-race stress, many athletes actually further complicate it. Some athletes make the mistake of putting off some decision making until these last few days, greatly increasing their stress level. Instead of relaxing and preparing themselves mentally for the race, they are running around trying to take care of last-minute details.

Some athletes spend a large portion of their time on the day before their race at the race exposition. They are so excited about being at their race, they want to hang out at the expo and take in the experience. They are on their feet and often in the hot sun for hours. Both of these are to be avoided, as they will leave you tired and dehydrated. We have even seen athletes get sunburned on the day before the race, which, of course, will negatively affect performance. Or worse yet, athletes make a change to their racing gear or race nutrition based on something they saw or experienced at the expo. These are all examples of what we consider to be "rookie mistakes."

Other athletes seem so nervous that they don't know what to do with themselves. They fill the void with extra training. Ouch! Another rookie mistake.

The training programs in chapters 6–9 show exactly what we should do in the days before our race. We want to do these light sessions and then spend the remainder of our time resting and gathering our strength, both physically and mentally. As we like to say, we want to be making deposits in our energy bank, not spending from it.

Plan for plenty of rest in the final couple of days. Get your feet up as much as possible. Stay out of the sun. Bring a good book, watch a positive movie, or listen to your favorite music. In short, find your calm.

The best way to head off any of these pre-race mistakes is to write out a two-day pre-race plan. We call this approach "The Count Down," because it starts two days before the race and then, in chronological order, counts down the planned events until the time of the actual race. It includes times for meals, sleep, training, registering for the race, equipment and bike drop-off, and so on. By making this plan and keeping to it, the athlete can be relaxed and confident going into the race.

We have successfully utilized this technique with many of the athletes we have worked with. It may sound like nothing more than a simple "to-do list," but it's actually a powerful tool to have you physically rested and mentally focused for a breakthrough race effort.

» *IRONFIT SUCCESS STORY:*
Damien Bullard

Damien Bullard is married with three children, has a demanding career as a self-employed automotive sales and finance trainer, and is a successful age group triathlete.

Damien first gave triathlon a try only three years ago. As is frequently the case, his first race was a local sprint. He enjoyed it so much he decided to do two triathlons the next summer. One race was the Cedar Beach Sprint Triathlon in Mount Sinai, New York; after that, he was hooked on the sport. As Damien puts it, "It was my second tri and the water was 52 degrees and I couldn't believe I got through it. I knew then I wanted to really try (pun intended)."

With the realization that his less-than-stellar training regimen was resulting in injuries and lack of consistency, Damien contacted us about coaching and has been successfully building his fitness and performances ever since.

As with many success stories, however, Damien has had more than his share of challenges along the way. A tumor was discovered in his bladder, resulting in two major surgeries. While many would have been derailed by such a challenge, Damien saw the positive in the experience and used it as a powerful source of motivation. As Damien says, "It has a huge impact on my state of mind and sense of mortality. It's scary as hell and for me it's made me want to live every day to the very best of my capability. Fitness is a huge part of that for me and the need to push my body to its maximum ability makes me feel alive and strong . . . strong enough to overcome anything."

Damien has done that and more. Practically every race he has run over the past year has been a new personal best, and as he heads into a new racing season, this trend will surely continue.

As with most successful triathletes, especially those with demanding career and family responsibilities, Damien has become a master at time management. He uses many of the "Big Five" approaches presented in chapter 1, especially "early bird" workouts. By training first thing in the day, he ensures he always gets his workout in, and it also makes him feel great for the remainder of the day.

Damien also has many of his own time management approaches as well. One great one is what he refers to as "getaway afternoon workouts." As the owner of his own business, he can sometimes plan in advance to block out an afternoon and leave his laptop and cell phone for his bike and the open road.

Watch for Damien Bullard at the races this year as he continues to build his performances, while overcoming any challenges along the way.

15

» Effective Goal Setting and Race Selection

Without goals, training has no direction.
—NATALIE COUGHLIN

Setting powerful goals and selecting the optimal races before starting your short course racing season can make the difference between success and failure.

We suggest planning ahead each race season to determine both your race goals and your race schedule before you even begin your race-specific training. In our experience, the most successful athletes are the ones who consistently do this every year.

Other athletes, who sort of "make it up as they go along," both in terms of goals and race schedule, waste a lot of time and effort and are usually less than fully satisfied with their racing results.

In this chapter we will explain the great motivating power of setting proper goals and provide guidance on how to establish the optimal goals for you. We will then present techniques for maximizing the power of your goals throughout your racing season. Finally, we will explain how best to select the optimal short course races that will maximize your chances for success.

Not only will the optimal triathlon or duathlon races vary from athlete to athlete, but a different set of criteria exists for an athlete's first triathlon or duathlon and subsequent races. Many additional factors need to be considered as well, including race date, location, expense, experience level, and the athlete's individual strengths and weaknesses.

As a first step, let's discuss how to establish powerful goals.

PRIMARY GOALS

We define a primary goal as the minimum goal that, in the mind of the athlete, constitutes success. In other words, if this goal is accomplished, you will generally come away from the race considering the entire experience to have been a success. Furthermore, you feel positive enough about it that you will be motivated and excited to continue to train and race.

Following are some examples of primary goals:

- **"Just Finish":** This is a very popular goal for many first-time triathletes and duathletes. They have never raced before, and if they can successfully prepare for and complete the race, they will consider the entire experience a success. This is a very appropriate and sensible primary goal for most athletes new to the sport. As we often advise first-time athletes: If you can finish the race healthy and with a smile on your face, it was a complete success.

- **Finish Time:** Many athletes have a finish time in mind that constitutes success—for example, completing a standard distance triathlon in less than 3 hours. This type of primary goal is reasonable as long as it is based on experience, past performance, and other supporting factors.

- **Break Personal Best:** The goal of improving on your previous best time can be another good primary goal. The only qualification for this one is that the race courses need to be fairly comparable. For example, if one course is extremely hilly and has a non-wetsuit swim, and the other is completely flat and has a wetsuit swim, this type of goal may not be as meaningful.

- **Top Percentage Finish:** Another popular way to express a primary goal is by a top percentage finish—for example, finishing in the top 20 percent or the top 50 percent. This goal measures success by how well you do compared to other athletes, as opposed to the clock (a time goal) or your past performances (a personal best goal).

- **Podium Finish and/or Win Age Group:** Winning your age group or a top three podium finish may be a good primary goal for an experienced elite-level athlete. Typically this goal should be for an athlete who has won and/or finished on the podium before, or at least come very close to doing so.

Consider the above possible primary goals, as well as others you may have in mind, and select the one that truly constitutes the minimum accomplishment in your mind that will constitute success. In other words, if you achieve your goal, you will feel positive enough about it that you will be motivated and excited to continue to train and race.

STRETCH GOALS

We define stretch goals as goals that are possible, but so challenging that they are not probable. In other words, if all goes perfectly according to plan throughout training and on race day, you feel that this goal can be accomplished. Achieving a stretch goal constitutes a major breakthrough of some type—one so significant that you will consider yourself at a new competitive level once it is accomplished.

An example of a stretch goal could be placing in the top three in your age group. Perhaps you have never placed in the top three in your age group before, but you have finished in the top ten, and now after reading this book and following the training plans, you feel that if everything goes completely as planned, you have a shot at achieving this for the first time.

Similarly, another example would be the stretch goal of winning your age group. You have never won before, but you have finished top three a couple of times and now you feel that if all goes according to plan, you may be able to break through and actually win the top spot.

We have even seen athletes who have established the stretch goal of beating their training buddy for the first time. Friendly competition can be a great motivation, so even this one can be a great stretch goal for some athletes.

Stretch goals can also be based on major breakthroughs in some of the areas discussed in primary goals; especially time goals and percentage finish goals. Stretch goals are not just for elite-level athletes at the front of the pack. They are for all athletes. The key is that they go much further than constituting the minimal level of what you will consider success. They signal a substantial breakthrough in performance.

GETTING THE MOST FROM YOUR GOALS

We don't want to set our primary and stretch goals at the beginning of the racing season and then only check back in on them in a few months to see how we did. We want to use our goals daily, weekly, and monthly to help drive our motivation for training and racing.

In the monthly training programs we design for our coached athletes, we continually post our athletes' primary and stretch goals right at the top throughout the competitive season. Every day when our athletes check their schedule for their daily training session, they will also be reminded of their goals. Likewise, every time we as coaches view or update their training, we are reminded of their goals. This is a powerful source of focus and motivation. Both coach and athlete are not just focused on what they are doing in the moment, but also focused on why they are doing it and what they plan to achieve as a result.

An example of how an athlete's goals appear at the top of his or her training schedule is as follows:

Goals: (1) **Primary:** New personal best time for standard distance triathlon @ New York City Triathlon–Standard Distance; (2) **Stretch:** Win age group @ New York City Triathlon

In the above example, this athlete's top two goals for the year concern his performance at the popular and competitive New York City Triathlon, which is a large standard distance race with thousands of competitors. The athlete's primary goal is to set a new personal best time for the standard distance, and his stretch goal is to win his age group. The power of the approach of listing these goals front and center at the top of this athlete's training schedule is that they will provide focus and motivation each and every day.

Another technique we encourage our athletes to embrace is what we call "posting your goals." This approach is simply to list your goals prominently on small signs and post them at locations in your home and workplace where they will keep you motivated throughout the season.

The following is an example of what a sign might look like for the athlete in the above example:

- NYC Triathlon

- Standard Distance PB

- Win Age Group

This sign has the targeted race listed at the top (i.e., the New York City Triathlon); the middle states his primary goal (i.e., to set a new personal best for the standard distance); and the bottom has his stretch goal (to win his age group).

One of the most productive places to post goals is on your bathroom mirror, as this is likely the first thing many athletes see each day. Other popular places include your work area or your workout area.

There is a wonderful motivating power of posting goals. It keeps us focused daily on what we want to achieve, and it helps us to make wise decisions each and every day that will positively affect our ability to achieve our goals.

RACE SELECTION

Now that we know how to set effective goals and how best to get the most from them, let's discuss race selection. We want both our goals and our selected races to work together to motivate and excite us.

Following is the criteria we suggest when selecting your race or races. These include the date of the race, the race location, the expense of the race, your strengths and weaknesses as they compare to the race course, and your overall experience level.

» Race Date

The date of the race is the most important consideration. We need to know the date so that we can back into when we should start our training program. For example, if we know the date of our triathlon is July 16 and we are using the 12-week standard distance training program in chapter 6, then we need to count back twelve weeks from our race date to determine our starting date. In this example that would be April 24, which means we need to be ready physically and mentally to begin training as of that date.

Once we have determined what this time period is, we need to check practically all aspects of our lives to make sure it's fully workable. Do you have any planned family or work-related activities during this time frame that will cause a conflict? Are there any other plans or events during this period that may cause an issue? This is the time to ask these questions to make sure that the race date is a good one for you.

Another important reason for selecting your race date early is the fact that many races have become so popular they sell out months in advance.

» Race Location

There is a big difference between flying internationally to a race and driving 30 minutes to race locally. The most important differences are expense (to be discussed in the next section), available time, equipment transport, and risk of error.

Do you have the time to fly across the country or internationally to attend a race? Doing so may require several days to get to the event, get settled in and acclimated, actually race the race, and then travel back home. Compare this to the other extreme. We have a great sprint race in our town where the starting line is three houses away from us. We can walk to the starting line before the race and walk home after the race (we will also run past our house twice during the race because we live on the course). Obviously, there could not be a more convenient race for us. Our example is, of course, extreme, but the majority of athletes in North America, Europe, and some other locations live close enough to drive to the race in the morning and then return back home by midday.

The other consideration to keep in mind when considering significant travel to a race is the risk of error. We find that the farther you travel, the greater the risk of something going wrong to spoil your racing experience. Flights get delayed or canceled, baggage gets lost, hotels lose reservations; you name it, it happens when you make big trips.

Two additional considerations for race location are climate and altitude. You will usually race best when the climate of the race is similar to where you have been training. Our bodies take time to acclimate to different weather conditions, so this should be considered. Similarly, altitude can be an issue. If you live and train at sea level, you will likely not race at your best at a significantly higher-altitude location.

» Expense

Closely related to location is expense. While race registration fees vary from race to race, it's the logistical expenses (e.g., cost of travel, hotel, meals) that make the greatest difference. Don't make the mistake of just comparing race fees. Consider all the expenses associated with a specific race.

Driving to and participating in a local sprint race could cost less than $100. However, traveling across the country or internationally can easily cost in the thousands of dollars. We advise our coached athletes to make these calculations in advance and to make sure that the races they select fit their budget.

» Strengths and Weaknesses

Race courses all differ in topographical features. Some have hilly and challenging bike courses, some have choppy non-wetsuit swims, and some are pancake-flat throughout. The features of the races you are considering should be part of your decision process.

If you are a weak swimmer, you may prefer a course with a calmer wetsuit-legal swim. If you are a strong cyclist, you may prefer a hilly bike course because you feel it's an advantage. The key point is that you consider the features of the course in relation to your own strengths and weaknesses and in conjunction with the goal setting process. You want to always select race courses that support your goals.

» Experience Level

Is this your first triathlon or duathlon, or have you been racing them for several years? If it's your first race, we suggest keeping it as simple as possible. You will need to concentrate on the task at hand, and the more distractions and complications, the greater the chance of something going wrong and spoiling the experience.

This relates to many of the factors we have discussed earlier. The more experienced you are, the more risk you are probably willing to accept when selecting your races in terms of location, travel time, and course topography. The less experienced you are, the more likely you are to benefit from eliminating as much of the risk as possible. For most "newbies," a good first race choice is usually a hassle-free local event.

We hope the above criteria will help you to select the optimal race for you.

» IRONFIT SUCCESS STORY:
Judi Germano

Judi Germano is married with two children, has a demanding career as an attorney specializing in cyber law, and is a fellow and adjunct professor at New York University. Judi is also a successful age group triathlete.

Judi's strength is the swim, and she is often first out of the water in her age group. As amazing as this is, it's even more amazing when you learn that Judi started swimming less than five years ago. In fact, she half-jokingly says that the triathlon accomplishment she is most proud of is to have learned how to "swim with my face in the water." She had dreamed about trying a triathlon for years, but didn't because her swimming was so weak—and she didn't even own a bike! Fortunately Judi met Melanie, and, as they say, the rest is history.

Judi continues to build her skills each year and consistently lowers her personal records for the standard and sprint distances, and long course distances as well. Judi credits having a coach and training plan as one of the main factors in her success.

(continued on next page)

(continued from previous page)

Judi says another of the greatest challenges for her was to overcome self-doubt. As she puts it, "I stopped listening to those negative messages and started training." Adding, "The training is not easy, but it is worth it. I am happier, stronger, and more efficient, and my family and work lives are the better for it."

As with most successful triathletes, especially those with demanding career and family responsibilities, Judi has become a master at time management. She uses many of the "Big Five" time management approaches presented in chapter 1, especially "early bird" workouts. As Judi says, "I complete my key workouts first thing in the morning, as early as necessary, before the calls and emails and other obligations (and distractions) of the day begin. It also means one shower and one time to deal with hair and makeup."

Judi also plans her bike routes well in advance. Instead of making her rides up as she goes, as many triathletes and duathletes do, she uses sources like www.map myride.com to map them out the night before. In addition to not wasting time or taking roads she may wish she hadn't, Judi finds this approach puts her in the right frame of mind before she goes to sleep, and then she wakes up eager and ready for her ride.

Judi also lays out all her workout clothing and gear, fills her bike bottles, and does any needed preparation the night before. This eliminates any delays in the morning and helps to get her out the door as quickly as possible.

Watch for Judi Germano at the races this year as she continues to achieve her goals and enjoy the endurance sports lifestyle.

» Off-Season and Maintenance Training

Success is not final, failure is not fatal. It is the courage to continue that counts.

—WINSTON CHURCHILL

How should you train during extended periods between races? In chapter 6 we provide guidance for athletes who want to compete in several races over a period of time and how they can combine the training programs in this book to accomplish that. But what if you want to have a longer period of several months between races? How should you train during that interim period?

It is very common for athletes to compete in short course races in the spring and summer months and then have an "off-season" that lasts for several months. Many are often confused by what to do during these months to stay in shape and be ready when the next season comes around.

During these periods it is easy for our training to become purposeless, and we may risk stopping altogether. This is, of course, not a good thing to do, as it will cause us to rapidly decondition.

We will lose most of our hard-earned fitness and likely gain unwanted weight. When the next racing season comes around, we will be starting from a very low level of fitness, and instead of focusing on building on our success from the previous year, we will just be trying to get back to where we started. It's common for injuries to occur during this type of situation as well, leading to further frustration.

The best alternative is to have an effective off-season training program for those extended periods when we are not preparing for a specific race. We want our off-season program to help us maintain our fitness gains, prepare us to be at a good starting point for the next season, and keep us healthy. One more consideration for most athletes in an off-season program is that they can accomplish all this with fewer training hours.

As you will recall from chapter 4, training volume is a function of training duration, intensity, and frequency.

$$Volume = Duration \times Frequency \times Intensity$$

A good off-season program usually includes decreases in two or more of the three variables. Our objective is to dial back our volume by enough to provide some relief, but not so much that we do not achieve our main objectives for the off-season.

Following are six programs that do exactly that. These programs can be used for any extended periods when you are not racing but desire to (1) maintain health and fitness, and (2) be ready to enter your next racing season at just the right level to begin race-focused training.

The six programs include Competitive, Intermediate, and "Just Finish" versions for triathletes, and Competitive, Intermediate, and "Just Finish" versions for duathletes.

Off-Season Program	Average Hours/Week
Competitive Triathlete	6–8
Intermediate Triathlete	5–6
"Just Finish" Triathlete	3–4
Competitive Duathlete	6–8
Intermediate Duathlete	4–6
"Just Finish" Duathlete	3–4

Each program is presented as a one-week training format. This weekly format is repeated throughout the off-season period until you are ready to transition into one of the specific programs presented in chapters 6–9. We will begin with the Competitive Triathlete off-season program.

COMPETITIVE TRIATHLETE OFF-SEASON PROGRAM

The Competitive Triathlete off-season program averages 6–8 hours of training per week, compared to the programs in chapters 6 and 7 for Competitive standard and sprint distance athletes, which average 10 and 9 hours, respectively. This program includes two swim sessions, three bike sessions (two of which are in the form of transition sessions), and three run sessions (plus one additional optional run as part of a transition session). The program also provides two Rest Day/Slide Days and several optional workout time ranges to provide great flexibility.

Note: Swim sessions 1–17 can be found on page 70.

COMPETITIVE TRIATHLETE
OFF-SEASON PROGRAM

All Weeks	Swim	Bike	Run
M	Rest Day/Slide Day	Rest Day/Slide Day	Rest Day/Slide Day
T	One of Swim Sessions 1–17	Off	45–60 min Z2
W	Off	Trans: 30–45 min Z2 (QC)	15 min Z2
R	One of Swim Sessions 1–17	30–60 min Z2	Off
F	Rest Day/Slide Day	Rest Day/Slide Day	Rest Day/Slide Day
S	Off	Trans: 1:00–1:15 hr Z2 (QC)	Optional: 0–30 min Z2
S	Off	Off	60–75 min Z1 to Z2
Totals: 6:00–8:00 hr	2:00 hr	2:00–3:00 hr	2:00–3:00 hr

INTERMEDIATE TRIATHLETE OFF-SEASON PROGRAM

The Intermediate Triathlete off-season program averages 5–6 hours of training per week, compared to the programs in chapters 6 and 7 for Intermediate standard and sprint distance athletes, which average 7.5 and 6.5 hours, respectively. This program includes two swim sessions, three bike sessions (two of which are in the form of transition sessions), and three run sessions (plus one additional optional run as part of a transition session). The program also provides two Rest Day/Slide Days and several optional workout time ranges to provide great flexibility.

Swim sessions 18–32 can be found on page 78.

INTERMEDIATE TRIATHLETE
OFF-SEASON PROGRAM

All Weeks	Swim	Bike	Run
M	Rest Day/Slide Day	Rest Day/Slide Day	Rest Day/Slide Day
T	One of Swim Sessions 18–32	Off	30–45 min Z2
W	Off	Trans: 30 min Z2 (QC)	15 min Z2
R	One of Swim Sessions 18–32	45 min Z2	Off
F	Rest Day/Slide Day	Rest Day/Slide Day	Rest Day/Slide Day
S	Off	Trans: 45–60 min Z2(QC)	Optional: 0–15 min Z2
S	Off	Off	45–60 min Z1 to Z2
Totals: 5:00–6:00 hr	1:30 hr	2:00–2:15 hr	1:30–2:15 hr

"JUST FINISH" TRIATHLETE OFF-SEASON PROGRAM

The "Just Finish" Triathlete off-season program averages 3–4 hours of training per week, compared to the programs in chapters 6 and 7 for "Just Finish" standard and sprint distance athletes, which average 5 and 4 hours, respectively. This program includes one swim session, two bike sessions, and two run sessions. The program also provides two Rest Day/Slide Days and several optional workout time ranges to provide greater flexibility.

Swim sessions 18–32 can be found on page 78.

"JUST FINISH" TRIATHLETE
OFF-SEASON PROGRAM

All Weeks	Swim	Bike	Run
M	Rest Day/Slide Day	Rest Day/Slide Day	Rest Day/Slide Day
T	Off	Off	30–45 min Z2
W	One of Swim Sessions 18–32	Off	Off
R	Off	30–45 min Z2	Off
F	Rest Day/Slide Day	Rest Day/Slide Day	Rest Day/Slide Day
S	Off	45–60 min Z2	Off
S	Off	Off	30–45 min Z1 to Z2
Totals: 3:00–4:00 hr	0:45 hr	1:15–1:45 hr	1:00–1:30 hr

COMPETITIVE DUATHLETE OFF-SEASON PROGRAM

The Competitive Duathlete off-season program averages 6–8 hours of training per week, compared to the programs in chapters 8 and 9 for Competitive standard and sprint distance duathletes, which average 10 and 9 hours, respectively. This program includes three bike sessions (plus one additional optional bike session) and three run sessions (plus one additional optional run as part of a transition session). The program also provides two Rest Day/Slide Days and several optional workout time ranges to provide great flexibility.

Note: The Wednesday transition session can be completed as a double or triple transition session if desired. (See page 19.)

COMPETITIVE DUATHLETE
OFF-SEASON PROGRAM

All Weeks	Bike	Run
M	Rest Day/Slide Day	Rest Day/Slide Day
T	Off	60 min Z2
W	Trans: 60 min Z2 (QC)	15–30 min Z2
R	60 min Z2	Off
F	Rest Day/Slide Day	Rest Day/Slide Day
S	Trans: 1:30–2:00 hr Z2 (QC)	Optional: 0–30 min Z2
S	Optional: 0–30 min Z1 (100+ RPM)	75–90 min Z1 to Z2
Totals: 6:00–8:00 hr	3:30–4:30 hr	2:30–3:30 hr

INTERMEDIATE DUATHLETE OFF-SEASON PROGRAM

The Intermediate Duathlete off-season program averages 4–6 hours of training per week, compared to the programs in chapters 8 and 9 for Intermediate standard and sprint distance duathletes, which average 7.5 and 6.5 hours, respectively. This program includes three bike sessions (one of which is in the form of a transition session) and three run sessions. The program also provides two Rest Day/ Slide Days and several optional workout time ranges to provide great flexibility.

Note: The Wednesday transition session can be completed as a double or triple transition session if desired. (See page 19.)

INTERMEDIATE DUATHLETE
OFF-SEASON PROGRAM

All Weeks	Bike	Run
M	Rest Day/Slide Day	Rest Day/Slide Day
T	Off	45–60 min Z2
W	Trans: 30 min Z2 (QC)	15–30 min Z2
R	45–60 min Z2	Off
F	Rest Day/Slide Day	Rest Day/Slide Day
S	45–90 min Z2	Off
S	Off	60–90 min Z1 to Z2
Totals: 4:00–6:00 hr	2:00–3:00 hr	2:00–3:00 hr

"JUST FINISH" DUATHLETE OFF-SEASON PROGRAM

The "Just Finish" Duathlete off-season program averages 3–4 hours of training per week, compared to the programs in chapters 8 and 9 for "Just Finish" standard and sprint distance duathletes, which average 5 and 4 hours, respectively. This program includes three bike sessions (one of which is in the form of a transition session) and three run sessions. The program also provides two Rest Day/Slide Days and several optional workout time ranges to provide great flexibility.

Note: The Wednesday transition session can be completed as a double or triple transition session if desired. (See page 19.)

"JUST FINISH" DUATHLETE
OFF-SEASON PROGRAM

All Weeks	Bike	Run
M	Rest Day/Slide Day	Rest Day/Slide Day
T	Off	30–45 min Z2
W	Trans: 15 min Z2 (QC)	15 min Z2
R	30–45 min Z1 to Z2	Off
F	Rest Day/Slide Day	Rest Day/Slide Day
S	45–60 min Z2	Off
S	Off	45–60 min Z1 to Z2
Totals: 3:00–4:00 hr	1:30–2:00 hr	1:30–2:00 hr

ADDITIONAL SUGGESTIONS FOR OFF-SEASON TRAINING

In addition to using the above off-season training programs, please also consider the following suggestions to maximize the benefits of your off-season training:

1. **Get Healthy:** If you have had a nagging injury that you couldn't seem to shake during the season, now is the time to seriously address it. You sure don't want to continue with it through the off-season and allow it to carry right through to the next competitive season. If you haven't already had the injury examined by your doctor, this should be done right away. Once you understand exactly what you are dealing with, work with your doctor to develop an action plan to get back to 100 percent good health. Consider rest if necessary, or cross-training if appropriate, to allow the issue to correct itself. Make sure you put injuries behind you in the off-season so you can start the next competitive season healthy and at your best.

2. **Stay Lean:** The off-season is a time when many athletes gain weight due to lower training volume. We want to head this off by adjusting our calorie intake to better match our reduced activity level. Adding a few pounds over the off-season is not a big problem, but anything more than that will make it harder to hit the ground running when you transition back into competitive mode—and it will increase the risk of injury when you do.

3. **Functional Strength and Core Training:** Strength and core training is usually the first training element to be dropped when things get busy during the competitive season. The off-season is the time to refocus on this important training element and take advantage of the reduction in training hours to make sure that you get your functional strength and core training in regularly. The off-season program in chapter 10 will serve this need well and have you stronger and more injury resistant when you are ready to transition back into the next competitive season.

4. **Improve Your Weakest Link:** If you have additional time beyond what is suggested in the above off-season programs, invest it in your weakest sport. As we like to say to our athletes, we want to turn our weaknesses into strengths and our strengths into weapons. Consider adding an extra session each week to your weakest sport. Also consider getting additional coaching in that area or perhaps attending a weekend clinic.

5. **Cross-Training Substitutions:** If you feel stale with any of the three sports, consider substituting in another suitable endurance activity to mix it up a bit and add some new challenge and excitement. Some of the best activities for this are mountain biking, cross-country skiing (including on an indoor cross-country ski machine), and the elliptical. Just one substitution a week can go a long way to the success and enjoyment of your off-season training.

6. **Give Back:** This one is for your mind and spirit. There are many ways to give back to the endurance sports community. Help to introduce others to the healthy endurance sports lifestyle. Many people secretly would love to do it but don't know where to start. Help to show them the way. You may very well change their lives. Also consider volunteering at an endurance sports event. You may be amazed at how motivated you become while you focus on helping and motivating others.

We hope the above off-season training programs and suggestions will help you to have a productive off-season, leading to a more successful next competitive season.

We also hope this book contributes to the success and enjoyment of your short course triathlon or duathlon journey. Keep up the great work, and we will see you at the finish line!

»APPENDIX A: SUGGESTED READING

The books listed here have been very helpful to us over the years and have provided a great deal of information to us as we compiled our research for this book. They may prove useful to you as well.

Be IronFit®: Time-Efficient Training Secrets for Ultimate Fitness, 2nd ed. Don Fink. Lyons Press, 2010.

The Big Book of Endurance Training and Racing. Philip Maffetone and Mark Allen. Skyhorse Publishing, 2010.

Core Performance Endurance. Mark Verstegen and Pete Williams. Rodale Inc., 2007.

Endurance Sports Nutrition: Strategies for Training, Racing, and Recovery, 2nd ed. Suzanne Girard Eberle, MS, RD. Human Kinetics, 2007.

Heart Rate Training. Roy Benson and Declan Connolly. Human Kinetics, 2011.

Instant Relief: Tell Me Where It Hurts and I'll Tell You What to Do. Peggy Brill and Susan Suffes. Bantam, 2007.

IronFit® Strength Training and Nutrition for Endurance Athletes. Don Fink and Melanie Fink. Lyons Press, 2013.

Lifestyle and Weight Management Consultant Manual. Richard T. Cotton. American Council on Exercise, 1996.

Personal Trainer Manual: The Resource for Fitness Professionals. Richard T. Cotton. American Council on Exercise, 1997.

The Power Meter Handbook: A User's Guide for Cyclists and Triathletes. Joe Friel. Velo Press, 2012.

Program Design for Personal Trainers: Bridging Theory into Application. Douglas S. Brooks, MS. Human Kinetics, 1997.

Sports Nutrition for Endurance Athletes, 2nd ed. Monique Ryan, MS, RD, LDN. Velo Press, 2007.

Training and Racing with a Power Meter, 2nd ed. Hunter Allen and Andrew Coggan, PhD. Velo Press, 2010.

Training Lactate Pulse-Rate. Peter G. J. M. Janssen. Polar Electro Oy, 1987.

The Triathlete's Training Bible. Joe Friel. Velo Press, 2009.

Triathlon Science. Joe Friel and Jim Vance. Human Kinetics, 2013.

» APPENDIX B: SUGGESTED WEBSITES

IronFit: www.IronFit.com

American Council on Exercise: www.acefitness.org

British Triathlon: www.britishtriathlon.org

Debra Trebitz: www.debratrebitzphotography.com

HITS Triathlon Series: www.hitstriathlonseries.com

Ironman 5150 Series: www.ironman.com

ITU World Triathlon Series: wtx.triathlon.org

James Mitchell: www.jamesmitchell.eu

Lose It: www.loseit.com

My Fitness Pal: www.myfitnesspal.com

Running in the USA: www.runningintheusa.com

Running Times magazine: www.runningtimes.com

Triathlete magazine: www.triathlete.com

Triathlon Australia: www.triathlon.org.au

Triathlon Canada: www.triathloncanada.com

Triathlon New Zealand: www.triathlon.org.nz

Tri Find: www.trifind.com

Tri Life Photos: www.trilifephotos.com

220 Triathlon: www.220triathlon.com

USA Track and Field (USATF): www.usatf.org

USA Triathlon: www.usatriathlon.org

US Masters Swimming: www.usms.com

Weight Watchers: www.weightwatchers.com

» APPENDIX C: GLOSSARY

Abs: Abdominal muscles.

Active Recovery: Lower-intensity running or cross-training sessions that allow the body to recover while continuing to build and/or maintain fitness.

Aerobic Energy System: An energy system that primarily uses oxygen and stored fat to power physical activity. This system can support activity for prolonged periods, as stored fat and oxygen are available in almost endless supply. Even a highly trained athlete with body fat percentages in the single digits has more than enough stored fat for several ultradistance races back-to-back.

Anaerobic Energy System: An energy system that primarily uses glycogen (stored sugar) to power physical activity. This system can support activity for relatively short periods of time, as the body stores sugar in relatively small quantities.

Basal Metabolic Rate (BMR): The number of calories needed to be consumed each day to allow our bodies to function normally and maintain current body weight. Active BMR is an athlete's BMR plus the additional calories needed to support normal daily activities, but not including calories used in training and racing.

Body Mass Index (BMI): A relative measure of body height to body weight for purposes of determining a healthy or non-healthy weight.

BOSU® Ball (acronym for "both sides utilized"): This is an inflated "half-ball" with a flat side and a half-dome side. This popular piece of equipment is primarily used to develop balance and stability on an uneven and unstable surface.

"Brick" Sessions: See Transition Sessions.

Calorie: A calorie is a basic unit of energy. Our bodies require energy to perform practically all functions and get this energy in the form of calories. Carbohydrates and proteins have about four calories per gram, while fat has about nine calories per gram.

Carbohydrate Loading: Various dietary approaches for the purpose of increasing glycogen stores prior to an endurance race.

Cooldown: Lower-intensity activity after training or racing to help the body to gradually prepare itself to stop or greatly reduce its level of physical activity.

Core Muscles: Includes abdominals, back, buttocks, pelvic floor, and hips.

Dumbbells: Handheld exercise weights available in various coatings from plastic to metal and various weights from 1 pound up to 50-plus pounds.

Electrolytes: Common examples of electrolytes are sodium, potassium, chloride, and carbon dioxide. They are needed by our cells to function properly and keep the body's fluids in balance.

Foam Roller: This piece of exercise equipment is made of hard foam and is usually 36 inches long and 6 inches around, with varying densities, and is used for self-myofascial release.

45-Minute Window: The time period of opportunity after a training session to jump-start the replenishment of glycogen stores.

Fueling: Within the context of endurance sports, this term refers to the process of consuming calories before, during, and after training and racing to build and maintain high levels of energy and to boost recovery.

Fueling Logistics: The means by which athletes access their needed calories during competition.

Glutes: Abbreviation for the gluteus maximus, medius, and minimus muscle group.

Glycogen: The form in which the body stores sugar (carbohydrates) for the purpose of powering muscle activity.

Heart Rate Zones: Heart-rate ranges expressed in terms of beats per minute (BPM) that correspond to the intensity levels of physical activities.

Higher-Intensity Repeats: Several consecutive higher-intensity efforts, separated by easy efforts in between.

Hill Repeats: This session is similar to Higher-Intensity Repeats. It includes several consecutive higher-intensity efforts up a hill, separated by easy efforts back down the hill to the starting point.

Hydrating: Within the context of endurance sports, this term refers to the process of drinking fluids before, during, and after training and racing to support optimal performance, safety, and good health.

Hydration Logistics: The means by which athletes access their needed fluids during competition.

Kettle Bells: These are handheld weights, but unlike dumbbells, the center of mass is extended beyond the hand. This facilitates ballistic and swinging movements. Like dumbbells, they are available in various coatings and weights.

Lactate Threshold: The heart rate level at which lactate begins to accumulate at a faster rate in the muscles than the body can clear it. Lactate is produced in our bodies when performing physical activity. The accumulation of lactate has a negative impact on the muscles' ability to perform.

Maximum Heart Rate (MHR): The highest heart rate attainable by a specific athlete, expressed in terms of beats per minute (BPM).

Medicine Ball: This is a round weighted ball with a rubberized or leather coating used in core and functional strength training exercises. It is available in various weights from 1 to 20 pounds.

Overload Principle: According to the American Council on Exercise: "One of the principles of human performance that states that beneficial adaptations occur in response to demands applied to the body at levels beyond a certain threshold (overload), but within the limits of tolerance and safety."

Quads: Abbreviation for the muscles of the quadriceps.

Reps or Repetitions: The number of times an exercise movement is repeated within an exercise set.

Rest Days: Days on which the athlete does no training activity at all, for the purpose of allowing the body to recover.

Sets: A specific grouping of repetitions of a specific exercise movement. Typically, there will be one to three sets of each exercise within a specific exercise program.

75-Minute Fueling Guideline: The approximate point in a workout when water alone is not enough for most athletes to maintain the same performance level. Adequate calories, in addition to hydration, are needed.

Stability Ball (aka Swiss Ball): This round inflated exercise ball is the most popular and widely used piece of core training equipment. It is important that it is properly sized to fit your height.

Stretch Cords and Resistance Tubing: These are rubber or plastic cords, usually with handles and available in various resistances.

Sweat Rate Test: A physical test performed by an athlete to help determine his or her hydration needs while training and racing.

T1: The transition between the swim and cycling phases of a triathlon.

T2: The transition between the cycling and running phases of a triathlon

Taper: A training period prior to a race in which the athlete does progressively less and less training volume as the race approaches. The purpose is to become fully rested and energized before the race, without losing fitness.

Targeted Ten: A 10- to 15-minute warm-up routine presented in this book that includes ten specific pre-exercise movements.

Training Volume: The combination of how long you train, how intense your effort level is while you train, and how frequently you train. Training volume can be expressed by the following equation: Training Volume = Duration x Intensity x Frequency.

Transition Sessions (aka "Brick" Sessions): Training sessions that involve two sports separated by a brief period for the athlete to change from the clothing and equipment of one sport to that of the other.

VO2 Max: A measure of an athlete's ability to process oxygen and convert it to energy.

Warm-up: Lower-intensity activity before training or racing to help the body gradually prepare itself for a higher level of physical activity.

Watts-Based Training: A training approach for cycling that involves measuring intensity by produced wattage.

» ACKNOWLEDGMENTS

We wish to thank the following individuals: Tim Beasant, M. Scott Boyles, Peggy Brill, Kellie Brown, Damien Bullard, Jackie Day, Bill Deimer, Stephen Grossman, Alice Hector, Yvonne Hernandez, Marienne Hill-Treadway, Peter Hyland, Lynn Kellogg, Laura Litwin, Steve Levine, Ed McEntee, Dave Mantle, Fred Marashi, Bryan Mendelson, James Mitchell, Soula Priovolos, Francis Quinn, Nataliya Schouten, Melissa and Cary Silverman, Debra Trebitz, and Susan Winkelried.

» INDEX

» ABOUT THE AUTHORS

Don Fink is an internationally known triathlon and running coach/trainer and author of the popular endurance sports training books: *Be IronFit: Time-Efficient Training Secrets for Ultimate Fitness* (2004); *Be IronFit, Second Edition* (2010); *Mastering the Marathon: Time-Efficient Training Secrets for the 40-plus Athlete* (2010); *IronFit Strength Training and Nutrition for Endurance Athletes (2013)*; *IronFit Secrets for Half Iron-Distance Triathlon Success (2013)*; *IronFit Triathlon Training for Women (2015)*; *Be IronFit, Third Edition* (2016); and *IronFit's Marathons After 40* (2017); all published by Globe Pequot. Among his credentials, Don is a Certified Personal Trainer by the American Council on Exercise (ACE) and he is a Professional Member of the National Strength and Conditioning Association (NSCA). Don and his wife, Melanie, train endurance athletes on five continents through their business: IronFit (www.IronFit.com). Don and Melanie have utilized their innovative approaches to coach hundreds of athletes to personal best times and breakthrough performances in triathlon, the marathon, and other sports.

In addition to being an endurance sports coach/trainer, Don Fink is an elite athlete. He has raced over 30 Ironman triathlons (2.4-mile swim, 112-mile bike, and 26.2-mile run) and has many age group victories and course records to his credit. Don's time of 9:08 at the 2004 Ironman Florida is one of the fastest times ever recorded by an athlete in the 45–49 age group.

Don Fink also placed in the top three overall in the 2002 Ultra Man World Championships (6.2-mile swim, 270-mile bike, and 52.4-mile run) on the Big Island of Hawaii.

Among **Melanie Fink**'s credentials, she is a Certified Personal Trainer by the American Council on Exercise (ACE) and former Regional Council Member of USA Triathlon Mid-Atlantic. Melanie co-authored the popular endurance sports training book: *IronFit Strength Training and Nutrition for Endurance Athletes* (2013); *IronFit Secrets for Half Iron-Distance Triathlon Success* (2013); *IronFit Triathlon Training for Women* (2015); *Be IronFit, Third Edition* (2016); and *IronFit's Marathons After 40* (2017), all published by Globe Pequot. In addition to being a sports coach/trainer and US Masters Level 2 Certified Swimming coach, Melanie Fink is an elite athlete. She has many age group and overall victories in triathlon and open water swimming competitions, has completed twelve Iron-distance triathlons (including the Hawaii Ironman twice), and completed Ultra Man Canada (6.2-mile swim, 270-mile bike, and 52.4-mile run) in Penticton, British Columbia.

Don and Melanie Fink live in Carroll County, New Hampshire.